Unarmed

But

Dangerous

Unarmed *But* Dangerous

Withering Attacks on All Things Phony, Foolish, and Fundamentally Wrong with America Today

H A L   C R O W T H E R

LONGSTREET PRESS, INC.
Atlanta, Georgia

Published by
LONGSTREET PRESS, INC.
A subsidiary of Cox Newspapers,
A division of Cox Enterprises, Inc.
2140 Newmarket Parkway
Suite 118
Marietta, GA 30067

Printed in the United States of America

1st printing, 1995

Library of Congress Catalog Card Number: 94-74239

ISBN: 1-56352-193-8

This book was printed by R.R. Donnelley & Sons, Harrisonburg, Virginia

Film Preparation by Holland Graphics, Inc., Mableton, GA

Book and jacket design by Jill Dible
Jacket photograph by Andrea Gomez

For Lee

"You can best serve civilization by being against what usually passes for it."

— Wendell Berry,
A Continuous Harmony

CONTENTS

FOREWORD

Hal Crowther quotes Rush Limbaugh inviting listeners to imagine him—Limbaugh—as a 303-pound cyst in a woman's abdomen: "Imagine me in this woman's abdomen as a cyst. Think of it." Thinking of it, Crowther notes, "Radio doesn't get much more postmodern than this. It's easier to imagine Rush Limbaugh as a world-record fibrous tumor than to imagine him as a star." Crowther characteristically takes off from there, sending up Limbaugh's "all-you-can-eat buffet of Cro-Magnon platitudes" and simultaneously, with the back of his hand, those "Manhattan mutants" who "honestly believed that Jim and Tammy Bakker were two male actors from Long Island doing an Emmy-winning sendup of Southern religion."

You can't help but think all's not lost in the world, if descriptions of its wrongs can be so hilarious. Was it Crowther who titled his column on children's butchering their parents "I Dismember Mama"? Kitty Kelley and Nancy Reagan are, convincingly, "sisters under the fur." He damns "our current series of designer wars." A German executive is a "Eurobigshot . . . He—four or five of him—was the worst person I ever encountered who wasn't actively trying to maim me."

It is a rare man who possesses both a passionate conscience and a brilliant wit. Crowther's conscience compels him to distinguish right from wrong, to honor the right, and to decry the wrong. He does so even here, in our "amnesiac culture constructed almost entirely by the lies and distortions of commerce." He does so even now, when "the things we have to swallow to live in the world keep staining our spirits." Hal Crowther is a wit who never lapses into cynicism or relativism; he is a powerful intellectual who is immune to "the latest mood in the faculty lounge." He is a man of honor who can't be bought.

Crowther's first-rate social criticism plots "the decline and fall of this hemorrhaging republic we call home," where corporate and personal greed and institutional deceit keep the underclass under. If he wrote abstractions, we wouldn't read him; instead, he presents the full spectacle of our culture. Here is Orrin Hatch fawning malignantly at the Clarence Thomas hearings, and a tobacco executive denying outright that the actor who died of lung cancer posed for the Marlboro Man. Here are homeless people sleeping on beaches, journalists obsequiously making love to power, gleeful crowds shouting at an execution, Native Americans denouncing the film *Black Robe* because it depicted 19th-century Native American culture as "violent," and Cambodian immigrants who, upon reflection, consider Cambodia safer.

What can a man of honor do but rage, rage against the dying of the light? Again and again Crowther's brilliant jeremiads rise to a pitch of outraged eloquence.

This is a thinker who loves truth. Unlike the trendiest professors, he believes there is such a thing: "We piece it together, scrap by hunch by painstaking reconstruction." He speaks the truth— "the simple facts of the case"—because today's journalism is tomorrow's history. He admires Carlyle; he admires Gibbon. "Should we pass this way without an honest clue about what went before us?"

The truth is the humanitarian's hope in "the hemorrhaging republic." For Crowther, though "fools and scoundrels lead multitudes to the precipice," though John Q. Public may look in the polls like "a vicious, amoral swine," nevertheless, the public, the multitude, can be aroused to right wrongs. We have a sense of good and evil, however vestigial. Why else would truth-telling work? Why cry in the wilderness?

Hal Crowther refers once, modestly, to "those of us who try to be fair." This begins to seem like a startling claim. Yet it is not too vaunting a claim for Crowther. From this "trying to be fair," all the rest springs.

— Annie Dillard

INTRODUCTION

"What I Do, I Think"

There may be those who believe that offering unsolicited opinion is a profession incompatible with humility. But humility, for a writer who worked the better part of his life in newsprint media, is sorting stacks of old columns and washing his hands every 10 minutes, as his life's work comes off on his fingers. If you haven't achieved perfect humility at 50, when half a dozen of your home boys have already died of natural causes, you're unusually stupid or pathetically hungry for something the world will never provide.

How do we choose a profession, those of us who have the privilege of choosing? I was cursed from birth with what Woody Allen, in *Stardust Memories*, calls "an inadequate denial mechanism." My own illusions were stillborn, and if I had a gift, it was a gift for seeing the structural flaws and stress fractures in the illusions of others. This is a gift that earns no gratitude.

"I had no more public spirit than a policeman or an archbishop," wrote H.L. Mencken. "But I was full of lust to function, and before I was 25 it was already plain that my functioning would take the form of a sharp and more or less truculent dissent from the mores of my country."

Mencken affected an urbane form of heartlessness. For his friend Ben Hecht he reserved his highest praise: "The spectacle of man's imbecility enchanted him." He boasted that his magazine, *The Smart Set*, would never "pretend that it was made sad by the sorrows of the world." But I was burdened with the one thing Mencken despised most of all, a missionary impulse—the bastard offspring of a fastidious Unitarian conscience and the promiscuous idealism of the '60s. Imbeciles don't enchant me; I can't pretend the world doesn't make me sad. I can't pretend it doesn't compel me to preach.

I wasn't born to be a journalist, with the sacred sense of vocation that grips poets and priests. I chose it by a process of elimination, and tried to abandon it on several occasions. But I'm nothing if not a contrarian. As the profession grew more cynical—about human nature and its own reponsibilities—I became less cynical. As its idealism waned, mine tended to wax. I don't laugh, as Mencken would have laughed, at the question the doctor, played by Anthony Hopkins, asks himself in *The Elephant Man*: "Am I a good man, or am I a bad man?"

These two essays add up to a sort of working philosophy. The first one is idealistic. The second one is realistic, and not intended to be dark.

Nothing but the Truth

I was moved by a piece I heard on NPR, about an old man in the California desert somewhere who has dedicated his life to preserving the memory of the famous Indian motorcycle. The reporter who visited the old guy described his place as a cross between a museum, a garage, a junkyard and a shrine. Working with salvaged parts and precious odds and ends that he acquires from dealers and collectors, manufacturing the rest bolt-by-bolt on his machine tools, this solitary perfectionist reconstructs Indians that are identical in every detail to the last ones manufactured, in the late 1930s.

Whether you could call any of his creations "authentic" or "original" Indians—or whether any such exist—is a matter of interpretation. The old man is in love with the *idea* of Indian motorcycles, a pure idea that has survived the perishable bolts and rings and sparkplugs because one man's faith is so strong.

The way this old-timer feels about his Indians is the way some of us old-timers feel about the truth. Even the way we deal with it is similar. We know truth is hard to locate and harder to certify. We don't expect to open a door and find a vintage, 1,000-pound truth just gleaming with chrome and wax and the original paint job. We piece it together, scrap by hunch by painstaking reconstruction. We break a drill press now and then, and sometimes it's years before we've built anything you could wheel out and ride.

"You call that thing the truth?" somebody will sneer, when we take the dustcloth off the best work we've managed so far. But that doesn't discourage us. Because it's the *idea* of the truth, regardless of the purity of any of its manifestations, that keeps us going. Like the old man in the desert, we find that it's more than enough.

Maybe it's a romantic conceit to suggest that in 30 years or so a couple of old prospectors like me will be out in the desert somewhere operating a little museum and junkyard dedicated to what's left of The Truth. ("Truth 20 miles, unpaved road ahead, four-wheel drive suggested.") Even in the United States a certain amount of truth has been manufactured since the 1930s, and products marketed under that label are still available everywhere. But the idea that we grew up with is fading, and other ideas have come forward to crowd it aside. The Indian motorcycle has no enemy but the passage of time; the truth has more implacable enemies than Salman Rushdie.

"There is something embarrassingly naive about talking about the truth," writes historian Dan T. Carter of Emory University. "In our time it's far more difficult to talk about the 'truth' than it is to discuss transsexual bestiality."

I've had a few months to think about an evening last spring when Dr. Carter and I served on a panel at Duke, a panel discussing "Interpretation, Revision and the Pursuit of Historic Truth." It was Dr. Carter who discovered that Forrest Carter, author of the inspirational bestseller *The Education of Little Tree* was not a Cherokee cowboy from Tennessee but a ferocious Alabama racist named Asa Carter, whose Ku Klux Klan strike force once castrated a 34-year-old black man in Birmingham.

When he published his research on Asa Carter in the *New York Times*, Dr. Carter was shocked to find that neither the publishers nor the readers of *Little Tree* were receptive to these revisionist truths. Schoolchildren cursed him for a liar and a cynic. The University of New Mexico Press denied everything, and literary critics weighed in with essays explaining the tenuous, virtually irrelevant connection between author and text.

Dr. Carter had collided head-on with the postmodernist reader-response theories that he had, he said, only half understood. By dismissing even eyewitness accounts as subjective interpretation and insisting that every text is meaningless until the reader interprets it, postmodernist theory appeared to confer carte blanche on anyone with a motive for erasing or revising the past or, like Asa

Carter and his Klan successor David Duke, for reinventing themselves entirely.

In his talk at Duke University, titled, "What Does It Mean to Tell the Truth in a Postmodernist World?" Dan Carter examined some of the alarming possibilities of Derrida and the postmodernists as interpreted by advertising, politics and weird tribes like the anti-Semites who refuse to acknowledge the Holocaust. He reserved his special contempt for the Judases in his own profession who conclude that "the search for truth is meaningless" and that traditional narrative history consists of little more than "wishes, daydreams, reveries" (Hayden White).

"I'm sure that most of you are at peace with the absolute indeterminacy of human knowledge about either the present or the past," Carter concluded. "For my part, however, I find that I am seized by a sense of vertigo as I face, in the words of American philosopher Richard Bernstein, the possibility that 'there may be nothing—not God, reason, philosophy, science or poetry—that answers to and satisfies our longing for ultimate constraints, for a stable and reliable rock upon which we can secure our thought and action.'"

Even at Duke, where several of the postmodernist heresies are said to flourish, it seemed impossible that anyone in the room could have failed to respond to the logic and passion of Dr. Carter's remarks. This assumption was naive. His applause had not yet died away (and this is what I remember most clearly) when a young woman in the front row stood up to put him in his place. A graduate student in English with the calm, untroubled confidence of a religious convert, she saw nothing but sentimentality and hardening arteries in Carter's conservative position.

"Don't you find the death of historical truth a little frightening?" I asked her.

"Don't you find it liberating?" she replied.

It doesn't surprise me that academics fail to consider how the world outside the academy might be affected if their journals and dissertations were taken seriously. They wouldn't deign to notice the foul things that come to feed on the carcass of this Truth they're so proud of slaying, creatures who erase the Holocaust, romanticize slavery, glorify war. How the denial of objective truth might affect the law, say, or journalism—humble trades that practice the rude science of cause and effect—I would not expect them to explore.

But I'm disappointed to find that all the clever flourishes and insights of their linguistic theories seem to reduce to a position as intellectually barren as "Hey, it's all relative, Mac, your guess is as good as mine." ("There is no difference between the signifier and the signified.") It's hard for me to see how such a banal, almost childish truism could achieve the force of theology in the academy.

And it's hard for me to see how they can be so cavalier with history. Literature, my own field of study, made an easy target for postmodernists. The truths of literature aren't trivial truths. But its sacred materials are too easily reduced to "texts," to artifacts that can be carved and parboiled and deconstructed according to the political fashions of the moment. Try telling a multicultural radical, gender division, that Nabokov isn't hard to read because he was white, male, privileged and European, but because of all the things he knew that she will never learn.

History is another matter. It is, as I wrote once, "a couple of critical inches closer to the jugular vein of civilization." If history is "daydreams and reveries," where does that leave journalism? Journalists are the field hands, the day laborers of recorded history. But our eight-hour shifts are critical. One hundred years from now, a reporter's handiwork is a primary source for a 21st-century Edward Gibbon. What happens if the reporter loses his faith, his vocation, his conscience?

We all know that history is selective, fragmented and provisional in many of the truths it tries to tell. This week Christians are celebrating a holiday based on events inseparable from the mythology of vanished religions that only scholars can name. Marguerite Yourcenar discovered that the indisputable history of the later Roman Empire, from the second through the fifth century, could probably be printed on a playing card.

But for every lie, for every silence, some horrible crime goes unremarked and unpunished, some dreadful mistake lies waiting to be repeated. This is no daydream. This is more than your point of view, your angle of vision. It matters, profoundly, just How It Was. Lee surrendered, not Grant. The smoke from Auschwitz carried an unbearable smell. Anne Boleyn's head was severed from her body. Between which two vertebrae the blade fell, that alone is a matter for conjecture.

Who fired the first shot, how tall was the general, was it raining? It all matters. It's my personal conviction that cruelty follows a lie, loves a lie, makes its nest in a lie. And I've never been able to divine any purpose in our individual human lives, unless it's to reduce the sum of human cruelty during the time when we're alive. That's reason enough to press for the truth, to expose falsehood, even to deplore ambiguity if it's thick enough for cruelty to hide behind it.

I've heard it said that standards of objective truth represent naked oppression, one class's heavy hand on the aspirations of another. I think it takes a lot of cynicism to believe that all human impulse, and all the language that expresses it, is related to the exercise of power and power alone. This is not only philistinism, to me, but a virulent strain of atheism. If I believed it I'd be subject to suicidal despair.

People who believe this must be very hungry, alienated people, and not especially good at making connections. I think that liberation from truth is the same as liberation from responsibility—an open invitation to all the ugliest things that adhere to human nature.

There was a time not long ago when you could say "truth" without blushing, pursue it without apology, tell it without footnotes, preach it without grandiloquence. Times have changed. The truth is attacked from one side by enemies with personal and political agendas, from the other side by enemies with Ph.D.s.

The hustlers and liars aren't the ones who worry me. Truth has survived millennia of liars. But universities confer, on just a few individuals in each generation, the time, privilege and resources to appreciate abstractions like The Truth. When this elite defects and adopts strange, myopic creeds, it weakens the covenant of civilization. It damages the pure idea of truth that has sustained our sorry race of monkeys for eons. It's the idea that matters. It matters as much as the *idea* of God, and is probably inseparable from it.

The Merchants of Meaning

You didn't have to be a sportswriter to suffer the maximum displacement from the San Francisco earthquake of 1989. But it helped. If you read the sports pages, you know that baseball writers in particular are obsessed with "history." In a 162-game baseball season, scarcely a day passes when a press-box poet somewhere doesn't invoke "the history of the game." I blush to think of the number of times I ended a sentence with that formula. I loved the sound of it, the sense of an ordered universe of facts and figures. The writers keep the faith and the statisticians keep the books, with a factual punctiliousness that puts accountants and scientists to shame. A Dominican boy with a three-day stubble glides to his right, the ball settles in his glove or glances off his knee, 50 men scribble in their notebooks and the incident is set forever in a dense matrix of history that goes back 100 years.

The last World Series that I can't remember was played in 1949. I've covered two Series from the press box and attended a half-dozen others. Larsen's perfect game, Mazeroski's homer and Mays' miracle catch occupy places in my brain that saner people reserve for wars, floods and divorces. With all that history behind me, I thought the 1989 World Series was more promising than most. In the playoffs the statistician/historians had a field day. Had any human being ever hit a baseball harder than Jose Canseco, whose 500-foot home run took an unearthly trajectory past the left field foul pole in Toronto's towering SkyDome, actually fooling the cameraman by landing two decks higher than all his experience allowed him to imagine?

A "historic World Series" they called it, the first ever played between league champions from opposite sides of San Francisco Bay. Then someone with a bigger bat than Jose Canseco's leveled everyone's illusions. As the players waited to take the field for the third game of the series, the earthquake rocked Candlestick Park as if it were a stadium made of cardboard instead of reinforced concrete; a few miles away it flattened automobiles and their occupants to a height of six inches.

"Stick that in your Baseball Encyclopedia," something deep down in the world told the World Series and its historians. In an instant we were reduced to responding to a legitimate argument that the rest of the Series should be canceled altogether and the World Championship left vacant for 1989—to a baseball man, a measure more radical and disturbing than canceling Christmas, Easter and the Fourth of July.

At this very moment hellfire preachers in storefronts and radio studios are trying to make moral sense of the earthquake for their congregations, insisting that San Francisco has been punished by the Lord for its sins of Sodom, which are countless. The question for me is how anyone could be on speaking terms with a deity who would incidentally crush a six-year-old boy (to extricate Julio Burumen from the I-880 rubble, doctors cut through a woman's body with a chainsaw and amputated his right leg at the knee) in order to get even with a sinner on the other side of town. But certain fundamentalists feed on intricate rationalizations, and on theologies of power and fear.

Some of them will emerge from the earthquake trauma more smug and self-righteous than they were before. Their faith is equipped with earthquake-proof shock absorbers, like the ones that keep San Francisco's high-rise office buildings from tumbling into the bay. The church of baseball has no such safeguards. The smaller and more tightly ordered your universe, the more exposed you feel when something cracks it open and you can hear the wind, and the faster the shock waves spread to the other assumptions that keep you cozy.

On one of the nights when I would have been watching the suspended World Series, my cousin and I sat up and reminisced about our own history, and the histories of our friends and families. She's a few years younger but we've both been married and divorced, settled and unsettled in many cities and with several inappropriate people, married again and become parents once each. We're no longer rookies in this league. As we told our stories, and perhaps with more pleasure and wonder told our friend's stories, we started to laugh helplessly at the wild plotlessness of it all, at the futility of trying to find any moral or pattern that could help the next generation of adults find its way. It was the usual litany of betrayals, abandonments, poor choices, failures, disasters, drugs, lost children, religious conversions, 12-step programs—the usual needing, breeding, bleeding with no more pattern than you find in the average swarm of gnats.

Please show me the meaning, the grand design behind all this pain and confusion, in some formula that won't make me laugh out loud. From our sample alone, setting aside the rest of the human race, it would take an idiot to argue that the wicked had been punished or the just rewarded, or even that important lessons were concealed in this chaos. An earthquake reminds us that most of the order and meaning in human lives is a product that we can purchase for our comfort and protection, like window stripping or aluminum siding.

Vendors range from the most cynical religious charlatans and self-help gurus to the most serious scholars and artists. My favorite novelist delivered a lecture explaining how art consists of imposing artificial order on the raw, formless stuff of our experience. Then you don't really believe, a disillusioned admirer asked her, in the kind of ordered universe that most fiction seems to reveal?

"Of course not," the author replied. "But I get the same comfort from writing it that I hope you get from reading it."

Few artists or other merchants of meaning will offer you such candor, or appreciate it. Not even the ones with the bleakest visions. In "The Gambler, The Nun and The Radio," Ernest Hemingway proposes religion, marijuana, economics, music, sex, alcohol, gambling, ambition, radios and bread as "the opium of the poor" or "the opium of the people"; he never suggests that literature itself is the opium of the literate.

Fiction at its best brings order and sanity to events where none had been visible to the naked eye, an alchemy that intoxicates its addicts and eases their pain. This is a critical function that artists share with priests, psychiatrists, journalists, historians and the architects of human-centered philosophies. Together we form a kind of Ministry of Order that faces its greatest challenge after earthquakes and hurricanes. You wonder how people can live on the San Andreas Fault after experiencing a 7.1-power earthquake, whether it takes wonderful courage or vegetable stupidity. They stay there thanks to the special amnesiac qualities of the human mind, and thanks to the rapid psychic reconstruction that this Ministry of Order engineers.

Physical reconstruction, with the bulldozers and cement mixers, is much less dramatic than the psychic kind, when all the pattern peddlers play their parts. Psychiatrists and sociologists keep struggling to place serial murderers and the Central Park rapists in some plausible human context; political writers keep writing as if the invisible virtues of prefab candidate A and the half-concealed vices of prefab candidate B added up to something that might alter our lives; novelists keep writing as if Jeanette's suicide or Eric's execution carried some message that would make it easier for the survivors to carry on; sportswriters go back to "baseball history" as if Canseco's power, Henderson's speed and Stewart's split-fingered fastball were forces to be measured against significant forces of the universe. Kids build castles of sand.

We all go back to our work with a little less conviction, but with relief. This is what we do; it's just as necessary and much more urgent than picking up the trash. The chaos, the randomness at the bottom of things is everyone's enemy, and nothing that human beings manufacture is more important than our illusion of order and purpose. But sometimes it's just as important, when arrogance and smugness get out of hand, for an earthquake to remind us that the comfort we manufacture is the only comfort we have.

I

If This Is a Culture, Wash the Petri Dish

It flatters me to be called a cultural pathologist. It has a serious ring to it, a professional gravity "columnist" lacks. Maybe at one time a cultural pathologist who practiced in America needed to be a shrewd and learned diagnostician. Today his specialty is more closely related to the trauma unit or the emergency room. The national rash has begun to look like gangrene—a cinch to diagnose, grievously hard to cure.

Neil Postman, a distinguished pathologist, raises the serious possibility of culture death in our time.

If we lose this patient, it's because our best tools are useless against the new infections. Journalist Roger Rosenblatt declared that irony has been dead since 1954, which would condemn many of us as necrophiliacs. But irony, according to Henry James, depends for its effects on some "positive other case"—some enduring standard of decency and integrity with which most readers are familiar. The positive other case has almost vanished in this society that elevates Geraldo Rivera and Howard Stern to positions of wealth and influence.

Most essays are triggered by something that happens to us, or by something we read. This one resulted from a gradual buildup of pressure on my gag reflex. And the pressure is building again.

Secrets of the Cultural Elite

When a population becomes distracted by trivia, when cultural life is redefined as a perpetual round of entertainments, when serious public conversation becomes a form of baby-talk, when, in short, a people become an audience and their public business a vaudeville act, then a nation finds itself at risk; culture-death is a clear possibility.

— Neil Postman, *Amusing Ourselves to Death*

The death of a culture is a lot like the death of a tree. There's no heart-stopping moment when the line on the monitor goes flat. Each season there are more dead limbs. The foliage grows mangy, the bark turns dry and scaly, creatures burrow deep inside and eat away at the heart. The tree's profile changes, its roots contract. And then one spring there are no new leaves.

Tree surgeons make a science of identifying patients that are past saving, and putting them out of their misery before that final, silent spring. There are no physicians to minister to a dying culture. Just a thousand diagnosticians, each pointing to a different symptom that indicates the end is near.

Pat Robertson preaches that an epidemic of homosexuality will usher in the final days; it says so in the Bible. Me, I began to say my kaddish for the culture when the vice president attacked the audience and producers of a silly television program as America's "cultural elite"—and the nation laughed for the wrong reasons. Mr. Quayle drew the usual catcalls for being so fatally uncool, and the media began a straight-faced debate about the political influence of Hollywood "elitists."

No one suggested that the American cultural spectrum might still stretch for some distance on the highbrow side of Murphy Brown. Or that out there, on that road less traveled, there might still be lonely bands of snobs who find bladder surgery a less painful experience than a half-hour of staccato closeups and actors with harsh urban accents shouting pseudo-hip one-liners over a laugh track.

In the spirit of full disclosure, I confess that I am one of those haughty ultra-elitists who fails to find cultural nourishment on network television. At the risk of some kind of cultural excommunication, I further confess that I haven't watched a commercial TV program in 15 or 16 years. But I've seen 60-second samples of these contemporary comedies during commercial breaks in the Braves' games, flying blind with my remote control. I thought this one Quayle immortalized was awful—banal, brassy, false-hearted and infuriating with some kind of insider smugness that I'm too far outside to understand. If this program is the guilty pleasure of the cultural elite, we are lost.

If this is snobbery, make the most of it. I don't apologize for despising television, I survived a five-year hitch as a television critic and I feel, like a member of Vietnam Veterans Against the War, that I earned the right to my opinion. Snobs and highbrows are easy targets to hit, but the word "snob" takes on a different meaning during a period of cultural disintegration. A snob may be someone who remembers standards and aesthetic principles that previous generations took seriously.

If you believe you have any taste, any discernment in any area, nurture it. Wear it proudly. Share it with your children. Don't be obnoxious about your standards, but be stubborn, be strict. Keep the flame alive. When a culture is in danger of dying, snobs are its most precious natural resource.

It surprises and amuses me to find myself on the upscale side of the cultural Great Divide. Backcountry-bred and culturally disadvantaged as a boy, I became, defensively, a determined lowbrow of a type common to ballparks and sports bars. My taste in music, running to blues and bluegrass, is distinctly blue-collar. Even as a salaried critic of cultural events I took an Everyman position that one well-stuffed shirt described as "belligerently proletarian."

I established my ground and held it. But the cultural water table keeps dropping and I find, like many of my friends and role models, that the low ground we held is becoming an aerie. We are becoming mandarins by default. Anyone who reads above the 12th-grade level and avoids "Geraldo!" has joined the new "cultural elite."

The reading and writing skills of the high school class of 1991 were the poorest in the history of the SAT examinations. With educational standards in free fall, with students increasingly segregated as much by class and income as they ever were by race, with politicians scheming to abandon public education, it's hard to see where a cultural renaissance is going to begin. Yesterday's outrage is tomorrow's commonplace. There are TV commercials in American classrooms now, and the president of Yale University quit his job to work for the man who put them there.

Sixty percent of American households purchased no books in 1991—not a cookbook, not a sex manual, nada. Of the 40 percent who were up to the challenge of printed material, only a third were up to anything besides "popular fiction"—the stuff with women in torn dresses on the cover and castles burning in the background. Only two percent of the books Americans purchased were texts that a sneering elitist like me would acknowledge as "books"—literature, poetry, art, history, non-tabloid biography.

America's literary and intellectual talent is aiming its best efforts at a tiny, shrinking fragment of the population. The largest single bloc of these readers, ominously, is "over 65." An impressive performance for a serious book is 30,000 copies sold. Others do better. Self-serving celebrity rubbish can be a gold mine; Lee Iacocca's autobiography, at 2.6 million was the best-selling general interest hardcover in recent history. Toxic neo-fascist rubbish sells almost as well, if it's written in a breezy, accessible style. *The Way Things Ought to Be*, a tract by radio hate-peddler Rush Limbaugh, recently became the best-selling hardback in Pocket Books' history— 725,000 copies. Cormac McCarthy, widely regarded as the most gifted American novelist, had published five novels before his total sales hit 30,000.

Thomas Jefferson based all his hopes for democracy on universal literacy. How could he foresee a republic that would founder not with illiterates but with aliterates—an American majority that can read, but chooses not to? In this ebb tide of civilization, this general rout, how much sympathy can we spare for the orphaned readers of *The New Yorker*? An era ended this summer when the last high-brow magazine to maintain itself in the marketplace was bound over to *Vanity Fair*'s Tina Brown, the crowned queen of celebrity journalism (the perfect oxymoron if there ever was one).

It was like hearing that your grandmother was going to pose for

Playboy—"Girls of the AARP." I don't know how much harm Brown can do. Some of *The New Yorker*'s profiles have been so long and boring I was sure they were a mad editor's joke on his readers, and at times the magazine's taste in fiction—variations on *Franny and Zooey*—seemed 30 years out of date (they told a friend of mine that they'd love to publish her stories if she'd write about a better class of people). But now this quiet, tasteful reading room designed by William Shawn is being redecorated by an editor whose famous covers featured nude, obese and pregnant celebrities, in all combinations.

To an alien cultural observer like the ones we used to meet on "Star Trek," America presents an almost unbroken landscape of vulgarity, venality and violence. The Three V's should be stamped on our coins, along with a new variation on the national motto: *E Pluribus Nihil*. Count on an elitist to remember his Latin.

It's no simple matter to assign blame for this terminal state of affairs, but it's easy to see who profits from it. TV at its lowest, with its daytime talk shows ("Oprah": Women whose best friends had bigger breasts) and sex-game shows that mate lowing Middle Americans as if they were so many cows or pigs, is so outrageously vulgar that it defies satire, beggars indignation. It's like the grossest Monster Baby/Elvis Lives supermarket tabloid come to life. It courts the brain-dead for profit and makes no pretense about it. But it's the music industry, where adults seldom trespass, that truly gets away with murder.

Everyone knows that teenagers, half mad with high-test hormones in the best of times, are angry, confused, alienated and imperiled in these times of imploding families and vanishing value systems. Probably the first measure of decency among adults is whether we try to help these kids or try to make money from their predicament. By that measure, music industry executives are heinous, heartless Fagins who hide behind the First Amendment.

Tipper Gore may be one of the most misunderstood prophets of her time. If you thought her campaign against rock lyrics was ridiculous, you haven't read enough of the lyrics. Employing and manufacturing "artists" who are too old to respond to this gibberish themselves, the swine who run these recording companies sell murder, misogyny, anarchy, rough sex, racism and perversion to 14-year-old nihilists. Crack dealers probably do less harm. Not 10 percent of these rabid lyrics represents honest political or artistic expression.

With that outburst I guess I reveal conclusively that I am not "with it," or anywhere near it. I suppose it's possible for a person my age to remain with it, to balance on the cutting edge. But a revealing measure of a culture's health, it seems to me, is how much you want to be with it. I want to be so far out of it that I can't even smell it decomposing.

You know those old guys you see sitting in parks, or eating in places where old people eat alone? They wear silk bow ties and nice suits cut in antique styles, like extras in Frank Capra movies from the '40s. They look a little foreign; I imagine that they've read Primo Levi and know everything about Rilke and Rachmaninoff, and don't give a damn about anything that's happened since the Second World War.

I want to be just like those guys. And I don't want to wait until I'm 70. I want to start now.

*I knew the guy. Even if he's a national celebrity who belongs to every-
one, a murder charge against someone with whom you've shared a
Heineken is a shock to the nervous system. Whatever happens to O.J.,
the media will never recover.*

The Simpsons: Sophocles on CNN

The Day of the Locust. Someone mentioned it, one of the TV voices
narrating the arrest of O.J. Simpson. Nathanael West concluded
his prophetic 1939 novel with an apocalyptic Hollywood riot. I
knew the police sirens, searchlights and mobs of chanting, star-
stoned savages reminded me of something. And where else, in history or literature, was there ever anything like this?

I dug through the archives yesterday, looking for a photo of O.J.
and me that was taken years ago at a benefit for public television in
Buffalo. If I published that picture now, implying that we were
thick as thieves, I suppose some hostile bastard would write in saying "It figures."

Never mind. I'd be flattered, even now, if Simpson recognized
my name. That's the way we all felt about him. There was only one
celebrity in Buffalo, and its other public figures—politicians, disc
jockeys, TV news anchors, hockey goalies, symphony conductors,
columnists—were thrilled to share his air supply and careful not to
use too much.

Jock-sniffing, the uncritical worship of celebrated athletes, is a
vice too common among journalists, not to mention businessmen and college presidents. Nearly every man who ever tried to
play these games stands in awe of people who could play one like
Simpson played football. Middle-aged men with big brains and
expensive educations turn into 10-year-olds when O.J. or
Michael Jordan walks into the room. We can't seem to help ourselves. But if you never met this man Simpson, there's a lot you
can't understand.

If the media ever raised up a deity who was born for the part, that
god was O.J. Simpson. He had all the charm the law allows, and he
was always generous with it. He wasn't just handsome, he was the
most handsome; not just a great athlete, but the greatest. And sweet?
When he smiled he looked like an orphan meeting Santa Claus.

He was irresistible. One of O.J.'s old Buffalo teammates, quarterback Jack Kemp, is currently running for president. An election that pitted Kemp against O.J. would end about the same as a footrace. Simpson might have been the first black president, if he'd ever lowered his sights to such a mean ambition. Jack Kemp would be the first to admit it.

We miss the point if we insist on Simpson's mediocrity as an actor and sportscaster, as if he was nothing more than a fading jock plugging products and turning mean. The man had a great human gift, a rare gift for engaging and enlarging lesser mortals. In O.J.'s presence, race was irrelevant. No one could see black and white when he hit the switch on that blinding grin.

I speak in the past tense, because this is a light that has been extinguished. Whatever happens to O.J. now, everyone who ever envied him will pity him or hate him. It's the kind of tragic fall the ancients understood better than we do. In Plutarch, the legendary wisdom of Solon the Lawgiver is established by his warning to Croesus, richest of all kings, whom Solon refuses to recognize as the happiest of all men:

"Our wisdom forbids us to grow insolent upon our present enjoyments, or to admire any man's happiness that may yet, in the course of time, suffer change." (Croesus lost his throne, his cities and all his gold, and barely saved himself from burning alive by relaying Solon's wisdom to his conqueror, Cyrus the Great.)

After months of the most outrageously prejudicial publicity in the history of American justice, what do we know for sure? The verdict is still out on O.J. Simpson. But the verdict is in on the rest of us.

We are a culture without a compass, a macabre reprise of 1st-century Rome when "Saturday Night Live" meant live lions regurgitating pieces of Christian children. We've completed the free fall from a society with discrete, private, meaningful lives, bounded by self-respect, to a vicarious universe ruled by tabloid television. Celebrities wax, wane, strip, mate, marry, quarrel, divorce, slay, gain and lose weight, give each other prizes, write books, commit suicide, spew thoughtless rubbish and tirelessly present themselves, without shame or intelligible context. We loll in the gallery like cretins at a Punch-and-Judy, cheering, jeering, hooting or gasping as the action strikes us.

When the thing called celebrity touches what we used to call hard news—where there's an unavoidable crossover—the vulgarity and irresponsibility defy comprehension. TV producers scramble like starving vultures to tear off some small bloody piece of this tragedy—a witness or false witness, a bit player, a rumor, a lie, a red herring—and turn it to their own advantage in the Nielsen overnights.

As I understand it, the Simpson case is tried and retried every day on "Geraldo!," "A Current Affair" and "Inside Edition." On "A Current Affair," "newsman" Jim Ryan sat fondling entrenching tools and knives with serrated blades, just to get his audience into a throat-cutting frame of mind. It can't get worse, though I know full well it will. I understand why Simpson might try to kill himself, if indeed he murdered his wife; what I can't understand is why Geraldo Rivera doesn't try to kill himself. How can you get up and look in the mirror, know that you're Geraldo and you'll always be Geraldo, and live with it? It's a twisted kind of courage.

No celebrity accused of a major felony could get an unbiased trial on Mars. In the Simpson case, pre-trial strategy consisted of media leaks by the prosecution and a saturation talk-show schedule for the defense—which now includes Alan Dershowitz and F. Lee Bailey, the most egregious grandstanders and self-promoters in the American Bar Association. But it would be against any lawyer's nature to deny his client the vivid forum tabloid television provides.

The trial itself will ring up record ratings for cable television. Everyone's working an angle, and that includes the people who are trying to turn the Simpson case into a national referendum on domestic violence. (Why not turn *The Oresteia* into a seminar on dysfunctional families?) Half of them sound as if they've been waiting restlessly, ever since the Bobbitt case deflated, for a nice high-profile family murder on which to hitch a ride. With Nicole Simpson scarcely buried, one ghastly twit declared that the Simpsons could do the same thing for domestic violence that Clarence Thomas and Anita Hill did for sexual harassment.

That's what I call therapeutic myopia, the same vulgar tunnel vision that compels fools to come out generalizing about Rwanda. And most of the national media picked up the same line without a murmur of reservation.

What a wretched time we live in, when a story with all the size, gore, horror and pathos of classical tragedy—someone must have mentioned *Othello*—is reduced to syndromes and symptoms and dissected by social workers between commercial breaks.

Tragedy is particular and personal, never symptomatic. No one but the principals can ever tell you what goes on in a marriage. Who was less typical of anything than the Simpsons—a famous black sex symbol, role model and folk hero and his blond homecoming queen from Beverly Hills?

Somehow we've produced a population so centerless, individually and collectively, that it clusters a quarter-billion strong around each horror or scandal that seizes its attention. ("Fed on lynchings, murder, sex crimes, explosions, wrecks, love nests, fires, miracles," as Nathanael West describes the dispossessed in *The Day of the Locust*.) The feeding circle forms and each component group feeds on the situation according to its needs.

At the center of this feeding frenzy is O.J. Simpson. Is it possible that a sunny, sweet-natured public man like O.J., the most beloved and assimilated African-American this side of Bill Cosby, could have committed a double murder so savage that a veteran homicide cop turned white at the scene of the crime?

I'd be a poor choice for the jury. I've admitted that this guy could have sold me a used racehorse, or a beach property in South Dakota. In an interview with *Sports Illustrated* two years ago—headlined "It's OK to be O.J."—he admitted with characteristic modesty, "I don't consider myself an actor." But if he was always a latent psycho with the potential to kill people, then he was the best actor I've ever met, and I've met a lot of them.

I've got a snapshot memory of O.J. leaning over the net wearing a white headband and a mammoth grin, after winning a tennis game from my Uncle Jack with an awkward but thunderous overhead smash. If you read his "suicide" letter, you have to concede that it's as touching and human as it is contradictory and puzzling.

We don't know who he is. But after all these trials by talk show we can't help speculating about pathology. If he did it, was there something about his life that made it more likely that he would do it, as opposed to you or me? Apparently possessiveness and jealousy and obsession were part of his marriage from the start. But isn't the classic wife-beater a powerless, thwarted male who plays the brutal tyrant in his own home because he carries no weight anywhere else?

In Simpson's life, on the other hand, there must have been times when his power seemed unlimited. The roar of the crowd is a devastating narcotic. Imagine the highs this man has known. If your head swelled the first time you were hailed by a half-dozen small-town cheerleaders, imagine 100,000 people screaming your name.

It distorts your self-image. It distorts your sense of reality. Athletes of the first rank are rarely turned away at any of the gates the rest of us find difficult of access or closed entirely.

If you factor in the personal magnetism everyone acknowledges, you have an outrageous possibility—that no one had ever said no to O.J. Simpson. Was this atrocity the result when someone did? If that turns out to be the case, then O.J. is our baby, our natural child. He belongs to all of us, just as Geraldo and Dershowitz belong to us, and Tonya Harding and Mike Tyson. We made him possible. Do we deny him now?

In 10 years, nobody will understand these distinctions between authentic and manufactured experience, or even between genius and celebrity. But maybe a Burchfield painting like "Orion in Winter" will still have the power to stop us in our tracks.

Disney's America

The night they opened the Andy Warhol Museum in Pittsburgh—billed as the largest space ever devoted to a single artist—I was literally, symbolically and deliberately moving in the opposite direction. I was driving south through the Smoky Mountain rain to Chattanooga for a second look at a touring exhibition of the paintings of the late Charles Burchfield.

Burchfield, one of the great solitary geniuses of American art, died in 1967 when Warhol's fame was at its zenith. He was also honored with his own museum, a modest facility compared with Pittsburgh's new Palace of Pop. It's in Buffalo, New York. Burchfield and Warhol have nothing else in common. In Burchfield's centennial retrospective, "The Sacred Woods," the best of his watercolors are haunted, visionary landscapes that nothing but a prime Van Gogh can rival. If they catch you in the right mood, they can change forever the way you look at nature.

The best of Andy Warhol, of course, looks best silkscreened on a T-shirt, employing a process not much different, nor more difficult, than the process Warhol employed to produce the original. The force behind Burchfield's exhibition is the passion of people who love painting and believe religiously that Burchfield will one day achieve the reputation he deserves. The force behind Warhol's new museum is the same hype he exploited to create himself in the first place—now urgently mobilized by mortified critics who know they overpraised him and lemming collectors who paid the ridiculous prices he once commanded.

Of the few American artists whose names have become household words, Warhol was the closest thing to an outright hoax. Another art note last month was that a Chicago businessman had purchased two dozen paintings by the executed serial killer John Gacy, for the purpose of burning them all. A shame, because anyone with a spark of real curiosity would rather see him burn

Warhol's paintings and hang Gacy's in Pittsburgh.

Robert Hughes said it best, in his celebrated essay on Warhol in *The New York Review of Books*, in 1982:

"The working-class kid who had spent so many thousands of hours gazing into the blue, anesthetizing glare of the TV screen, like Narcissus into his pool, realized that the cultural moment of the mid-Sixties favored a walking void. Television was producing an affectless culture. Warhol set out to become one of its affectless heroes. . . . His silence became a Rorschach blot onto which critics who admired the idea of political art—but would not have been seen dead within a hundred paces of a realist painting—could project their expectations."

When he had dismissed the myth of Warhol's "art," Hughes moved on to the moral void that was exposed when the once-liberal Warhol, sniffing out imperial connections and fat commissions, became a sycophantic courtier to the Shah and Shahbanou of Iran and then to Nancy Reagan.

Hughes hammered home his contempt with such huge nails— Warhol was "the semi-official portraitist to the Peacock Throne" and "Bernini to Reagan's Urban VIII"—a more delicate reputation might have perished from its wounds. But satire is like a rare orchid in America, and celebrity is kudzu.

Celebrity (in Hughes' words): "The ruling passion of Warhol's career, the object of his fixated attention—the state of being well-known for well-knownness." Celebrity was Warhol's art, his only art, and it has not abandoned him. A dozen years after Hughes' apparent *coup de grace*, eight years after Warhol's death, his fame is still sufficient to launch a museum, dwarf any mild curiosity about the Burchfield show and completely upstage the National Gallery's current retrospective for Willem de Kooning, arguably America's greatest living painter.

It sounds almost precious, at this point, to complain that our largest museum for a single artist is dedicated to an artist who never really existed. It's like complaining that great writers starve while Robert James Waller sells his cheap tricks by the millions. Inauthenticity is the cultural heritage we leave our children. Andy Warhol was no painter, but he looks better and better as a prophet of our times. He could see the void opening when other cultural opportunists and horse traders were still kidding themselves about marching in the avant garde.

Warhol mocked and swindled them, and impudently accepted the adulation that was not his due. He never lied to them. When he said of his art, "There's nothing behind it," when he said, "It's so boring painting the same picture over and over," he was indulging himself in the delicious pleasure of telling the bald truth and letting the listener deceive himself.

Warhol's prediction of 15 minutes' fame for every living soul has become the central truth of the Age of Media. His contempt for the public that pampered him was summed up by an observation on the mass media and their consumers: "If it moves, they'll watch it."

It isn't among cultural institutions that the Andy Warhol Museum takes its place in society, but among celebrity monuments — Graceland, Dollywood, Twitty City. It's a tourist attraction. As tourists get harder to attract, harder to lure away from TV and computer screens and onto the actual asphalt highway, even the fine arts are learning that it's celebrity and publicity, not authenticity, that keep the turnstiles humming.

Restraints are few, and crumbling everywhere. Perhaps the most depressing tourist attraction ever proposed is the ersatz empire called Disney's America, a historical theme park the Disney juggernaut planned to build just three miles from the Manassas battlefield in Northern Virginia. If you know that beautiful rolling countryside—and if you ever viewed it from a stationary position in one of the 10-mile traffic jams that already torment motorists near the Washington beltway—you suspect that someone in Richmond had been bribed or gone insane.

What Disney World has done for Central Florida—about what General Sherman did for Georgia—Disney's America could do for Northern Virginia. The site is surrounded by a dozen *actual* Civil War battlefields, and Virginia is the most history-haunted state I ever lived in. From those facts I calculated that the Disney obscenity would be built over the dead bodies of every unreconstructed Confederate in the Old Dominion—a possible voting majority. But Virginia's governor welcomed Disney with open arms, and its legislature set aside $163 million to help Mickey and the gang turn the Civil War into pony rides and video arcades.

Most of the organized resistance came from a fighting rear guard of 30 historians led by the illustrious Shelby Foote, who charged that Disney will do to history "what they have already done to the animal kingdom—sentimentalize it out of recognition."

The historians were not expected to prevail. The Disneyfication of America, inauthenticity's Final Solution, rolls over history, art, literature, science and nature like a bulldozer over wildflowers.

Theme parks always bewildered me. Why captive animals, mechanical animals and cartoon animals when real, wild animals are still available? In Rocky Mountain National Park a couple of years ago, I sat all afternoon in the center of a herd of elk, as comfortable as Adam in Eden. When you choose Disney World for your children's vacation instead of the Grand Tetons, the Great Smokies or the Outer Banks, it seems to me that you risk marking them for life with a certain kind of inferiority—a weakness for fakery they may not overcome.

An increasing, alarming number of intelligent people seem deaf to the kind of argument I'm trying to make. Deaf, in other words, to the distinction between authentic and manufactured experience. When I say that I see no virtue in virtual reality until we've exhausted actual reality, they respond as if I'm trying to deliver some kind of Luddite *bon mot*. But I'm serious. I read in a literate computer column about little truck stops on the information highway called gopher holes, where some hacker has created imaginary villages and landscapes. Fine, I thought, but who has time for this stuff when there are so many actual villages and landscapes we'll never see?

I'm incorrigible this way. I was in the hospital last week, and lying there in bed I couldn't help thinking that television was a wonderful invention for invalids, shut-ins and the very old—and totally irrelevant, or worse, for everyone else. You don't have to watch soap opera for five minutes (and it's all soap opera, "LA Law" and the rest) to see what's going on. This is not entertainment. This is an artificial alternative to having a life. This is a crude emotional prosthesis.

Who will stand up for the real thing? Historians may never outflank Disney, and Burchfield's museum will never attract as many customers as Warhol's. But the fight is a good fight, and its rallying cry was written years ago by Shelby Foote's best friend, the late Walker Percy.

"In such a time as this, a time of pollution and corruption of meaning," Percy wrote, "it is no wonder that the posture the novelist often finds natural is that of derision, mockery, subversion and assault—to assault the benumbed sensibility of the poor media consumer because anything other than assault and satire can only be understood as a confirmation of the current corrupted meaning of such honorable old words as love, truth, beauty, life. . . . There may be times when the greatest service a novelist can do his fellow man is to follow General Patton's injunction: Attack, attack, attack. Attack the fake in the name of the real."

The gauntlet is down. Don't be tempted to dismiss these battles as cultural catfights pitting educated elitists against the poor tube-tortured proletarians. A human life is what a human being experiences and remembers. If everything you experience and remember is a third-hand, third-rate product concocted by hucksters reaching for your wallet, you've been cheated of your birthright. You aren't living half the life you deserve.

I know she wins a battle every time one of us writes about her. But what pathologist can resist a walking social disease? This greedy little hooker is the first celebrity whose identity is determined solely by audience response, calculated hourly. Among those who insist on taking her seriously—or sexually—you will find the most gullible individuals in the world.

The Trojan Whore

Obviously, she's an orphan, or a foundling. She wouldn't do this to her mama. That's one of the generous things I think when I think about Madonna, and the most miserable thing about living in America is that you can't help thinking about Madonna, at least fleetingly, at least once a week.

If there's a mother hiding somewhere, looking for a reason to live, Madonna has published the book that will kill her. God rest your soul, Mrs. Ciccone. All of us who have daughters will experience *Sex*, a runaway bestseller, as a cautionary tale. What cruelty, what repression, what iron Victorian code, what phalanx of severe nuns, what combination of psychological train wrecks could produce a 34-year-old woman who could produce a book like this one?

No, of course I didn't buy it. Anyone who buys it should be ashamed of himself, when $50 will keep 10 Somalians alive for a week. My daughter, who has connections, borrowed a copy for me so I could write this without being accused of guesswork and groundless overreaction. She brought it to me in the equivalent of a brown-paper wrapper, and we opened it and briefly discussed its contents. I should add that my daughter is not exactly a chip off the old block when it comes to cultural assumptions. She has been known to defend Madonna.

"What do you think?" I asked her, running my thumb over a page of lurid, grainy photographs that will one day find their niche as postcards in Tijuana.

"This is really disgusting," she said, and I nodded my agreement. (A woman psychologist in Raleigh said, "Madonna's trying to shock people by conveying that women can misuse power like men have stereotypically.")

"How about the—uh—text?" I pursued.

"She sounds like a really stupid, horny 14-year-old," said my daughter, who's about halfway to a B. A. in psychology.

That's what I love about my daughter, her unfailing generosity. This was, I think, the first time that she and I ever formed a cultural consensus.

The photography by fashion specialist Steven Meisel is derivative and forgettable—it unintentionally captures the musty-sweat-sock flavor of one of those soiled magazines you might see poking out of a booth in a 42nd Street peep-show arcade. Madonna's erotic imagination, undeniably active, doesn't seem especially creative. Maybe we could blame this on Warner Books, those prudes, who refused to run photographs of Madonna having sex with children, animals (they hedged here) or religious ornaments. Santa Claus, his elves and his reindeer will have to wait for *Sex, Volume Two*. The tough question is, what audience is Warner trying to reach with this material? Whose fantasies, besides Madonna's, does a book like this service?

Your run-of-the-mill heterosexual male is definitely out of the loop here, though many of them are too gullible and media-managed to understand it. This is not a boy-girl thing. Though some men will pay to see almost any woman undressed, who would pay a premium to see Madonna? I rate this woman just on the high side of homely. "Rather plain-looking" was a wire-service reporter's chivalrous assessment. She's in great physical condition—admirers always mention her devotion to aerobics—but so are Mary Lou Retton and Martina Navratilova, and their agents aren't fielding any offers from *Penthouse*. In the world of commerce, sex is all sizzle and no steak. All pizzazz. You're as sexy as you insist on being. And Madonna literally exploded onto the scene, 10 years ago, grabbing her crotch on stage at the Paradise Garage.

Granted, beauty is in the eye of the beholder. My taste runs to Claire Bloom in her first bloom. But even now, with Claire pushing 62, I'd rather watch Claire Bloom water her delphiniums than watch Madonna . . . well, never mind.

An erotic fantasy? How about a Yeats scholar in a demure wool dress, whispering something mildly suggestive in my ear as we pass on the library steps? That's my idea of meltdown. The exact opposite effect would be achieved—as Madonna must know—by a gum-chewing amazon in an iron brassiere making a grab for my zipper.

With her clothes on, Madonna reminds me of the tough, chain-smoking older sister who used to stand in the back of Larry's on 11th Street, heating the calzone. If you've ever fantasized about the calzone cook naked, sweating back there by the ovens, *Sex* is the book you've been looking for.

I don't claim to represent the sexual mainstream, but I claim to be closer to the mainstream than the boys who will be "reading" this book behind locked doors. It comes down to the question of what sex is, or at its best ought to be. Eroticism comes from the tension between the primal and the public self, between our animal natures and our civilized veneer. We take the public stuff off together, along with our clothes, and the shock of this intimacy is the great mystery of sex. An erotic relationship is based on the complicity of lovers who know that other shocking possibility in each other.

Without mystery, without modesty, without delicacy, we're the same as farm animals. The same, to put it bluntly, as Madonna. She must have paid a personal price, sexually, for the kind of notoriety she enjoys. Whatever she's lost, she hopes we'll lose it too. She knows she's an enemy of sex. The latest incarnation of Madonna—Eros '92—represents sex as war, sex as guerrilla theater, sex as felonious assault. No doubt Madonna, at least in person, could create a regular epidemic of impotence.

Is that good? Someone must think so. For heterosexuals Madonna is the poisoned candy, she's the Trojan Whore.

If this is a sex goddess, Ross Perot is a populist. I think of Madonna as Roboslut, an alien programmed to conquer the earth by attacking our reproductive psychology. Her greatest support comes from gay and feminist factions and from academics, who love to write books like the upcoming *The Madonna Connection: Representational Politics, Subcultural Identities and Cultural Theory* (Westview Press) and say things like "I really think that what Madonna's been trying to promote is a different worldview."

This rooting section turns its back on some serious contradictions. There will always be feminists to admire a woman who uses men like cigarettes. They salute Madonna for doing exactly what she pleases in a world dominated by men—but she has enough money to build a university and *this*, this book, is what she pleases. Dropping your knickers and your self-respect in exchange for money or power is a strategy many women have tried before. No one called them feminists.

As I understand it, she courts the gay community with codes and symbols that only homosexuals comprehend. But doesn't an act like hers lend credence to that homophobe chestnut, "It isn't what they do that bothers me, it's the way they carry on about it"? This is hardly sex in proportion, sex in its proper place. As for the pop academics, their gibberish has reached a point where they mostly deserve our sympathy. No doubt Madonna's material makes for more exciting research than Edith Wharton's letters to her aunt.

Another grim possibility is that I'm just as gullible as these academics, making much of an over-exposed exhibitionist and reading motives into a mind where there's nothing at all except Blond Ambition. This may be just another American entrepreneur like Mike Milken or Donald Trump. When you've found an easy way to make a lot of money, like selling junk bonds or showing your tush, it's hard to know when to quit.

Let's say that Madonna develops a product and puts it on the shelves. If it moves, she makes more of it. That's the American way. And that takes the moral onus off this nasty Catholic school-girl and puts it back on the rest of us, where it probably belongs. The bestseller list must be one measure of a nation's taste, its cultural vitality, its moral fiber. At the moment, the two hottest properties in publishing are *Sex* and *The Way Things Ought to Be*, by Rush Limbaugh.

Opposite ends of the cultural spectrum? More like two dramatic symptoms of the same disease. Prurience and prejudice are a knock-out combination at the cash register, even when the public has seen the same buttocks and heard the same buncombe a thousand times before.

My theory is that these books would sell just as well if their formats were reversed—if one of them offered Madonna's foreign policy and economic programs, and the other offered a 300-pound rightwinger dirty-dancing in a teddy or hanging naked from the ceiling in chains. Both authors got rich and famous for being preposterous, which means literally, in Latin, "with the hindside in front." Why shouldn't they sell it both ways?

Everybody's heard it—you see one, you've seen them all. But up until now, who had seen enough of them to be sure?

When Privates Go Public

You can go broke betting that the mass media have bottomed out. There's no natural law, no theoretical bungee cord to save a media culture in free fall. We can only watch in wonder as it plummets, giggling, to unimaginable depths. December's outrage is January's cliche. Standards that took 100 years to establish themselves have been eradicated in a matter of months.

It's a time of despair for journalists, a time of challenge for social historians and cultural anthropologists. No one can predict the outcome. The real game is to fix the point where it all turned around—the point where America had matured as much as it could with the materials at hand, and suddenly reversed itself and raced headlong back through simpering adolescence and gibbering infancy toward the silence of the womb.

That's one way to introduce the Bobbitts of Virginia, the Samson and Delilah of our tabloid twilight, the couple that stole the word "penis" from Dr. Ruth and put it on CNN. If I still feel a twinge of discomfort when I type the word, excuse my age. No one outside the medical profession ever used this word until I was over 40 (in private most of us lapsed into the vernacular, where other words prevailed).

The Bobbitt story, a grisly footnote to the gender wars, ought to have been one of those eight-line curiosities—quints in Tunisia, salmonella in Terre Haute—that the night wire editor stacks in a column on page six. But its timing was perfect, for the Bobbitts. Whatever they've suffered, their futures are bright. Books and TV movies will keep them visible for years and financially secure for any reasonable lifetime. This is a nation where the most certain path to wealth is to do anything ostentatiously dreadful that doesn't take you to the gas chamber.

An atrocity that took a fraction of a second to perform receives more coverage than Bosnia, Somalia and health-care reform combined. None of the traditional mandarins of the media had the courage or good taste to ignore it. *The New Yorker* commissioned a profile of Lorena Bobbitt—a manicurist—by Gay Talese, God help us all. Imagine 20,000 words, in pokerfaced Talese, on a woman who tossed a severed penis out the window of her car. The *Washington Post*, scrambling for an interview with Mrs. Bobbitt, was aghast to discover that she'd negotiated exclusive rights with one of its own reporters who was moonlighting for *Vanity Fair*.

The laughter, the taunting and the traffic in sick comedy have been inexcusable, and the women I respect the most are the ones who acknowledged that first. If the victim had been a mutilated woman—even a woman as unappetizing as John Bobbitt—scarcely a man in this country would have been gross enough to laugh at her. Even Howard Stern and Andrew Dice Clay would have held their tongues.

Any woman who's still laughing, well, she scares me. If you hate men that much, don't pretend to tolerate us anymore. We respect your rage, but please keep your distance.

Most of us didn't suspect that much anger. But I'm not sure it's female anger, morbid curiosity or even the deep Freudian undertow that keeps the Bobbitt case in the spotlight.

Maybe it's just the penis.

"Penility is in," wrote art critic Paul Richard, reviewing a show in Washington that included 100 images of the male sex organ.

If we're regressing back through every phase that precedes maturity, we must be fixated in that self-fondling, unfocused masturbatory phase when your own equipment is the center of your universe. Or maybe a bored nation turns to its genitals during the last stages of culture death, when people actually complain that there's nothing on TV. We've all experienced those moments when there's no one to talk to, nothing to read, nothing much to do or look at. Sometimes Mother Nature, in a playful mood, will remind us that we were born with a home entertainment center that requires no cassettes.

One way or the other, we find ourselves in a New Age kindergarten where teacher never says no, never says "Put that away" or "Cover that up." Indecent exposure has become a career strategy. In a society where wealth confers status, our children get weird messages. Two of America's most spectacularly wealthy entertainers have had their sex organs photographed—Madonna for soft-porno street sales, Michael Jackson by the police, to compare with the descriptions of children who accuse him of sexual abuse. Howard Stern earns over a million a month for saying the same things on the radio that horny 12-year-olds say to each other while they're shooting baskets.

On "NYPD Blue," a popular TV cop show, the standard contract compels cast members of both sexes to remove their pants on command. "Blue" offers a Tush of the Week surprise to feed America's passion for naked cops.

TV has regressed almost to the diaper phase of sexual incontinence. On *one* quick channel scan a few weeks ago, I saw a "Donahue" promo for "Sex at the Office" (with a secretary disrobing), Morton Downey teasing hardcore porn star Porsche Lynn (who kept her dignity), a network affiliate investigating "Sexercise" on its "Eyewitness News," and a promo for an "Eye-to-Eye" show on men who work for lecherous women, with CBS anchorwoman Connie Chung.

Even worse, though no actual sex organs appear on camera, are the pitiful sexual confessions that run all day long on the geek shows with Phil and Oprah and their legion of imitators. Are we supposed to feel sorry for a North Carolina schoolteacher who might be fired for describing his extramarital affairs (his wife's idea of marriage counseling) on "The Montel Williams Show," in a wig and false mustache?

I say sack the fool. Not for his morals—who wouldn't be tempted to cheat on a wife who watches Montel Williams?—but for his crimes against human dignity.

These aren't moral issues. Someone else's sexuality, as long as it involves consenting adults, is someone else's business. In a culture that can't keep its drawers up, the real casualty is dignity.

Dignity is the main thing that separates people from gibbons. It's the thing no one can starve or beat out of you. You can only sell it or give it away. A naked slave in chains can carry himself with more dignity than a teacher in a wig on "The Montel Williams Show."

It isn't nakedness that robs you of your dignity. Look at the ancient Greeks, or the Bushmen of the Kalahari. It's your attitude toward your nakedness, and the nakedness of others. Maybe the best measure of a society's sexual dignity is commercial. Where voyeurism and prurience are big business, expect an adolescent population that smirks and hoots and hollers every time a zipper comes down.

I'd enjoy a debate on the subject of modesty—whether it's an essential component of human dignity, or a separate virtue. I'm conservative, but I think the question's open. Nudists have always perplexed me. Solitary nudism seems normal and desirable. But the group varieties always struck me as cultish and forced, and sort of aggressively eccentric.

But the one thing you can say for the nudists, they sure take the humor out of sex organs. The second time through, a nudist magazine is like a seed catalog. The silliness is over—and so is the thrill.

In a culture of exhibitionists and peeping toms, dignity goes first and eroticism soon after. Adults who live in an infantile society, where nothing is private, struggle to preserve their private fantasies. Eroticism was so much easier for the Victorians.

In the gallery of 100 phalli, the art critic Paul Richard learned the lesson of the nudist camps:

"Long before one leaves this show," he wrote, "penises begin to look as interesting as earlobes."

It isn't just penises. Watching Robert Altman's film *Short Cuts*, I was unsophisticated enough to register some shock when the buck-naked Julianne Moore, exposed from the navel down, delivers a three-minute speech to an unflinching camera.

It's a strange experience for those of us who grew up in another era. Here, in living color, was the sexual ornament of a beautiful actress that I would once have paid dearly to see in a grainy black-and-white snapshot. It seized my middle-aged attention. But sure enough, in two minutes, it might as well have been her earlobe.

I'd like to think that Altman, a filmmaker I admire, was making a snide comment about voyeurism. Probably he was just trying to sell some tickets. But the experiment was devastating.

It will take a real anthropologist, a 21st-century Margaret Mead, to tell the story of a society that destroyed the only mystery worth preserving—the erotic, romantic sexuality that's the best thing life offers most of us.

It isn't for kids. Media that treat us like children seem to be turning us into children. When we can't call these things our "privates" anymore, we've robbed them of their power. We may as well leave the future of the race to the test tubes and turkey basters.

This piece became a great disappointment to me. It's essentially pro-Cobain, or at least pro-tolerance. I wrote it hoping to bridge a generation gap. I didn't set out to make nasty points about the attention spans or reading skills of grunge-rock fans. I made those points in spite of myself, when angry letters from young people proved that most of them read only the first six paragraphs, or missed the point entirely.

The Beautiful and Damned

The suicide of a rock musician named Kurt Cobain meant a little less than nothing to me. When I read in some magazine that his death was getting "the JFK treatment" on MTV, I probably stooped to one of those contemptuous snorts that cynics of colliding generations use to condescend to each other.

It goes without saying that I didn't relate to his music, what little I'd heard. More to the point, I don't relate to junkies. When I was Cobain's age—27—I knew a lot of druggies who abused their brains, but back then most of us were pretty squeamish about our bodies. Needle addiction horrifies me. I suppose it seems tame, at least in the beginning, to kids who think tattoos and body-piercing are a part of growing up—a little strategic self-mutilation lets Mom and Dad know that curfews and family picnics are history.

Maybe my first reaction was closer to disgust than compassion. From my point of view, this was a boy who made megamillions whining about the soullessness of a mercenary society. And at an age most of us would kill to regain for an hour, all he could buy with his money was a one-way ride on what Joan Baez, in a dirge for Janis Joplin, called "the mainline rail."

So what do you expect from a paleolithic fossil who quotes Joan Baez albums? People who remember the Depression, the Second World War, Vietnam and 40 years of playing "chicken" with H-bombs—people whose friends are recovering from mastectomies and multiple bypasses—have a hard time sympathizing with the crushing angst of Generation X.

Somebody informed me quite earnestly that Cobain's was the first generation of Americans who can't expect as much affluence as their parents. My tears failed to flow. As I recall the '60s, a lot of us made a political decision to lower our economic expectations.

Some of us succeeded, too.

There may be a yawning perception gap here. There's a whopping distaste factor, too—a trash factor. Cobain's wife Courtney Love, another junkie who fronts for a rock band with the lyrical name of Hole, was booked for heroin possession the day before he shot himself. Her public farewell to her husband was incoherent and toilet-mouthed. Worst of all, there's a baby girl 19 months old who will be turned over to an agency if her mother is convicted.

Luckily, I'm not so old that my prejudices are harder than my arteries. I was having mean, ungenerous reactions to this MTV death; at the same time I was reading Jeffrey Meyers' new biography of Scott Fitzgerald.

I've made more difficult connections. This one jumped right at me. Their ages, the premature success and adulation, the addiction and self-destruction, the mental breakdowns and suicide attempts, the identification with the *zeitgeist* of a wounded generation. Even the two little girls with the same name—Frances—dragged along in their parents' chaotic wakes.

If Scott and Zelda Fitzgerald were the doomed darlings of the Jazz Age, Kurt and Courtney are a kind of shock-theater parody set in the Grunge Age. But they're kids, not cartoons. I can't dismiss their pain because they treated it with a habit that makes me sick.

Fitzgerald and Cobain both climbed the charts at the age of 24, Fitzgerald with *This Side of Paradise* and Cobain with a band called Nirvana. In those days before MTV, more young people read novels. Both artists traded on disillusionment. Fitzgerald spoke to, and for, the Lost Generation of young Americans who believed that civilization could never recover from Verdun. According to journalists and publicists, Kurt Cobain was the spokesman for another embittered generation. The Bust Generation might have called itself the Lost Generation if no one had reminded them that the name was taken.

Two doomed, sensitive young men with their wild and crazy ladies. It's an understatement to say that they both dealt badly with their fame. They were insecure exhibitionists and hopeless addicts. Cobain's poison was heroin, Fitzgerald's was alcohol.

Grunge-rock fans probably laugh at the idea that people in their great-grandparents' generation could raise any serious hell. How many Jazz Age survivors remain to tell the tale? But Scott Fitzgerald, in a candid letter to one of his Princeton professors, sounds more like Axl Rose than Edmund Wilson.

"For me," he wrote, "outside interests generally mean women, liquor or some form of exhibitionism."

Scott and Zelda committed adultery, popped pills, exposed their private parts, lived in a haze of hangovers and invented varieties of disreputable behavior that young Americans have been imitating ever since. Kurt Cobain would have no problem understanding Zelda, explaining to a friend why she drank: "Because the world is chaos and when I drink I'm chaotic."

The Fitzgeralds and the characters in their fiction were role models for several generations, mine included. I did the Doomed Sensitive Young Man to the best of my abilities—reckless drinking, notions of picturesque suffering and plenty of self-absorbed, self-destructive theatrics.

So did a lot of others, men and women. We ought to be honest enough to acknowledge that the differences between Cobain and Fitzgerald—between Cobain and ourselves—were differences more of style than of substance. Style and, of course, class. Scott went to Princeton, he favored tuxedos and white suits, he dumped his daughter with English nannies instead of unemployed musicians. Cobain with his needles, his guns, his ragged fans and his rude, sad lyrics seems to come from way off on the other side of the tracks. But it's mostly the world that has changed, not the kind of young person who wins all its prizes and chokes on them.

Why is it so hard for the middle-aged to be generous about Kurt Cobain? Part of it is the parental frustration of The Catcher in the Rye who has missed another one. Each generation of kids seems paralyzed when its culture heroes self-destruct. But at our age we've seen so many promising lives swept over this same Niagara that we can't understand why they never read the 50-foot sign that reads "Danger: Cataract Ahead." How big does the sign have to be?

But a bigger part of it is the age-old problem of communication between individuals at different stages of their lives. Successful communication depends on mutual respect, and it requires a lot of character to take young people seriously when they treat us as if Alzheimer's strikes at 35.

Each generation rebels the same way, and part of the rebellion is refusing to believe that the previous generation was ever young—that it was ever anything but gray and cautious and boring.

We *are* gray and cautious and boring, even boring to ourselves sometimes, because we learned long ago that you can only take so many risks and expect to survive. But we remember everything—especially those of us in the middle. A lot of the adults who were offended by my wild beard, faded overalls and radical opinions on the Vietnam war are still alive, and maybe still offended. But now I have a daughter in Generation X, with a pierced nose and a tattoo.

It's hard not to grin when young people find cosmic revelation in trivial insights we filed away 20 years ago. It's hard not to scream when they wound themselves making the same mistakes we made in 1965, and described to them in detail.

It's really hard to bend over backwards to understand someone who assumes that you're rigid and stupid. But if you don't try, you prove you're rigid and stupid. I was dumbfounded by a journalist who kept comparing Kurt Cobain to John Lennon, and then quoted some of his favorite lyrics by Cobain: "And I forget just why I taste/ Oh yeah, I guess it makes me smile/ I found it hard, it was hard to find/ Oh well, whatever, never mind."

To me, of course, those lines are an insult to John Lennon, and a comment on the steady decline of SAT scores in America. But I called a friend who runs a record company, and asked him if these lyrics were deliberately coded to confuse the enemy—in this case, me.

He patiently explained that most of the rock songs Cobain wrote depend on the music and the emotive qualities of the singer's voice; the lyrics can't be separated from their musical context without losing a lot of their punch. I listened to *Nevermind* and I think I get it. You certainly know what each song is about, if you pay attention. It's something like the experience of nonrepresentational art.

My friend in the music business, who's only a few years older than the deceased, rates Cobain "at the top of the heap" for his generation, a genuine original who managed to maintain artistic control in spite of his personal torments. Cobain, he says, was never a punk nihilist, but an individual with a social conscience and causes he believed in.

That would make Cobain a better citizen than the apolitical Fitzgerald, whose sadness never attached itself to anything too specific. All these labels like grunge, slacker, punk—even junkie—may be pretty useless when it comes to bringing an actual human being into focus.

We need to keep listening to each other's music, even if it doesn't make much sense at first. I concede that the kids who believed in Nirvana have suffered a lot of emotional damage from disintegrating families and absent parents, and the cumulative effect of cradle-to-grave television may be too awful to contemplate.

But I still think the experience of each generation, as it tries to establish and define itself, is much the same—or more the same than different. There's always the sleaziness, the cheap, nasty, venal, predatory quality of life as we find it, what Fitzgerald called "the foul dust" that floated in the wake of Jay Gatsby's dreams. Survival means learning to hate what's hateful, and not to hate yourself. Some of the best, in 1920 or 1994, fail to learn and end up falling on their swords.

II

The Media — Distemper Decimates the Watchdogs

It's late in the game when the network elephants like Dan Rather, Ted Koppel and Tom Brokaw go around sounding the alarm, warning graduating classes that journalism is no longer an honorable profession. Then Dan goes back and sits down next to Connie Chung. He hopes you'll remember that he was a real reporter once, and he hopes history will be kinder to his memory if he confesses now.

Adam Gopnik characterizes the fashionable style in journalism as "abstract aggression divorced from any real wisdom or any real moral experience." Between gratuitous aggression and celebrity-fawning there's a shrinking middle ground. Here in what was once the world's most fertile media environment, a toxic wasteland spreads as far as the eye can see. The contamination has occurred so rapidly that definitive postmortems for the free press have yet to be written.

What happened? Economics, for one thing—a monopoly of megacorporations eliminated wildcat independents and placed 70 percent of America's information flow at the mercy of two dozen imperial CEOs. But it was a general decline in literacy, the legacy of failing schools and universal television, that made the pander's path too easy and lucrative to resist. Supermarket tabloids have always done it—fed a passive audience of subliterates from a limited menu of its favorite junk foods. Fat profits, low overhead. "Why not us?" the mainstream media asked themselves. O.J. and the Bobbits lured them past the point of no return. What will replace journalism? In the 21st century who will remember that there were heroes in our lost profession, and sages too?

*After a thorough initiation in the heart of the establishment, I took up
"alternative" journalism when I was almost too old to appreciate some of
its eccentricities. But it was the best decision I ever made, next to marrying my second wife. This piece isn't meant to be self-righteous, but to
illustrate some of the gross discrepancies, in the contemporary media,
between resources and achievement.*

In the Rearview Mirror

Ten years doesn't sound like much anymore. I'll bet I've seen ten
years go by on a single bottle of vermouth. But it's a long time in
the life of a publication—it covers the entire lifespan, or at least
the useful lifespan, of most. Celebrating the tenth anniversary of
this unique experiment we call *The Independent*, immortalized by
the Republican right as "left-wing attack media from hell," it's natural for the publisher to roust out the most venerable specimen on
the premises and ask him to provide historical perspective.

Can I finish my coffee first? I feel like Punxsutawney Phil,
snatched from the back of that warm burrow in Pennsylvania,
blinded by the lights and cameras and obliged to prophesy on an
empty stomach. Our methods are about equally scientific. I have a
better record, I think, but Phil has a better agent and better teeth.

In 1983 I had my original hair in its original color, and arthritis
was just a word our parents used. I looked better then, I could run
faster. But I didn't feel so good. Nineteen eighty-three was a year of
the Reagan recession, when 3,000 people queued in a parking lot
in 20-degree weather to apply for 100 apprenticeships in a Pennsylvania refinery. It was the year Ed Meese, a fat crook stuffing himself
at the public trough, said that he'd never seen a hungry child in
America.

It was the year Interior Secretary James Watt, whom I had
immortalized as "this mental, physical and moral Caliban, this
piece of genetic rubbish," finally lost his job for making fun of disabled veterans at a businessman's breakfast. (Let us never forget
Reagan appointee Eileen Gardner, special assistant to the Secretary
of Education, who was forced to resign because of a paper on the
handicapped she had written for the Heritage Foundation "think
tank": "They falsely assume that the lottery of life has penalized

them at random," philosophized Frau Gardner. "This is not so. Nothing comes to an individual that he has not, at some point in his development, summoned.")

It was the year my father died, suddenly. Maybe I was in no mood to humor these gargoyles of the victorious Right. One of my columns about Reaganism bore the headline, "Springtime for Hitler."

When I think of 1983 and all the hideous hungry things that had already come twisting, chewing and clawing their way out of the national woodwork, it doesn't seem possible that the ones who summoned them to feed—a party with no plan but plunder—could have won two more presidential landslides. In 1983 the United States was entering a decade of dismal reaction, gross selfishness and self-deception and unprecedented public and private dishonesty. It was a decade in which we lost so much blood, so much of our moral and material capital, that there may be no treatment for the national anemia. I don't anticipate a quick recovery. I've just about been able to convince myself that the bleeding has stopped.

I wish I could believe that this decade of embarrassment has been a decade of hard lessons well learned. But most Americans, with the permafrost brains of the Cold War, were ready to spend our last nickel to destroy the Soviet Union, right up to the day it disappeared. Offered a new enemy, any enemy at all, they emptied their pockets again on cue, no questions.

What happened in Grenada, Panama, Kuwait? New weapons were tested, defense contracts were justified, gross policy mistakes and deceptions were erased by brute force; approval polls were boosted, domestic disaster was expelled from the evening news, hapless locals were slaughtered. History will remember Desert Storm as the first war where "friendly fire" killed more Americans than the enemy—and as the war where the press was reduced to a camel caravan of docile ruminants, bearing heavy loads of propaganda across the desert waste.

It's what happening to my own business that hurts me the most. In a technical sense the whole profession has been revolutionized. In 1983 the tool of my trade was an old Royal manual that already had seen 20 years of service. In 1987 they sneaked a computer terminal into my office overnight, but I made them tear it out. Today I sit, rebellion crushed, wearing out the "Delete" key on a Compaq laptop.

CNN and the satellite system bring us live images from any-where on the planet, cable and minicam technologies offer electronic journalists an arsenal of options that were only experimental in 1983. I could go on, but that stuff bores me. The point is that high-tech hasn't brought us happiness or higher levels of achievement.

It certainly hasn't brought us respect. In polls that ask "Who do you trust?" the free press ranks dead last among traditional American institutions. In one poll journalism emerged as the second most despised profession in America—only Congressmen were considered lower forms of life. The majority seems to hate us even more for our best work, which threatens its illusions, than for the sleazy work we produce too often when we try to pander to its tastes.

In 1993, only 28 percent of adults under 35 read newspapers. It was 67 percent as recently as 1965. There's a general perception that journalists have reached a crossroads, and that none of the options look too promising. The dean of the Columbia School of Journalism, Joan Konner, writes in a letter to the school's alumni, "There is a mindless mechanism at work in the business as a whole. News is made up of habit, competition, and lack of individual power."

I could have told the dean that it's also made up of purposeful handouts from public relations specialists, who now outnumber professional journalists 150,000 to 130,000 and provide at least 40 percent of all the information we perceive as news.

It looks like a losing battle. In their powerful new alliance with politicians, the elite "spin doctors" of public relations have all but stripped the press of the interpretive function that was its most significant contribution to popular democracy.

"Ross Perot changed the system," writes PR guru Bob Dilenschneider, former president of the notorious Hill and Knowlton influence factory. "He went above the media. He's created a totally new system for communicating."

Perot's success was not lost on President Clinton, whose doctors are developing new techniques for bypassing the press corps and presenting his spin-crafted messages undiluted by interpretation. After the flogging they gave him during the primaries, it's kind of hard to blame Clinton for getting even with the media. But the trend is ominous.

Thanks to NBC News, this perception that the press is superfluous has been compounded by the impression that we're outright charlatans. The rigged truck explosion on "Dateline NBC" was the first scandal that ever got a network news president fired almost overnight. But the biggest joke of all was the shock and outrage expressed by his boss, NBC president Robert Wright. According to TV historian Ken Auletta, it was Wright, shortly after he arrived at NBC from General Electric, who suggested that network stars like Bill Cosby and Don Johnson should be drafted to host news documentaries.

That gives you some idea of NBC's current commitment to journalistic excellence. Michael Gartner, the unfortunate news chief, was a newspaperman NBC hired to cut costs. I doubt that he understood some of the cost-cutting tricks his producers were inventing. Two weeks after the truck fiasco, NBC was caught faking footage of dead fish in a mismanaged national forest.

Of course this stuff has been going on for years. TV news operates on simple principles: If there are no visuals, forget the story; if the visuals are weak, try to hype them up. Why do you think you never heard of the S&L scandal until they'd practically hijacked Fort Knox? White-collar crime is impervious to film.

I laughed out loud at the ultimate in "Eyewitness News" enterprise, when a reporter and a cameramen in Bemidji, Minn., were indicted as a result of their hard-hitting series on teenage drinking. Apparently they rounded up some minors, bought them two cases of beer and rented them a cabin. News of the '90s. It wasn't even an NBC affiliate.

Seventy percent of Americans get all the news they need from TV; when TV and newspapers disagree, 56 percent say they trust the TV version, only 22 percent trust print. Make no mistake about the pecking order. The power of the press is going to TV, and TV news is going to the devil.

The networks are getting out of the news-gathering business, as the cost-cutters close the foreign bureaus and try to buy cheap from freelance retailers. The newspaper business, dominated by giant chains, is taking the same route. Gannett employs no foreign correspondents and neither do Newhouse, Thomson or Ingersoll. Like foreign correspondents, investigative reporters are viewed as luxuries by the new press barons. They're no longer cost-effective.

There go the two most glamorous careers in journalism. At *The Independent*, where we reckon we've won more national awards per

budget dollar than any publication in history, we sometimes wonder if we're really *that* good. We're just five or six neurotics taking
their medication and trying hard. Maybe we win because the big
guys aren't trying at all anymore.

If that's true, there's a grim explanation from Ben Bagdikian,
whose book *The Media Monopoly* revealed that 70 percent of our
sources of information are controlled by 20 conglomerates.

"The media are no longer neutral agents selling space and time
to merchants," Bagdikian writes, "but vital instruments needed by
major corporations to maintain their economic and political
power."

At this point someone always pesters me for the good news, as if
there's bound to be some. When they won't back off, I tell them
the future might belong to micromedia—alternative tabloids, cable
access commandos, FM radio militia, desktop pamphleteers. A guy
jumped up and told me I was thinking too small and too low-tech,
that national computer bulletin boards were already replacing conventional media as a source of free-flowing, untainted information.

It sounded promising. But the cyberspace pioneers seem to have
the same problem as my micromedia, a problem of primary
access—access to presidents, generals, battlefields, boardrooms.
With all the open channels and overflowing databases in the
world, it still takes trained people to dig out the facts and recognize
them. It still takes a professional class of educated hunter-gatherers.

"Truth cops," idealists like me used to call them, before we realized that truth cops might be even more unpopular than traffic
cops. If publishers and advertisers can't afford them and citizens
don't believe them, what are we going to do about Thomas Jefferson's warning?

"Were it left to me to decide whether we should have a government without newspapers or newspapers without a government,"
Jefferson wrote, "I should not hesitate to prefer the latter."

To most Americans TV is as essential as electricity or running water, and my phobia is a weird elitist affectation. But E.B. White prophesied in 1938 that civilization would "rise or fall" on this invention, and I see no evidence that it's rising. On the fire side of the argument: I discovered after writing this essay that not only Franklin and Jefferson but Benjamin Thompson (look him up), the third great American genius of the 18th century, had played a pioneering role in fireplace design.

The Fire Sermon

One character of Truffaut's attributes the popularity of television to the fact that "people seem to want moving images after dinner" and not enough homes have fireplaces anymore.

— Frank Rowsome Jr., *The Bright and Glowing Place*

It was a cold Friday night, the last day of November. My wife was out of town and I'd just cashed a paycheck, so it was one of those rare evenings when I could do anything I felt like doing, within the limits imposed by my age, imagination, physical condition and good reputation.

I did what I always do, on these wild nights of unrestricted freedom. I built myself a roaring fire, stacked up some tapes—Patsy Cline, Lyle Lovett, Guy Clark, Django Reinhardt, Kate Wolf, Paul Simon ancient and current—and ate my dinner by firelight. Then I poured another glass of wine, settled my animals in their favorite positions around the hearth and stared at my fire for another three hours. I dozed. When I woke up at 3 a.m. the ashes were almost cold, and it was December.

I haven't always been this much of a hellraiser, just the last four or five years. Even when I was inclined toward more aerobic entertainments, I always saved some choice winter evenings for the best show in town. When the prairie dogs hibernate and December winds come moaning around the old bunkhouse, a cowboy turns to his woodpile. A fire may be the one thing in nature that's simultaneously a stimulant and a sedative. It stirs the memory and the imagination, suspends time, cleans old connections that have rusted.

A fire is the best friend and the last refuge of the weary, outraged eye. It's the only visual delicacy that hoboes in a train yard, huddled around an oil drum, share on equal terms with a duchess in her grand salon.

"Those who have been blind from birth are unlikely to care strongly about open fires," writes Frank Rowsome Jr. in *The Bright and Glowing Place*, a definitive manual of fire worship. "No wonder, because fires seem to have been created to be stared at. On its domestic stage a fire puts on a show of great sophistication, for the main outlines of the plot are comfortably familiar but the dialogue is always fresh and new. I have been attending this theater for more than half a century and have never once seen the same performance repeated.

"Visually a fire shares with composers like Bach and Haydn the intellectually satisfying device of richly embroidered variations on simple themes. This is a visual device nature is fond of; one thinks of the varied linear motions within a waterfall, a willow tree dancing in light airs, the rip of breakers coming diagonally to a long beach, and the spumy assaults of an ocean swell on a rocky coast.

"But the fire has still another appeal to the eye. These are the incandescent forms and structures at the heart of an established blaze that are so seductive to our imaginations, luminous caves and shimmering temples, a glowing Rorschach challenge we can rarely resist studying."

Fire has held its audience—spellbound—for at least 750,000 years, according to Rowsome the fire scholar. For eons it faced no competition in the field of home entertainment. From the dawn of literacy it existed in symbiosis with reading, the greatest of all the pleasures that transcend the flesh, because the hearthside was the only place with enough light and heat to sustain the evening reader (legend has Abraham Lincoln reading Seneca and doing sums by firelight, but he didn't have my trifocals and 700/20 vision). The radio and the phonograph only enhanced, added new dimensions to the fireside experience.

Only in my own lifetime has the fire lost most of its market share—to the medium that invented "market share" and that threatens, in a few accelerated decades, to reverse the process of human evolution. It isn't really my fire-gazing or its sedentary, slothful character that sets me apart: It's that other slothful medium

I failed to consider. There aren't as many of us, anymore, who come home on a cold winter evening and check the woodpile instead of the *TV Guide*.

I haven't checked the *TV Guide* since 1975, about the last time my "On the Air" column appeared in the entertainment pages of the *Buffalo Evening News*. I'm grateful now for my early, reluctant career as a TV critic because it inoculated me for life against any possibility of acquiring that lethal habit, as a straight shot of Wild Turkey is supposed to turn a six-year-old into a lifelong teetotaler (they say it worked for Billy Graham).

Militant videophobes used to be attacked as snobs and elitists, but now we're so rare and isolated that most people merely question our grip on reality.

When friends quarrel over "Twin Peaks," or someone at the office tells me that the real story is the goofy way TV news is covering Our Boys in the Desert, I might say "Really?" and my eyes will light up with such an innocent, Martian curiosity that they think I'm putting them on. Fifteen years' exile from commercial television gives me a Rip Van Winkle perspective that someone, somewhere has to maintain. Sometimes when I'm watching a ballgame, I'll pilot my remote control across 30 cable channels in a vain attempt to avoid commercials.

The landscape that greets me is post-apocalyptic. The gunshots, the sirens, the tires squealing, the infernal hammering music, the heartless sound of laugh tracks where nothing is funny, the vertigo of microsecond video-montage, the braying, posturing pitchmen and "hosts," the high-tech teeth—if you don't eat some of this every day, you can't bear five minutes of it. To me it's like a few seconds in hell. I grip the insidious little remote device like the safety bar on a roller-coaster car, in a kind of terror that it will never bring me back to Shea Stadium.

I wish I were exaggerating. If you think I'm exaggerating grossly, you've watched too much TV. People get used to anything—to the elevated train that thunders past their windows every five minutes, to a paper plant that almost suffocates out-of-towners. A smoker doesn't realize that his hair and clothes can stink up half a room. And the average American will watch 20,000 hours of television before he graduates from high school, according to Neil Postman, and 5,000 hours before kindergarten.

It's ridiculous to pretend that this saturation hasn't had a profound effect, almost certainly a negative effect, on the basic structural integrity of the human mind. The prophet Postman (*Amusing Ourselves to Death*), who likes to remind us that it takes more brain power to eat than to watch TV, claims that one American in 10 can now expect to spend time in a mental institution—an amazing figure by pre-television standards. There are new studies showing that Americans consume more medication, therapy and hospitalization for mental disorders every year, and that more work days are lost.

That's hard evidence that this country is simply cracking up, and I grinned at one writer's suggestion that it's the economic pressure of the current recession that's doing it to us. If drug abuse and mental illness are epidemics, why not take a look at the single most schizophrenic, bizarre, mind-rending new thing that recent generations of Americans have had in common since their childhood? If there were no other factors, just the vertiginous speed and racket of television would render it hostile to our sanity. The difference between my fire and a sitcom is the difference between Beethoven and 2 Live Crew, the difference between a hot bath and a root canal.

The week after Simon and Schuster (a publishing house so venal that insiders call it Simon's Shoe Store, according to Calvin Trillin) absorbed a $300,000 loss to reject his novel *American Psycho* as simply too sick and disgusting to publish, 26-year-old author Bret Easton Ellis turned up in the *New York Times* with a general lament for his bewildered generation:

"Our style is assimilation, our attitude reaction, even if some rebelliousness remains . . . we are clueless yet wizened, too unopinionated to voice concern, purposefully enigmatic and indecisive."

Ellis's complaint, subtitled "Adrift in a Pop Landscape," was a quavering whine of self-pity from a generation that sees itself swallowed whole by a poisonous culture. But his frames of reference were TV, movies and rock music—he never mentioned a book—and he never suggested that his toxic exposure to "junk culture" was in any way voluntary.

In fact, aging sanely means outgrowing the ephemera of popular culture, not clinging desperately to the thin slice of it that colored "your generation." Junk culture is easy to avoid; the covers of supermarket tabloids are my only exposure. I may be a prematurely old man huddled by the fire, but I'm not "too unopinionated to voice concern." Just say no, Mr. Ellis. You'd be surprised to see how your spirit, like a smoker's lungs, will regenerate if you just let it breathe.

Of course Ellis expressed his angst by writing the first mainstream "snuff novel," about a stockbroker who skins women alive and has sex with their severed heads. As Dolly Parton said to a fan who wanted to know her bra size, "Wouldn't your Mama be proud of you."

If only this poor kid's parents had set him down by the fire—or maybe thrown him into it, after all. As opposed to its electronic successor, which seems to increase anger, isolation and alienation, fire is credited with the socialization of primitive man, with the bonding and sharing that generated the first speech, laughter, ritual and song. Fire isn't just a solo activity. It was Thoreau, a famous solitary, who observed that a fire was the most tolerable third party.

What wood fires took a million years to establish, the cathode-ray tube has undermined in four decades. The damage isn't totaled yet; we won't know how much we've lost until we see the kinds of leaders, artists and thinkers the new order produces.

The early returns don't encourage me. Benjamin Franklin (the famous Franklin stove) and Thomas Jefferson were American geniuses who broke new ground in fireplace design; Lincoln nearly burned himself to read. Theodore Roosevelt was a campfire fanatic; radio broadcast FDR's Fireside Chats, which old-timers remember with affection. Now we have presidents who don't read books and children who can't. We have, in the political generation nurtured by television, Dan Quayle and David Duke.

I don't blame it all on TV. But fire-gazers produced all the world's great literature, from Homer to Faulkner and Joyce. TV produced Bret Easton Ellis.

At this point Rush Limbaugh's worldly success has been so great that we can suspend our pity for his personal shortcomings. Liberals waste their hatred on this human geyser of yahoo resentments and misinformation. He's only an entertainer working an audience. It's the audience—its size and its sentiments—that's truly frightening.

Rush to Ignorance

"I tried to imagine myself as a cyst in this woman's abdomen. The cyst weighed 303 pounds and I go about 310, it wouldn't be much of a squeeze. Imagine me in this woman's abdomen as a cyst. Think of it."

Radio doesn't get any more postmodern than this. It's easier to imagine Rush Limbaugh as a world-record fibrous tumor than to imagine him as a star, the king (Farouk?) of talk radio, a man who rages against reason on 426 stations and commands $25,000 for a personal appearance. Limbaugh's rapid success at acquiring stations, sponsors and listeners has generated major profiles by *Time*, "60 Minutes" and the *New York Times*.

They treated him with a mixture of alarm and respect that persuaded me, against my better judgment, to tune in this latest in a long line of right-wing rabble-rousers and hear what, if anything, he has added to the tradition.

Not a whole lot, from where I sit. Maybe I caught him on an off day. Here was this loud guy, with a plaintive note in his voice that almost made you want to help him, suffering through the usual tortures of talk-radio personalities with too much time to fill. He was trying to make points out of pointless news items. Among the repetitions and unearned exclamations he sounded earnest, halting, a little slow for a man who says he fights the Left with half his brain tied behind his back, to make it fair. This was a day when he should have untied the other half.

His meditation on the Guinness cyst, the only apolitical monologue Limbaugh offered, was the show's brightest moment. Where was the flash, the "irresistible" panache I read about in *Time*? I tuned in to hear the devil dancing and I found a stammering, under-rehearsed after-dinner speaker with one eye on the clock. Here, it seemed to me, was still another example of self-promotion so successful that the reputation dwarfed the product.

Maybe it's just that we don't find his opinions so astonishing, here in North Carolina. We've been listening to this stuff half our lives. On WPTF in Raleigh, the same station that carries Limbaugh five days a week, they used to have a resident reactionary, Bob Kwesell, who worked the same afternoon air shift. Kwesell was the exact same size, shape, volume and political coloration as Rush Limbaugh. He was even a nice guy off the air, as Limbaugh is alleged to be. When I was at WPTF doing radio commentary from my own political perspective, Bob and I used to joke in the men's room about the uptight WPTF employees who thought they had to act as if they were on his side or mine, and seemed to expect us to close like pit bulls in the hall.

Limbaugh, like Kwesell and our beloved Sen. Jesse Helms, dispenses the familiar poison in its most unadulterated form. Egocentric, ethnocentric and phallocentric, this decadent yahoo "conservatism" is the defiant bellow of a certain kind of cornered white male who imagines that his grandfather ruled the earth, before things began to go wrong. Subject him to misfortune or humiliation and this creature strikes like a mongoose, never at the cynical politicians or corporations that might have caused his troubles but at the vulnerable bottom of the pecking order, the half-imagined "welfare cheaters" (black) and their liberal patrons (white, but thin and with glasses).

This sad stuff is so old they find it scrawled on the walls of caves, down here where I live. If there's anything original about Rush Limbaugh, it isn't his rhetoric. The big question of whether he's kidding, and how much, plays better in New York than in Raleigh. Bombast and verbal extravagance ("Here with talent on loan from God, serving humanity simply by opening his mouth . . .") are a part of the act that even his callers must recognize as show business. "Rush to Excellence" is the slogan for his stage shows. But if you think Limbaugh is pulling your leg when he says "The new home of communism in the world is the American environmental movement," you've been spending too much time at symphony benefits and save-the-whale fundraisers. You are out of touch.

"I attack the absurd by being absurd," Limbaugh told the reporter from *Time*. This means one thing to him, another to the New York-based editors of *Time* and "60 Minutes," who honestly believed that

Jim and Tammy Bakker were two male actors from Long Island doing an Emmy-winning sendup of southern religion. I saved the column by a New York critic arguing, in all sincerity, that professional wrestling was "a brilliant parody of male violence." These Manhattan mutants are as dangerous, in their ignorance and influence, as Rush Limbaugh. His audience self-selects exactly like the audience for pro wrestling. People who relish tongue-in-cheek don't listen to Limbaugh, or wouldn't listen with amusement for more than five minutes. Monotony annihilates the ironical interloper. Wrestlers change costumes and Limbaugh coins new adjectives, but it's the same moves over and over.

The audience has to believe. Whatever Limbaugh may be thinking, with the aid of "the largest hypothalamus in North American," 90 percent of his listeners—8 million a week—are true believers. You don't have to listen very long to understand that. Many of the callers are weird cases. Yesterday there was a man who wanted to restore respect for Gerald Ford, and a woman whose Halloween project was a right-to-life House of Horrors with a skinned squirrel to represent a bloody fetus (even Limbaugh seemed amazed by her). These are disadvantaged individuals starving for sympathy. Limbaugh's share of the dialogue, when he isn't boasting, cackling or playing "Monster Mash," is an all-you-can-eat buffet of their favorite Cro-Magnon platitudes, served with an authoritative display of utter nonsense about economics and foreign policy—classic talk radio.

He sounds like he means it. And because they believe, and because there are so many of them, Limbaugh may not be exaggerating—too much—when he calls himself "the most dangerous man in America." How can I, for one, take him lightly when I've spent years of my life and hundreds of thousands of words fighting against every misguided notion he seems to cherish? This is a man who hates the Clean Air Act, who rails against environmentalism as the work of Bolsheviks and witches, who ridicules George Bush for "caving in" on civil rights and the environment.

"If you want to know what's on the minds of voters, listen to David Duke," Limbaugh said yesterday. In his most alarming, self-revealing tirade, he called for "a strong leader who won't apologize, who won't knuckle under to the socialist commune-out-of-work libbers (near incoherence here) and femi-nazis . . ." It was a cry of pure longing for a fascist messiah.

Whatever he intends, Rush Limbaugh provides phone sex for bigots and a nurturing environment for the most destructive strains of ignorance on the American fringe. You can't dismiss his program as a carnival of harmless sound and fury, as professional wrestling for the ear. Free speech isn't the issue. I'd march in the rain to keep the fascist Left from silencing Rush Limbaugh—I hope he'd do the same for me—and I'm no stranger to many of the conservative impulses that move him. It's a question of his conscience. What strange fire is he feeding, what service is he providing for these callers of his, with his racial slurs ("I didn't want to talk to some Jamaican clerk") and his audible 300-pound sighs? In a country overrun with rapists, what kind of man earns a living by putting up pornographic billboards?

He'll drive you crazy, but you can't cast Rush Limbaugh as the Devil Himself. It's too easy to psychoanalyze someone—someone like me—who makes himself so vulnerable. But he is vulnerable. This is a 40-year-old man who's 100 pounds overweight, who's been fired a lot and divorced twice, who has no kids, who lives alone and admitted to the *New York Times* that he's lonely in New York and would like to make some friends. About women he says, on the air, "I'm totally confused and I admit it."

That comes across on the air. The social life can be painful for a 310-pound bachelor who makes a living trashing the aspirations of women and minorities. Why not blame the liberals, the Gary Harts and the demon Kennedys who seem to get every woman they want, one way or the other? Why not run a little clubhouse of the airwaves where you can share your anger with other men who feel left out? Most of Limbaugh's listeners are male. With or without the financial success that eases the pain for Limbaugh, white guys with his background often embrace the ungenerous politics of the frothing right fringe.

These are the dead-end politics of born losers—sore losers. It would be too neat to go back to that cyst and to wrap this up by calling Limbaugh a 300-pound malignant growth in America's belly. He's not, really. He's a tiny reflection of something much bigger and more frightening that's been growing there for a long, long time.

American civilization began to hemorrhage critically when salesmen and politicians decided that persuasion was all passion and technique, and entirely independent of the truth. How does a humble columnist restrain himself from fighting fire with fire?

The Howling

Most speeches by business leaders have a peculiar retro flavor, as if the wisdom of the boardroom had been gleaned from self-help and motivational manuals that were 10 years out of date. Even the most successful, least sentimental of these white men in dark suits seem to tithe to the Church of the Obvious and elevate platitude to the dignity of scripture. Ross Perot was no exception. But last week in Richmond a captain of industry got my attention with an insight that deserves a wider audience.

"Finding common ground" was the text of an address by John Clendenin, CEO of Bell South, to a group of foundation directors who were meeting to make a post-election reassessment of their missions. The session was closed to the public and especially to the press, so ethically I can't quote Clendenin or even subject him to close paraphrase. But what he told them, in the simplest terms, is that the first responsibility of the leaders in every community is to find the common ground, the consensus that will reconcile apparent enemies and unite them in a common purpose.

This task is especially urgent in the aftermath of an election, Clendenin argued, because the belligerent rhetoric of political candidates leaves the impression that America is a battleground of feuding factions and hereditary enemies that could explode like Beirut or Sarajevo. In fact, he reminded us, the common ground shared by most Americans is extensive, and the gulfs that seem to yawn in election years are mostly hot air and hallucination.

This was a sober voice from the center with a message that brought me up short. Who shares the blame for turning up the heat? Like many journalists trained in polemic and prone to indignation, I notice that election years bring out the strengths in my prose and the weakness in my character. I get caught up in this ugliness, I respond to the vicious lunges of Republican Rottweilers with superheated invective of my own. I get military, I burn bridges. I brandish my vocabulary like a sword.

I am not a healer. I forget, like almost everyone else, that most of the dragons we slay are chimeras, spawned during the primaries and fated to vanish in a puff of smoke on Election Day, whether we slay them or not. Few of us are as stupid as Patrick Buchanan, the fascist Don Quixote who imagines the drums and flags of an American Holy War where there is nothing but a sullen minority of religious Neanderthals nursing ancient grudges in the dark. But most of us, at some point, mistake the rhetoric for the reality.

We fail to see that this is not a struggle for America's soul between Buchanan and Jesse Helms at one pole and Ice-T or Karen Finley at the other. It's a struggle by three-quarters of the population, on their common ground near the center, to do their work and heal their wounds in spite of the terrible howling that drifts in from the fringe.

Working closer to the howling, I'm more easily distracted than a corporate executive or a philanthropist. But maybe I have a better background for understanding the process that poisoned the well of political discourse in this country, and opened distances that seem unbridgeable between groups that seem indistinguishable.

Civility and rational debate began to disappear from political campaigns when candidates began to entrust their fortunes to the flourishing neo-science of advertising and public relations. Politics in this country have always been coarse and emotional. But anyone who believes that American politicians have always comported themselves like mad dogs and strip-show barkers isn't familiar with the Lincoln-Douglas debates, conducted 134 years ago in the elegant syntax of the Roman Senate.

The influence of advertising on politics may go back 100 years. But it's only in the past 25 years, as video gadgetry evolved into the salesman's nuclear weapon, that free elections have been subordinated to the same sordid sleight-of-hand that drives the consumer treadmill.

The evil that we've wrought is in the nature of The Beast itself, the capitalist tool that has almost outgrown capitalism. At the risk of embracing the obvious, I need your agreement that the purpose of advertising is never to tell you the truth, unless it's absolutely unavoidable. The genius of advertising is not to inform your judgment but to suspend it. Over your lifetime it's a brainwashing, *1984* process of convincing you that all cigarette smokers are healthy and attractive, that beer drinking is a virile outdoor activity, that soft drinks and sex are linked inextricably. But its immediate purpose is to push you toward one irresistible impulse, one irrevocable act—buying a product, pulling a certain lever on the voting machine.

When the products are candidates, the media warlocks know it's easier to make a demon of the other candidate than to make a hero of their own. So the rhetoric that drives our elections is hostile, misleading, divisive and superficial by design.

The long-term effect of these tactics, on the voter, is low retention and disorientation. I've heard repeatedly that 1992 was the exception to the rule, that Ross Perot helped to hold us to the issues, that more information and more intelligent media coverage were available.

"The mood was entirely different this year," Clinton ad director Mandy Grunwald told David Von Drehle of the *Washington Post.* "People were so much more serious and so much more cynical. People were paying attention. They were desperate for information."

Unfortunately, an election-eve survey conducted at the University of Massachusetts doesn't support this portrait of an informed and discerning electorate. The UMass survey of likely voters, coast to coast, revealed almost total ignorance of all relevant issues, and even basic facts about the United States. Most respondents said that foreign aid and welfare, in that order, were larger budget items than defense. In fact, military spending—a fifth of the entire pie—eats up three times more tax dollars than welfare (five percent) and foreign aid (one percent) combined. The only "facts" most voters were sure of were the ones the campaigns had been feeding them: Clinton is a draft-dodger, he raised taxes 128 times, etc.

The only questions most voters answered correctly? They knew which TV character was insulted by Dan Quayle, and they knew the name of the President's dog.

Whatever actual information the candidates provided, it had vanished by the time the voters went to the polls. Which is, I think, the idea. The manipulated voter/consumer is left with nothing but vague resentments, and in the worst cases unfocused rage. The Republicans' "family values" crusade, an unholy collaboration between cynical media professionals and the religious right, was one of the most frightening examples of "wedge" campaigning ever embraced by a major party. It employed the dangerous language of civil war and ethnic cleansing, and all for what? To re-elect two schmucks with double-digit IQs who never belonged on any party's "A Team" in the first place.

The good news was that it didn't work. While there's no evidence that voters saw through it in any meaningful way, there's ample evidence that they ignored it. And now we have, in George Bush, the first high-profile martyr to the slash-and-burn philosophy of modern media science. His handlers whispered in his ears and blew on his trembling muzzle, and this reluctant pit bull charged into the ring with all the heart he could muster, and all the meanness. It worked against Michael Dukakis, a very reluctant dog himself. But this time jaw-weary George lost his election, his self-respect and whatever place in history he might have coveted, outside the gallery of one-term curiosities.

His fate might serve as a warning. As for the winning candidate, Bill Clinton, he employed every bit as much state-of-the-art media science as the Republicans, make no mistake. The morning after the election, the networks offered us a sports-page postmortem explaining how Clinton's media team executed its winning game plan.

But thanks to an easy case, the economy, and an easy target in the White House, Clinton prevailed with relatively little blood on his hands. He's in a position to de-escalate the war of angry words, to turn down the heat. He could take the high road altogether and declare a ceasefire.

I'd be willing, with certain assurances, to abide by the terms of the ceasefire myself. But it's probably quixotic to think that we could turn back the clock. Our economy is driven by an engine built of lies and tricks, an engine so powerful that it propels us, probably against our basic instincts, through an endless cycle of superfluous consumption. Politicians can see where the power lies, and they know just how much it costs.

The best hope, probably a faint one, is an immediate and drastic legal curb on campaign spending, so that none of these hungry candidates will be able to afford Ed Rollins or Roger Ailes. The issue is critical. How are we expected to find the common ground, when the basic business of democracy is conducted by mercenaries who draw hugh salaries for their uncanny ability to destroy that common ground, or to hide it from us?

Twenty years ago the "journalism" of supermarket tabloids was a tired joke; now it rules the marketplace. After the indignities he's suffered as president, the misfortunes of Clinton the candidate sound like history lessons. But a medium without scruples is a lethal weapon for the unscrupulous.

A Septic Emergency

Everybody needs groceries, right? Most of us can't feed ourselves with the things that grow and graze on our acre lots at the edge of town. That puts almost everyone in the supermarket at one time or another, angling a grocery cart into the checkout chute and looking around for something to amuse us while the guy ahead of us in line tries to pass a third-party check on an out-of-state bank.

We can't just double-time through the checkout lane with our eyes closed, holding our noses. So we all know what's there. More than billboards, more than prime-time television, the checkout lane is the universal information station.

Those of us in the information business are naturally alarmed by the publications we find in the racks above the conveyor belt. That doesn't mean we aren't amused. "Elvis had sex with his mother," was a headline last week. "Bigfoot is the father of my child" has become a cliché. (For an insider's view of the supermarket tabloid business, fictionalized, try Francine Prose's excellent novel *Bigfoot Dreams*.)

But Elvis is dead—the tabloids' denials notwithstanding—and Bigfoot is even less sensitive about his reputation. What's alarming is that real, living people can find themselves in the tabloids, which make no attempt whatsoever to provide you with accurate information about these people. Their only motivation is to catch your eye and stimulate your sick curiosity until you buy the magazine.

In a free country, some argue, this is all right in its place. Most of the stories are so ridiculous that tabloids use their lack of credibility as a defense—"Come on, no one believes this stuff"—when someone sues them for libel. Most of the staple celebrities who fill the tabloids' pages are cynical, publicity-starved vermin delighted to see their faces at the supermarket, even implicated in sex triangles with Geraldo and Pee Wee Herman.

But what happens when the cesspool press forgets its place? Yesterday, sheepishly, for the first time in my life, I picked up one of these magazines and brought it home. I hesitate to reprint this stuff. But now that tabloid scandal has spilled over into the "legitimate" media to such a toxic extent—I think of a ruptured septic tank and crews in rubber boots and coveralls cleaning up—maybe it's time to deal with it head-on.

"Bill Clinton's Four-In-A-Bed Sex Orgies With Street Hookers" was the banner headline that caught my eye. "And he's the father of my child, claims ghetto gal he had sex with 13 times," runs the subhead, on the cover of a magazine called *Globe*. Inside, there are accounts of the Arkansas governor enjoying standup sex behind a tree in the park and picking up squads of hookers for round-robin orgies at his mother's place in the country. There's a quote from someone identified as "a black activist": "Bill Clinton has been with enough black women to cast a Tarzan movie." Three pictures of the governor's "love child" by a black prostitute are included in the four-page spread.

It's hard to come to grips with the logic of an industry whose only logic is excess. In the two weeks since *The Star*, another scandal sheet, paid Gennifer Flowers to confess to a 12-year affair with Gov. Clinton, the presidential candidate has been accused of having sex with everyone except Elvis and Bigfoot, and they aren't taking calls. People who think it's funny tell us that this is just the gutter press waging a typical circulation war. Bill Clinton is a hot cover subject. *The Star* stole a lot of readers with the Gennifer Flowers confession and its competitors are scrambling to catch up, in a racket where anything goes.

I think that's politically naive. I don't know who's responsible for publishing *Globe*—I couldn't find a masthead and I assume all the bylines are pseudonyms—but I think we can take it for granted that they don't want Bill Clinton in the White House. This emphasis on black sex partners, for a candidate who relies on the support of white Southerners, is sufficient to convince me that there's a method in their madness.

You can imagine the ecstasy among Republican campaign thugs, watching the Democrats' most plausible presidential candidate replace Pee Wee Herman in that gallery of shame between the disposable razors and *Soap Opera Digest*. When you're talking about reckless character assassination linked to political advantage, you're closing in on libel law and the principle of "malice afore-thought." It's hard for any of us who have been caught in the coils of major libel suits to understand how something like *Globe's* assault on Gov. Clinton could have appeared in print anywhere.

I once wrote that a certain broadcasting executive was a devious and abusive employer and a shady, irresponsible businessman. This was true, to put it mildly, but it took nine years and a fortune in legal fees to sort the thing out and prove it to a jury. If the man had been more of a Grade-A public figure—someone like Clinton who has sought and found a place in the public eye—could I have written with impunity that he had sex with nuns, vegetables, his retarded twin sister and his pet ferret Rocky?

Libel standards for supermarket journalism are so radically different from the rules the rest of us live with, the law must subscribe to the popular belief that "the supes" are a twilight world of bovine, half-literate readers and strange feral reporters in leisure suits and gold chains—an alternate world that never touches the real world at any point.

This view is inadequate; the only evidence you need is the way the Gennifer Flowers story has permeated the mainstream media and possibly changed the course of a presidential election. There is no Berlin wall between the most septic supermarket sleaze and the "respectable" media. If there ever was one, it lies in ruins. Actor Warren Beatty made this point a few years ago, speaking to an audience of mainstream newspaper editors. You ask, why Warren Beatty and not, say, Noam Chomsky? Beatty might have wondered himself, because he asked these august journalists if they really thought the public made any clear distinction, as we of the press do, between tabloid news in the supermarket and "real news" at the newsstand.

A telling point; a crushing point. My guess is that a majority of Americans would be unaware that there are two kinds of publications peddling news—one that really means it and another that's only fooling. I'm sure they don't understand that the tabloids themselves come in several grades of seriousness. At "the top" are the celebrity scandal sheets that actually check some of their stories and take their own photos. In the middle are the Elvis-lives, UFO, Bigfoot, miracle-diet rags. At the bottom of—can we call it "the puking order"?—are the tabs that feature goiters shaped like

Gandhi and retouched photos of lizard-faced ladies and snakes that swallowed babies.

No doubt there are even subtler gradations of this toxic waste. And all of it is moving uptown, seeping into the wells and reservoirs that supply most of the nation's information. I hate to blame the contamination on television, my favorite scapegoat, but its fingerprints are everywhere.

TV is the medium where news and entertainment have completely interpenetrated. Daytime freak shows like "Geraldo!" and "Sally Jessy Raphael" are actually a step down for a tabloid heroine like Gennifer Flowers. She's waiting for a call from Diane Sawyer or Barbara Walters, and her hopes should be high. Barbara has just booked the woman Mike Tyson raped. Marla Maples and Donna Rice were both honored with prime-time interviews by these "anchor-level" network journalists, who pressed them greedily for intimate details of their rich and famous sex lives (in the strange argot of TV news, "anchor-level" means the top, but we all know that anchors function by burying themselves in the mud).

Television makes a supermarket audience feel right at home. Geraldo and Sally Jessy service the goiter-and-gangrene crowd; Liz-Elvis-Bigfoot readers enjoy "Entertainment Tonight" and "Lifestyles of the Rich and Famous"; current scandal and gossip, the *National Enquirer* beat, is handled by network magazine shows with anchor-level hosts. And once a tabloid story appears on any of these shows, with their enormous national audiences, it becomes news enough to be picked up by legitimate print media. This is the incredible food chain that disseminates malicious gossip and deliberate slander.

I don't defend the scruples of the print media. Since we've been forced to compete for survival against broadcasters who regard news and entertainment as interchangeable "product" with a dollar value, it's been all downhill. *People* plunges to new depths every week. Newspapers are full of celebrities and frivolous features, and always have been. But at least they try to keep their news and entertainment separate. There's no Diane Sawyer doing Marla Maples on Tuesday night and Helmut Kohl on Thursday. No one ever confused Walter Lippmann with Walter Winchell.

In the general confusion, which is probably the collapse of the last standards the media have pretended to maintain, a slime-coated monster has lurched up from the basement. Unfettered by fact, libel law, ethics, common courtesy or common decency, The Thing From The Checkout Counter gives unscrupulous campaign operatives, among others, a lethal weapon to use against their enemies. And as we know from the repentant deathbed confession of the late Lee Atwater, there's no weapon the new breed of campaign thugs wouldn't use to win.

I don't think Gov. Clinton was a random victim. I think the monster was programmed, and I think it's highly suspicious that a similar rumor about George Bush (a mistress, not standup sex in the park or orgies with hookers) got nowhere with the mainstream press when a tabloid printed it in 1988.

It seems to me that if even one American believes the cover story in *Globe*, a crime of some kind has been committed. I suspect that the damage has been done. And the victim, whatever his shortcomings, is a former Rhodes Scholar with an 11-year-old daughter who goes to the supermarket. You wonder why there are no decent candidates for office? Who in his right mind would subject himself, or herself, to this?

This sordid catfight between Kitty and the Queen makes a logical bridge to the next chapter, which argues that politics, entertainment and the media have melted into each other and become a single industry.

Twisted Sisters

Now that the Middle East has just about exhausted our national attention span, it's a nasty book about the ex-Regent, Nancy Reagan, that distracts America from its economic emergency. There's no reason to read this book by Kitty Kelley, a kind of strip miner of celebrity scandal whose ore trucks arrive, heavy laden, every couple of years. I don't dismiss the importance of the subject, the only important one Kelley has ever approached with her dynamite and steam shovels; Nancy Reagan was arguably the most powerful individual in the United States for a decade. Kelley's book is superfluous because there's nothing in it—nothing that matters—that's new.

Naturally decent people are offended by these stories that embarrass an old woman, now that her power has vanished. Kelley's most scandalous suggestion, that Mrs. Reagan played geriatric sex games in the White House with a decrepit crooner, is so sad and grotesque that it shames the writer as much as the Regent, even if she's guilty as charged. But the national tragedy is that no one was interested in hearing or publishing any of these stories 10 years ago, when the scandal might have helped to terminate the ruinous reign of this truly dreadful woman.

My personal collection of Reagan anecdotes goes back to the '60s, when Ronnie and Nancy ruled California and I was writing magazine articles about education, which they opposed. I picked up a lot more stories, ranging from good-as-gold to bitchy gossip, from Reagan neighbors and acquaintances when I worked in LA. Reagan lore was idle amusement. In those days every journalist in the country would have laughed at you if you had predicted that Nancy and her movie-star marionette were an act that would one day play the White House.

When the impossible came to pass, I did what little I could to arouse the countryside. I passed along the worst stories the editors and lawyers would allow, and ungallantly referred to Mrs. Reagan as "a vulgar shrew" and an "anorexic voodoo doll," among other titles of respect. I could do it with a clear conscience because I knew for certain that she was awful—and because she was so powerful.

Some journalists have a different response to power. The one great pleasure of the current scandal is watching Mrs. Reagan's former sycophants mount a self-righteous chorus against the "irresponsible and unethical" journalism of Kitty Kelley. But which is the more despicable impulse in a reporter, to kick the mighty when they're down or to kiss their rings when they're mighty? George Will, for one, still seems to think it impresses us to hear that he, unlike the pariah Kitty Kelley, knows Nancy personally. Of course it's more gracious of him to stick by Mrs. Reagan than to renounce her, after eating all her sorbet and cold soups. But how can this fellow still go around collecting honorary degrees when he's been dead wrong about everything—the Reagans, Gorbachev, the economy, the Cold War, you name it—for most of his professional life? Don't you have to bat even .200 to stay in the major leagues where he plays?

The only honest thing Will could say now is "I'm sorry, I got a whiff of raw power and I lost my head. She made a stooge of me." But more substantial journalists fell under Nancy's spell, the notorious adoring "gaze" that became her trademark. *Time* offered one of the most comprehensive and balanced assessments of Kelley's book; but I know from an eyewitness that Time Inc. Editor-in-Chief Jason McManus once rose up in indignation to defend his friend Nancy against raffish press types who were poking fun.

These powerful journalists had access to most of the material that's making a rich woman of Kitty Kelley. The information was out there. But the Reagan phenomenon was a kind of national hypnosis, reaching way beyond the moral and intellectual paralysis that seized immediate victims of Nancy's famous gaze. Waves of damaging memoirs and reassessments, followed by the S&L scandal and the near-collapse of the Reaganized economy, have silenced and disillusioned all but the most diehard partisans of the Reagan Revolution. But no one can dismiss the terrifying achievement of those intrepid image artists who took Twilight in Palm Springs and packaged it as Morning in America.

The Reagan Revolution was a media revolution, in every sense—the coming-of-age of the image industry on its final frontier, power politics. Reagan's was the first all-video presidency, as Kuwait was the first all-video war. It was the first successful political movement based on neither a program nor a personality, but on a marketing concept.

"What if we tried something like an American royal family?" one Republican said to another while poor Jimmy Carter was still grappling with the Ayatollah. "Glamorous but wholesome, rich but not too chic. She'd be sort of prim and lacquered, formal; he'd be tall and dim like Prince Philip, you know, conservative, with just a whiff of the stables."

"Where would we find an act like that?"

"Hollywood."

"Actors?"

"Kind of, yeah."

"But it's the queen who has to carry the ball."

"That's OK, too."

It was a loathsome idea whose time had come. Carter never knew what hit him. New information suggests that Reagan's campaign manager, the mysterious William Casey, may have sewn up the 1980 election with direct meddling in the Iranian hostage crisis, a crystal-clear case of high treason if it's true. But once established, the Hollywood monarchy was a concept that worked like a charm—exactly like a charm, and more than a charm. Like a narcotic. Americans seemed to believe in these mediocre performers and their patriotic pageant out of a terrible need to believe, a deeper need than anyone had anticipated.

The trouble was that the roles they played bore no relation to the Reagans themselves, a discrepancy that became painfully obvious when their reign was ended and their image-handlers let them fall. Whether Mrs. Reagan had been what was once known as a tramp isn't really relevant to those of us who relish her discomfort, and neither is the certainty that she was a vulgar, shallow, benighted arriviste. What matters is the overwhelming evidence of her meanness, the utter lack of magnanimity that colors every aspect of her life. Don't let them try to pass her off as a flawed but sensitive gentlewoman victimized by this envious and avaricious guttersnipe from the tabloid press. Nancy Reagan and Kitty Kelley are refugees from the same celebrity cesspool. They worked the same circus. They even shared an interest in Frank Sinatra.

As you read more about them, the more they sound like sisters—

two razor-clawed kittens from the same ferocious litter. Ambitious, ruthless women who left a lot of bodies in their wakes. They lied, invented and reinvented themselves, changed identities when it seemed expedient. Very little that they say about themselves is true. The only difference is that Nancy is older; in her day it took sex and men—a man, preferably—to get a hungry woman what she wanted. Women are making progress when someone of Kelley's generation can claw her way up on energy and intimidation alone.

These women are pure products of the image industry, and sisters under the fur. Even sillier than the scenario of the Queen and the Guttersnipe is the notion that Kelley has committed some unpardonable sin against her profession with a book that contains as much gossip and innuendo as truth. How can you compromise the profession of celebrity journalism, where the basic assumption is that no one but a libel lawyer worries about the truth because none of it matters anyway? Kelley belongs to a sorry sisterhood of affluent journalists—Tina Brown, Liz Smith, Barbara Walters, Diane Sawyer, Connie Chung—who lost their honor and vocation following dollar signs down that dismal dirt road. But somehow her specialty of digging up skeletons and embarrassing the powerful seems more like journalism, to me, than most of the uncritical star-fawning that magazines and networks sell as news.

The whole business is disgusting, but people have it backwards. It isn't this redundant, malicious book that's the crying shame, it's the fact that there was a woman in the White House who provided true grist for such a mill as Kitty Kelley's. Kelley isn't selling half the falsehoods the Reagans were selling, and when it comes to harm done there's no comparison. When the final bill is tallied, what Nancy Reagan sold us will hurt almost everyone in this country—all but the wealthiest one percent, whose income increased 49.8 percent while she was queen. What Kitty Kelley sells hurts only a handful, and most of them deserve it.

The only final appeal is to common decency. And that, I'm afraid, is a court where Nancy Reagan has no right to appear.

III

$\mathscr{P}$olitics — Waiting for the Visigoths

Ask the man in the street what's lower than a journalist, and in most cases he'll say a congressman. The press and the political fraternity are America's evil twins. Democracy depended on them, and on a balance of power between them; they were entrusted with roles of leadership and responsible public service. They both wear masks of public virtue. But they both sold out cheap, and if they truly hate each other it's because each sees its corruption mirrored in the other.

The media and the politicians play the same game now, one for profit and the other for power. It's the game of pandering to the public, exploiting its ignorance, prospering from darkness instead of trying to shed some light. In private, both camps probably curse the public, which bares its teeth and then sells its votes for candy that melts in its hand—for gimmicks as transparently insincere as a "Contract with America" that never mentions campaign reform. But it may not be possible to serve democracy honestly, without condescension, in a nation where 75 percent of the population believes in angels.

The most frustrating thing about covering politics is the idiot assumption that everything you write is connected to some partisan agenda. Anyone who attempts to be objective will be reviled and eventually ostracized by both camps, Left and Right. To me this exile is the last place of honor in a republic of partisans and panders. I was raised by liberal Republicans who believed government should be as compassionate as it could afford to be, with the emphasis on "afford." That still makes sense to me. Now there are no liberals left in the Republican Party and very few true conservatives—just pseudo-intellectual bullies like this Gingrich who play carelessly with the fires of fascism and xenophobia.

I never thought I'd live to see Richard Nixon eulogized as a hero by any-one but Bebe Rebozo or Robert Vesco. His posthumous rehabilitation was the most alarming symptom—so far—of our national amnesia.

Kicking Nixon: A Dog's Life

We used to have terrible fights over Richard Nixon. We: my grand-father, in his 80s, and my father, late 50s, two lifelong Republicans, friends of free enterprise and enemies of FDR; my brother, just home from Vietnam and already a member of Vets Against the War, the only registered Independent in Allegany County; me, late 20s, already peddling opinions for a living, freshly radicalized by the war, Kent State and New York City. My mother usually stayed in the kitchen when the bull elephants began to trumpet. But she had the satisfaction of being the first one in the family to say the war was crazy—back in 1966—and of seeing both her sons convert-ed to her point of view.

The most violent arguments occurred in 1971, when it was uncertain whether Nixon and Kissinger would end the war in Viet-nam or turn it into World War III. According to my father, the old Red-baiter was just the man to negotiate an honorable peace with the communists. My brother and I thought he was just the man to work some political angle that would cost another 40,000 lives.

We'd all be drinking whiskey. Sundays were the worst, when cocktail hour lasted several hours while the roast was in the oven. Through the first drink, the Republicans would listen restlessly while my brother castigated Nixon and the generals. A tour of combat duty gave him the right. But after two drinks they reverted to the surly old Cold Warriors we knew so well.

We were—we are—a demonstrative race. Sometimes we escalat-ed until my mother threatened to call the police. I regret some of the things I said about my family. I don't regret anything I said about Richard Nixon. I'd say I owe him nothing, but maybe I owe him the first argument the younger generation ever won in that house. My father, who had voted for every Republican since Alf Landon, admitted years later that he voted for George McGovern in 1972.

A few months later Watergate ended all the arguments. It wasn't the magnitude of the scandal. History will probably decide that both Reagan and Bush perjured themselves more profoundly and committed worse crimes against the public trust. It was the voice of Nixon himself, on the tapes.

Up to that time, most Americans conceded their president at least a superficial superiority, a median respect for the law of the land, for fair play and common decency. Yet here, indicted by his own words, was a treacherous, paranoid, profane, bigoted, absolutely ruthless and lawless hypocrite whose personal standards fell far below the ones most Americans set for themselves and their neighbors.

It isn't what he did, it's what he turned out to be. We learned that Nixon had no shame, no scruples, no class. He was a petty, ranting tyrant attended by thugs and sycophants. Half the time he sounded out of his head. He took my inexperienced cynicism and turned it from an attitude into an abiding conviction. America's faith in its institutions was permanently damaged 20 years ago—not by Nixon's crimes but by his crumminess.

One of the few decencies we still observe in this country is a reluctance to speak ill of the dead. I respect it. But spare me this amnesia, this impulse to rehabilitate, to forgive, to revise the record on Richard Nixon. I'm holding a newspaper with Nixon's funeral headlined as "A hero's tribute." I remember my favorite line from Hunter Thompson: "If there were a god, Richard Nixon would be somewhere off the coast of Easter Island in the belly of a hammerhead shark."

President Clinton asked us to "assemble to pay homage" to Richard Nixon. He must have been kidding. Forgiving is one thing, forgetting is another. A history that resurrects Nixon is as corrupt as one that denies Auschwitz or asserts that slavery had its sweet side.

But Nixon, whose attitude toward winning was similar to the one that makes Bobby Knight and Tonya Harding as great as they are, understood one thing about winners who end up in the White House. They acquire immunities. The republic is bursting with closet monarchists who hate to see even the most wretched president fall from grace.

Reagan and Bush raised bungling and arrogance almost to the level of treason, but no one wanted to indict them when the evidence finally surfaced. Nixon calculated that Watergate would be forgiven, too; he just overestimated the monarchist factor. But no one complained much when he was pardoned. And as long as his lawyers fight further tape releases, he's still scrapping for his place in history, from beyond the grave.

Presiding at Nixon's funeral, Bill Clinton could take comfort from the odds that he, too, will be acclaimed when he lies in his coffin. In the meantime, thanks to Nixon, he stumbles through minefields of cynicism and suspicion that will maim every presidency until Watergate is forgotten.

Nixon's mother named him for Richard I of England, the legendary Lionheart. But in many ways her boy favored Richard III, another formidable scrapper, to whom history has been less kind. It's easy to imagine Nixon bawling "I am not a crookback!"

He wasn't pretty, inside or outside. It was often said in reference to Nixon that a man's character is stamped on his face. At his darkest Nixon was a gargoyle. The jowly scowl, baroque proboscis and five-o'clock shadow inspired some of the most extravagant caricature ever inflicted on a politician. But it's significant that actual photographs, from certain periods in his life, appear to libel him more cruelly than any hostile artist.

Nixon was elected in 1968, the year of the assassinations, the most desperate, confusing year most of us can remember, when it seemed as if American civilization must be coming to an end. We almost avoided him. He was elected by seven-tenths of a percentage point, in that bizarre year when segregationist Democrats seceded behind George Wallace and moderates voted for Nixon because Hubert Humphrey couldn't repudiate Johnson's war.

"Nixon's victory was the nation's concession of defeat," Garry Wills wrote in Nixon Agonistes, "an admission that we have no politics left but the old individualism, a web of myths that have lost their magic."

The obvious achievements, demonstrating farsightedness at times, are beside the point. Nixon was blessed with analytical intelligence as well as animal cunning. Wouldn't Hubert Humphrey or George McGovern have gone to China, if the opportunity had presented itself? Nixon loved foreign policy because it yielded easy points with historians, while domestic reform was thankless drudgery.

Once he told Time's Hugh Sidey, "I always felt that the country can more or less take care of itself." Give Bill Clinton credit for taking the opposite tack, to almost no applause.

From the beginning Nixon stooped to reptilian depths of political expediency. His early career as a junior Joe McCarthy ought to have been sufficient to seal his fate wherever decent people keep the ledgers. "Of course I knew Jerry Voorhis wasn't a communist," he admitted to a supporter of his first political victim, "but I had to win. The important thing is to win."

That deadly pragmatism surfaced first when Nixon, the son of devout Quaker pacifists, enlisted in the Navy to protect his political prospects. It gave him a distinct advantage over people with principles. The only thing he clearly believed in was a moldy myth served up by Horatio Alger. He was Alger's boy of lowly origins prevailing against a sneering world of privileged Ivy Leaguers. American history became the psychodrama of Nixon's personal redemption.

His was a long, messy, distinctly American life that exposed one of the worms at the core of the American system of government. Presidents are not selected from the general population, but from a very small pool of ego-mutants whose megalomania is sometimes tempered by altruism or public spirit. But sometimes it isn't. The long run for the White House favors drab, driven little men like Nixon and Bush, pure self-believers unencumbered by principles or ideology.

The theme of most of the eulogies was Nixon's phenomenal resilience, his "dogged determination." In fact he was hounded—dogged—by canine metaphors.

"One doesn't like to feel embarrassed by a candidate," Garry Wills observed. "That must explain a good deal of the popular antipathy to Nixon. One is *embarrassed* to keep meeting the dog one kicked yesterday."

Nixon was like a sled dog who finishes the last 100 miles of the Iditarod race with a broken leg. It takes a hell of a dog, but not necessarily a good dog; not necessarily a dog that won't take your hand off, or eat its own puppies in a flash.

It isn't as if he ever had a cause, a constituency or anything to offer except his own miserable ambition. The American Dream of rising in the world has always been vulnerable to the question, "Rising to what?" Fixed on a worthless goal, persistence is a worthless virtue. The Iditarod finish line means nothing to a dog, and

Nixon's only goal—a place in history for Richard Nixon—meant nothing to anyone but Nixon.

Just a month ago he was dragging himself around Moscow, a mangy old hound still sniffing hopefully at the hydrant of history. Dogged he was, as indomitable as he was incorrigible. But sometimes he looked more like a drugged greyhound chasing an artificial rabbit. The pursuit of political advantage was the only game he knew.

Remember *Our Gang*? It was a wild satire by Philip Roth, a book we'd call savage if its target had been anyone less reprehensible. The last chapter is titled "On the Comeback Trail; Or, Tricky in Hell." The assassinated president, Trick E. Dixon, is running against Satan for president of Hell.

Is that beyond the pale, or dead on the mark and very funny? I calculate that Nixon has been gone for two weeks now. Wherever he is, by now he knows half the precinct captains and all the loopholes for slush funds. Whoever's in charge there would be crazy to ignore him.

How do we fight against amnesia, except to write the truth and hope that some small fraction of it will survive us? If Nixon was a hero, maybe Ronald Reagan was the Messiah. Mt. Rushmore? Don't count him out.

Go Tell It on the Mountain

I'm all in favor of putting Ronald Reagan on Mt. Rushmore. I would send money, and take up a collection at work. I want him up there. I want him next to Thomas Jefferson, so the president who learned six languages will be cheek-by-granite jowl with the president who needed a teleprompter to handle one. R. Emmett Tyrrell, the crackpot right-wing editor who's behind this crusade, has promised that no dangerous drilling or dynamiting would be necessary; giant pieces of Reagan's face could be cast in cement and glued to the mountain next to the sculptures of Washington, Lincoln, Jefferson and Theodore Roosevelt.

That's fine, but a little drilling and blasting wouldn't bother me either. What if a few pieces of Washington and Lincoln are lost in Reagan's facelift? I love it. And why stop with Reagan? It's a big mountain. There's room for the other giants of popular culture, for Hulk Hogan, Morton Downey and Madonna. Stick them all up there, until Rushmore is covered with wart-size faces, like pips on a colossal blackberry. Let the great broken stone faces weep rubble among the warts. Let's do the same thing to their mountain that we've done to their republic.

Maybe you sense that I feel something less than religious reverence for Mt. Rushmore. It's true, I share the view of the Sioux Indians from whom the sacred Black Hills were stolen. Indians hate the huge faces, and regard the mountain as a symbol of oppression and broken treaties.

But I know many Americans take Mt. Rushmore seriously, and drive long distances in their campers to show it to their children. Maybe Tyrrell's absurd project and the absurd possibilities in its execution will help to wake them from the coma that began in 1980. Maybe only a great symbolic humiliation—the world howling at a 50-ton cement pompadour amidst the rubble of Rushmore—will wake them to the real humiliation, the comic disaster that was Ronald Reagan.

I'm too young to remember his movies. Like most Americans born in the '40s, I met him first on the General Electric Theater, where he was marking time as an appliance salesman before the political winds began to fill his sails. His was a dignified pitch—TV in general was more dignified in those days—and he was a handsome, reassuring presence even then. But my real introduction came in 1970, when I was assigned to cover the battle between Angela Davis, the black Marxist philosopher, and the conservative Board of Regents that was determined to end her teaching career in the state of California. I started out dead neutral. Within a week Gov. Reagan had turned me into a raging radical. One of my stories had to be rewritten three times because I was too sarcastic at Reagan's expense.

"What do you want me to say?" I blustered at the tired editor who shook his head as he handed back my second version. "This man is the governor of California and he's so stupid he doesn't even understand that he's a racist. He doesn't even know what it means."

When I was out of earshot, I know my editors commiserated: "Lou, they're sending us kids so green they think you have to be smart to be governor of California."

There's a myth that it's the overprivileged, overeducated young people who generate contempt for authority figures. The truth is that young people who spend their formative years in college and graduate school, as opposed to the real world of power and commerce, will tend to overrate the intelligence of the people in charge. The profession of journalism is the only sure antidote for this academic innocence, and Ronald Reagan was my coming of age. Once I knew him, I watched with guilty fascination as his hour came round—not so much a swift rise, in his case, as a standing rooted while the nation slipped back to the place where he was.

Jerzy Kosinski had predicted it all in his novel *Being There*, a fable about a dimwitted gardener named Chance who proves that a perfect fool is the perfect candidate for president of the United States. Peter Sellers played Chance in the movie. We were held in suspense, as readers and as citizens, waiting for Chance and Reagan to stumble and betray their utter incomprehension. And of course they did, repeatedly and flagrantly, but it only added to their mystique and their distance from ordinary men. In the book it was funny.

Chance knew one thing, gardens. Reagan knew one thing, cameras. "Photo opportunity" replaced "equal opportunity" in the living language of our land. At first there was widespread alarm and astonishment that an ignorant actor from the wild right fringe had landed a role so far beyond his skills. But a population softened by decades of television was ready for its first camera-trained president. The chemistry between them resembled hypnosis. They suspended all judgment. Without even asking, he received credit for every benefaction—for warm weather, for fine sunsets—and impunity from every disaster. They called it Teflon, but it was sorcery, blackest magic. It was the old centripetal force between performer and audience, between preacher and congregation, transformed by a new technology into a new and terrible power.

At the center of it he stood and waved. Ronald Reagan. Was he the worst of all possible presidents? He delegated justice to a neo-fascist crony with sticky fingers, civil rights to bigots, foreign policy to psychopathic Marines and gunrunners. He ignored the environment, neglected the poor and nearly bankrupted the country by opening the treasury to the Pentagon and all the corporate thieves who feed there. His few ideas were bloody-minded or outdated and his speeches were comic masterpieces of patriotic buncombe and booster-club patois. I withheld a final judgment. We judge all public figures through a prism of our own prejudices, and some things seemed to go well in spite of Ronald Reagan. In every popular history we read of simple men who grew in office.

Then came his final television interview as president, on CBS' "60 Minutes." He chose the medium he knows and loves best to offer the nation a parting shot on the subject of civil rights.

"Sometimes I wonder if they [black leaders] really want what they say they want," he told Mike Wallace. "Because some of those leaders are doing very well leading organizations based on keeping alive the feeling that they're victims of prejudice."

There's no appropriate response to such a statement. No point, really, in noting that the net worth of the average white family in America is 12 times the net worth of an average household of blacks—$40,000 to $3,400—or that unemployment among blacks has doubled since Reagan fired Angela Davis 20 years ago; that racial incidents in an average year have tripled since 1980 and that life expectancy for blacks has actually dropped, for the first time in a century. Those are just facts. Reagan's remarks to Mike Wallace raised a simple question: Of what country was he president?

"Reagan's attitude resembles the easy-going acceptance by the Aztec emperor Montezuma of the invasion of the Spanish conquistadors in 1519," wrote one stunned historian, the late Barbara Tuchman. But the media, fast in the grip of the national hypnosis, took little notice.

"He left Washington as the most popular president of the postwar era, and the first in 28 years to complete his term with his head held high, unburdened by defeat or disgrace," a wire service poet eulogized. That same week Ollie North went on trial, Justice Department straight arrows refused to exit without reminding us that Ed Meese should have gone to jail, and the General Accounting Office issued an unprecedented report warning George Bush that the Reagan years had all but bankrupted the federal government.

"Win one for the Gippet [sic]," the President told the champion Notre Dame football team, muffing the one line that he had delivered a half a million times. And then made his exit with a 68 percent approval rating, the highest any president has achieved.

We aren't a nation gone deaf and blind so much as a nation in denial. If Reagan is what all the evidence insists he is, what are we? If all we ask of a leader is a smile, a wave and high spirits, couldn't we substitute videotape and keep the Gipper forever, as *Doonesbury* suggested?

Meanwhile the man who knows no history will write his memoirs, with the help of some poor ghost, for a fee of $5 million. The man who never wrote or conceived of a line of his own speeches will make speeches for $50,000 apiece, and his wife will get $30,000. Money they can leave to heirs they almost never see.

History will judge us harshly for this burlesque. No prince will come to wake us from our trance. Nothing releases us but the bitter truth, proclaimed out loud—the president of the United States was a dunce, and a dunce much past his prime, which wasn't much of a prime. He was a dunce of such proportions that the mediocrity historians attribute to Jimmy Carter now seems an impossible dream.

Goodbye President Chance. May you be immortalized in cement, your natural element. Our instant Ozymandias. You were the first President to serve without a clue. Let us pray, gazing into the vacant blue eyes of Dan Quayle—Alfred E. Neuman's handsome little brother—that you weren't the first of many.

George McGovern told me that Jesse Helms has diminished the U.S. Senate more than any man living or dead. In the political kennel, there is no dog so old and mean and stupid that it will not have its day.

Here You Come Again

Every few years the political universe shifts a few degrees to the right and the national media rediscover Jesse Helms. Astonishment is followed by angry editorials and wild stabs at psychobiography. My God, he's *still* there. Bleeding-heart New Yorkers volunteer for Peace Corps assignments in darkest Charlotte. A Georgetown hostess asks me where I'm from and then asks me how I find the stomach to stay.

Rediscovering Jesse is like rediscovering the La Brea tar pits. These are ugly, ancient things that don't go away. But unlike Los Angeles, which built a modern city around its tar pits, North Carolina has made no effort to conceal or improve upon the sticky black hole of Jesse's ignorance, where the fossilized remains of his Cenozoic ancestors lie entombed. If anything we treat him like a tourist attraction.

We appreciate the nation's sympathy. We deserve it. But it's not as if Jesse Helms floats up in front of the sun every morning like the Goodyear blimp and casts a fist-shaped shadow from Murphy to Manteo; the air temperature drops a few degrees, birds cease their song, blue-tick hounds howl mournfully, liberals slink off to their secular prayers behind locked doors.

It's not like that at all. The chorus of amazement that accompanies each rediscovery actually tickles most of us. We get to be experts again, we take calls from out-of-state reporters who were in high school the last time Jesse was discovered. I've had my fun. For a while I wore a Jesse Helms watch someone gave me. It told time in reverse, of course, counterclockwise. Once I called Helms "a mascot, a huge old pit bull, useless and vicious, that sits in its own mess at the end of a tow-truck chain and snarls at everything that moves."

I received the great compliment of seeing that image stolen without apology by the *New York Times*, which probably thinks no one writing down here reads the *Times* or understands copyright.

Another time I compared Jesse to Grendel, but his brain trust at the Congressional Club probably told him I meant Fred Grendle, who runs the feed store up on Rte. 158 between Oxford and Berea.

Jesse's such a wonderful foil and such a gifted comedian in his own right, it's a good thing humorless liberals break in from time to time to remind us that life with Jesse isn't all songs and skits.

If Jesse and the segregationists hadn't bushwhacked Sen. Frank Porter Graham in 1950, North Carolina might now be a state everyone could be proud of, with real pride instead of the chamber of commerce variety. Instead of a backsliding contradiction of a state where pockets of progress and talent are surrounded by a wilderness of reaction and racial resentment, and where nearly a million people live below the poverty line.

Nelson Mandela might have been out of prison 10 years earlier, if Helms and other racists hadn't sent South Africa the quasi-official message that a lot of Americans thought Mandela was right where he belonged. Jesse's the one who would need bodyguards if he ever visited El Salvador or Nicaragua (or Fire Island).

There are checkpoints on the highway to heaven where the angels will take a hard look at that thing old Jesse calls his soul. But what he's selling in 1994 is mainly nostalgia. Nostalgia for the good old days when a Coke cost a nickel, everybody was a Baptist who talked like Sam Ervin and weird sex was anything you did with the lights on. When you could sit on your porch and talk to someone across the street, with no traffic to drown out your voices.

Most of us from small towns feel this same sense of loss and displacement. Unfortunately, Jesse's customers are all white people, and in North Carolina white nostalgia for the good old days usually includes nostalgia for separate rest rooms and lunch counters.

A vote for Jesse Helms is a vote for their ancestors. North Carolina has been begging for Disney's historical theme park. But our senator is a walking theme park with two themes, Jim Crow and the Cold War.

They were the pole stars of his life. In each case containment was the thing. A man could get a good night's sleep if he knew the colored and the communists were in their proper places, on the other side of the tracks and the other side of the world. But it took a viable threat to keep them in their place.

This world that produced Jesse Helms sounds prehistoric, to most of us here on the threshold of the 21st century. Does the last prominent relic of the old Jim Crow/John Birch South pose a viable threat to the security of America?

I don't think so. Aside from his refreshing sense of humor (who else could have added "garden-variety lesbian" to the Senate lexicon), there's no compelling evidence to refute the theory that Jesse is a moron. Think of Forrest Gump's cranky older brother, with a toothache.

In the flexible profession of politics, he's the rarest thing of all, a flatliner—a man who has practiced politics for 50 years with no discernible learning curve. It isn't very likely that Sen. Helms is a satanic hypocrite. He's mastered a kind of hit-and-run style, wise-cracking out of closing elevators and car windows. But when you trap him in front of a microphone, he's a tongue-tied, slightly bewildered old guy who sounds about as cerebral as most of his true believers.

Making Jesse chairman of the Senate Foreign Relations Committee is a comic inspiration, like naming Barney Fife to direct the FBI. Who said Republicans have no sense of humor? Who said history has no sense of humor?

If Ollie North were elected president, of course, he and Jesse and a Republican Congress might get a lot of people killed, and 40 years of diplomacy undone in six months. But that's an unlikely scenario. Even as chairman, Helms will offer little more than his usual noise and nuisance. Many Senate Republicans, including several members of the Foreign Relations Committee, find Jesse's crackpot foreign policy (invade Cuba now!) much less appetizing than Bill Clinton's.

In this period of national realignment and right-wing evangelism, Jesse Helms may be the best thing the poor liberals and moderates have left in their arsenal. His national approval rating, 13 percent, is a third of Clinton's worst ever. The country isn't going back where Jesse is—there are too many young people and nonwhites who will never figure out where he is, or where he's been.

He serves the nation as a kind of navigational marker, a fixed thing to steer away from if you want to keep yourself from grounding on dangerous shoals. The whole political spectrum has shifted to the Right dramatically, but as long as Jesse lives we can always find Too Far.

If only all the reactionaries were like Jesse Helms, painted purple with a big necklace fashioned from the jawbones of civil rights workers and Latin-American peasants. If only they were all Macy's Parade-size and trailing long kite-tails of errors, absurdities and unbelievable quotes on everything from art to apartheid.

It's the camouflaged ones, the ones who all seem to look alike and think alike, the consumer Christians with identical Lite-Right lives who scare the daylights out of me. Who can tell them from ordinary citizens until some door slams shut and they've got us? Jesse's not the problem. You can see him coming from 100 miles away.

The most lucid things about politics are usually written before the election. Afterwards, despair or elation may throw the best of us off balance.

Swallow the Leader

"The essential safeguard against the tyranny of arbitrary officials is to be found in applying steadfastly the liberal conception of the official as a man with specific rights and duties, rather than as a man touched with the divinity that hedges the King."

— Walter Lippmann, *The Good Society*

The confetti was still aloft in Atlanta when the first wave of nonsense went out over the wires. Typical of the vacant fustian and deliberately misleading mind-candy that passes for commentary on the editorial pages of this benighted republic is the so-called "leadership" question. Michael Dukakis was still waving and smiling his tight little smile when the first headline appeared over the byline of one of Washington's most reliably irrelevant insiders: "Dukakis can manage—but can he lead us?"

A rule of thumb in presidential debates is that anyone who brings ups "leadership" or "experience" is either an idiot or a partisan with a secret agenda. Leadership is a much-abused, manipulative buzzword that exploits a childish people who long for a forceful father figure. In politics it means the same as "charisma." And charisma, as near as I can figure, is simply the force that guides the bullet to its target.

The Kennedys had it, Martin Luther King had it, Malcolm X had it. Ronald Reagan and George Wallace had some, but not enough to create a perfect bull's-eye.

God save us all from charisma. Americans are a wild, violent, contrary people. The flip side of our adulation is hatred, the companion of our worship is murderous wrath. Ask Yoko Ono about charisma in America. Consider dangerous jobs. You might think that policemen or convenience store clerks run the highest risk of being murdered. But the most dangerous job in the United States is President, with a murder for every 47 man-years on the job. The celebrity machinery makes any president a target, but a president who commands emotional responses has a life expectancy measured in months. I never thought that a Jesse Jackson presidency would be dangerous for America; I know it would be dangerous for Rev. Jackson, and so does he.

"Magnetism" has a grim history among us chronic regicides. Maybe we can begin to do without it. Since authentic personal magnetism is rarely visible through the image machinery that surrounds the modern candidate, what we're really considering is whether the candidate has qualities that can be manipulated to create the appearance of leadership. But when a president who appears to be leading has no idea where he's going, the situation is analogous to the migration of the lemmings, or the Charge of the Light Brigade. That was the hard lesson we learned from Ronald Reagan.

Leaders will play different roles in the 21st century. We won't need heroes, or orators who make us rage and weep. There'll be no place for war chiefs, Sun Kings, Divine Emperors, Royal Highnesses. In successful societies inspiration will be a controlled substance. In a crowded world, nationalism creates nothing but widows and deserts. Iran's Khomeini has been a charismatic leader, one of the last if we're lucky.

We won't need leaders to mobilize us, because there's nowhere for us to go. No more frontiers. Gov. Dukakis dressed it up rhetorically when he spoke of "the next frontier," but he was acknowledging that all further frontiers are symbolic or internal. "Frontier" is a word that has a special effect on Americans; I doubt that politicians in other countries use it at all.

A lot of Americans still talk about "presidential timber," which means a tall handsome man they can shout for and shoot at. But the leaders of the next century are going to be managers, mediators and technocrats. The old challenge was to make a nation grow, and growl at its neighbors on cue; the new challenge is to make it function. A nation still pining for Davy Crockett will be a nation on the outside looking in.

The gravest of all America's problems is its untamable irrationality. One part of our American heritage is madness. What nation so loves its guns, its drugs, its pseudoscience, its crazy religions, its wildest dreams? Where else are there astrologers in the royal palace, or attempts to bring an obese, drug-addicted rock star back from the dead? Yesterday on color TV—cable channel 5—I saw a big plain country woman in a yellow silk cocktail dress holding up her nail-punctured palms to the camera. She wasn't selling just the stigmata of Christ crucified, but his actual bleeding wounds, from nails the size of railroad spikes. The camera dropped down across yards of yellow silk and there on each instep, just above her dyed-to-match yellow pumps, were the nail wounds that completed the crucifixion. An organ played. An evangelist shouted "Praise Jesus!" Poor vacant country Christians filed by her lowing gently and shaking their heads with wonder. On color TV, in a nation with 99 percent literacy.

Anyone who watched the Democratic convention understands that wound-gazing is closer to the center than to the periphery of the American experience. After two days in Atlanta, a virgin convention correspondent called to complain that he's never seen people to match these delegates, and that his stomach would never weather New Orleans if indeed the Republicans were worse. I told him to think like an anthropologist; there is nothing left on earth, as H.L. Mencken reported 70 years ago, to rival the silliness of an American political convention. It's never been clear whether delegates are drugged with amphetamines, pre-programmed like daytime TV audiences or handpicked for their silliness and mindless enthusiasm.

Into this landscape of delirium marched the accountant, the Greek in the gray flannel suit. Michael Dukakis has never kindled a fire in any heart but the heart of Mrs. Dukakis, and even this lady treats him a little like Blondie treats Dagwood. Even in the giddy atmosphere of Atlanta, the convention's enthusiasm for its nominee seemed a little half-hearted or forced. Even "Duke," the nickname they love to call him, has a bite of irony matched against the macho memories of John Wayne and Edwin Donald Snider.

No passions will slay him, if he becomes president of the United States, nor will they elevate him to the comic Throne of Ronald. He doesn't appeal to the dark, wound-gazing side of the American psyche, the same side that promotes a foreign policy of excessive pride and paranoia, a domestic policy of mistrust and callous self-interest.

Dukakis made his reputation with competence, which even his enemies seem to grant him, and which ought to be something of a selling point after the Reagan debacle. After what's gone down in this country for the past eight years, we don't need a leader as much as we need a good plumber. We need a president who's learned a trade, not a president who's learned a role. Let him lead us nowhere. Let him take out his tools and do his job.

I detested George Bush, probably because his goofy patrician innocence masked Washington's most perfect moral vacuum. This is a dour post-election piece, but I like it because it has a hero, a villain, and a moral.

Class Distinctions

There was a time when I believed that great coincidences were especially arranged to catch my attention. There's still such a thing as a coincidence I can't resist.

On November 8, 1988, George Bush was elected president of the United States, and Kingman Brewster died of a brain hemorrhage in England. Two Yale men of the '40s, two New England aristocrats with distinguished service records as naval aviators in World War II. Former ambassadors who had been featured on the cover of *Newsweek* and caricatured in *Doonesbury*. A pair of tall, athletic men whose clothing, bearing and haircuts would always proclaim them Ivy Leaguers of a certain vintage. In a herd of their kind, at a summer place in Maine or on the Vineyard, they'd have looked as much alike as two stripes on a club tie.

Two men with nothing in common. The Nov. 9 news stories on Bush's triumph and Brewster's death reminded me of one of the key philosophical debates of the '60s, that decade in which Brewster figured so prominently while Bush was characteristically invisible. Where could a young man of principle work most effectively, we asked ourselves earnestly and ingenuously—inside or outside the system? It was a big question. We all agreed that great changes were necessary. It was a question of methods. Some favored law school and ringing doorbells, some favored civil disobedience and guerrilla warfare. Patience versus passion.

Kingman Brewster, born and nurtured in the bosom of the American establishment, grew restless in there. A student of the law and something of a prodigy in legal education, he was a full professor at Harvard Law School at the age of 34. Yale trustees didn't smell any subversive qualities when they hired him as the university's 17th president in 1963. But the '60s had a way of testing and defining people. Brewster turned Yale upside down. His new admissions director recruited minorities aggressively and rejected the under-qualified sons of alumni. In 1969, the 268-year-old university admitted its first women undergraduates. And in 1970, caught between conservative alumni and a militant student consensus against the war in Vietnam, Brewster sided with his students. After he led a Yale contingent of 1200 antiwar demonstrators to Washington, Vice President Spiro Agnew called for his resignation. Conservatives reviled him as a cowardly administrator caving in to campus radicals. When he resigned in 1977 to serve as Jimmy Carter's ambassador to Great Britain, Brewster joked that his departure would give Yale's fund drive a $100-million shot in the arm.

Where was George? He was in Texas, running for a Senate seat as an archenemy of Martin Luther King and the Civil Rights act of 1964. Adapting easily to the John Birch politics of West Texas, where he made a modest fortune in the oil business, Bush campaigned far to the right of his own father, a former Republican senator who supported civil rights, opposed Joe McCarthy and criticized Vietnam policy. As a Texas congressman in 1968, Bush tried to gut the fair housing bill. Wherever America tried to move forward, he was there, in his quiet way, trying to push her back. Defeated by Lloyd Bentsen in another Senate race in 1970, he was recruited by Richard Nixon for a series of dirty jobs, including ambassador to the U.N. (which he had savaged as a right-wing congressman and where he passionately defended the Taiwanese while Nixon and Kissinger, unbeknownst to Bush, were dealing with the communists to sell them out).

From that triumph he went on to chair the shellshocked Republican National Committee at the height of Watergate, leaving "I have absolutely total confidence as to his integrity" as his tribute to a president who would resign a few days later. Again he never complained about being kept in the dark. "He'll do anything for the cause," Nixon told H.R. Haldeman. Gerald Ford rewarded George with the CIA, again at the most demoralized point in its history. One of his appointees at the Company was the now-legendary hardliner Richard Pipes, who said that all we needed to survive a nuclear war was "enough shovels." Immune to embarrassment or irony, Bush even accepted an appointment as envoy to Red China. In 1980 Ronald Reagan found him more than eager to change a few stripes and accept the most thankless job of all.

The remarkable record of George Bush is a record of unquestioning adherence to "the system" however and wherever he found it. It's a

record of defending every failed and contradictory policy from Tai-
wan and Vietnam through Nicaragua, and staunchly defending
every liar and villain—Nixon, Ed Meese, Ray Donovan, Ollie
North, John Poindexter, even Ferdinand Marcos ("We love your
adherence to democratic principles"—1981)—who was attached to
the party he served. As a perfect tool of the most devious American president and then of the most slow-witted, and about the only
major tool that one inherited from the other, George Bush left a
record of stone-blind loyalty that may never be challenged.

There must be a moral here. The man who served folly faithfully
and shrank from any dissent has been elected president of the
United States. The man who had a quarrel of conscience with the
establishment and removed himself from its center to its far
perimeter has died, if you will, in exile. No one would say in disgrace. At his death Brewster was master of University College,
Oxford, the oldest college in the English-speaking world, 450 years
older than Yale. His Oxford appointment was a great honor. But
Brewster's voluntary expatriation, at an age when most men cling
to home, could be taken as a comment on the society he left
behind. Even Yale has changed a lot. Measured against the 1200
antiwar demonstrators in 1970 is an astonishing statistic: in 1985,
one-third of Yale's graduating class applied to work at a single
investment bank, First Boston.

To the class of 1985, the story of George Bush and Kingman
Brewster may have a simple and obvious moral: Don't bite the hand
that feeds you. To the Yale class of 1969, the Brewster class that
included *Doonesbury* creator Garry Trudeau, the moral may be something quite different. The question of inside vs. outside was based on
the old criterion of achievement—not on power, acquisition or fluc-
tuations in the human stock market that the United States has
become. It can be argued forcefully that George Bush, at 64, has
accomplished absolutely nothing except America's most impressive
resumé. Brewster left his permanent mark on the educational establishment, especially on the elitist education that still seems to produce most of our political leaders. Much more to the point, he died
at peace with the mirror on his wall. It might not occur to the class
of '85, but it would certainly occur to the class of '69 to ask which
was more valuable to a man, the White House or his self-respect.

They might seriously question the value of working inside a system that rewards a tractable, obsequious flunky ("No imagination

or originality," said his prep school English teacher; "Few ideological or intellectual beliefs at all," added *Time*) and turns its back on a man so far superior in intellect, independence and integrity that even the President-elect would wave away the comparison. There are few specimens who've been stewing inside the establishment quite as long as George Bush. But even a few years inside seems to leave the would-be best and brightest looking like Cornish game hens that were broiled too close to the flame. After two or three terms of Bush and Dan Quayle, the next generation may begin to question whether this system we've created is capable of supporting intelligent life.

Who would join a revolution against poor old George Bush? Some of the overheated political rhetoric of the '60s embarrasses me now, almost as much as the nonsense of secret societies that we children went through with such straight faces, imagining that we were cutting great figures. We were more likely to protest the invasion of Laos than the hazing at Lambda Chi. But patterns emerge early, and it's often true that the boy is the father to the man. Kingman Brewster launched an audacious attack on Yale's ancient senior societies when he was editor of the *Yale Daily News*. One superficial thing that he and George Bush didn't have in common was membership in ultra-exclusive (and increasingly embarrassing) Skull and Bones. When the members came to get him for initiation, Brewster hid himself in a basement bathroom. When his turn came, of course, George Bush went right along.

Anything we write about an incumbent president dates very rapidly. This is a recent attempt to understand why so many Americans hate this curious man so violently.

Clinton Groans on the Rack

The only thing certain about the friendly invasion of Haiti is that it will turn out badly for President Clinton. If the operation reduces American anxieties and even brings some small measure of security and sanity into the lives of Haitians, Jimmy Carter gets a Nobel Peace Prize. Jean-Bertrand Aristide gets a media whitewash and a second chance, Colin Powell gets a blank check to run for national office. The president gets another dunce-cap as a bungler who was saved by cooler heads.

If Haiti turns into a debacle, Clinton gets all the blame, for blundering into a situation so volatile that no one could save him. What curse is on this man? History will say almost nothing of his immediate predecessors, save that they achieved moments of great popularity by invading small nations and smashing them flat. But when Clinton rattles his saber—out of misguided idealism or a burning desire to be praised by someone, anyone—this nation of knee-jerk belligerents turns its back in disgust.

Who wrote the script? It's like a Jerry Lewis movie where the hero can't take a step left, right, backward or forward without falling on his face. But like much of the Lewis *oeuvre*, it exhausts its humor quickly. Trip a man three times and it's comedy; trip him ten times and it's cruelty.

How bad can it get? The Haitian adventure united Democrats and Republicans in North Carolina's congressional delegation for what must be the first time in history—all in opposition, of course. Jimmy Carter, fresh off the plane from Port-au-Prince, summoned CNN to the White House (the Lincoln bedroom) and explained why the president, in the event of success in Haiti, deserves no credit whatsoever. On the editorial pages, the bloody beaks of hawks and doves pecked with equal ferocity at the man who can do no right.

Does Bill Clinton have a right to be paranoid? Paula Jones and the Whitewater investigation may cost him most of a million dollars in legal fees, a sum about equal to the Clintons' net worth. Since the last time a Democrat held the White House, the Republican opposition has lost its ideological rudder and degenerated into a fierce polyglot rabble united in nothing but their determination to destroy a Democratic president.

Far from dissociating themselves, national Republican leaders march hand-in-claw with media cutthroats who smear Clinton so outrageously that any acknowledgement of their charges would dishonor the presidency. Courtesy of the "Christian" Right, Hillary Clinton has heard herself accused of the murder of Vincent Foster. The Clintons have been portrayed as the godparents of some kind of redneck Mafia that buried its critics and turncoats in shallow graves all over Arkansas.

According to the *The New York Review of Books*, "the principal adversary of the President of the United States" is talk-show titan Rush Limbaugh, who practiced his own version of Christian charity by calling Clinton's daughter Chelsea "the family dog." Though his liberal detractors (see FAIR's "The Way Things Aren't") have documented hundreds of egregious factual errors in Limbaugh's broadcasts, he reaches a radio audience of 20 million scary "dittoheads" who bristle at the suggestion that his rabble-rousing monologues are rarely anchored in reality. One loyal dittohead is his personal friend William Bennett, would-be-president and author of a best-selling book on personal morality.

Limbaugh has never pretended to journalistic standards, but equally rabid Clinton-haters at *The American Spectator* and *Human Events* carry press cards without apology. The so-called straight press, caught in its own lazy slide toward tabloid irrelevance, sponges up stories from the mud-wrestling media more carelessly than ever before, and mocks the president when he objects.

Is Bill Clinton justified in describing himself, after only 20 months in office, as "the most maligned of modern presidents"? Is Richard Nixon so quickly replaced? I keep seeing articles denying that this abuse is unusual. They quote savage attacks on FDR and Harry Truman by right-wing publishers, and note the fact that Ronald Reagan, at this same stage in his first administration, scored worse than Clinton in the Gallup Poll's love/hate ratings.

These same don't-worry-be-happy writers tell me that the religious right is a paper tiger, and that man-haters carry no weight in the women's movement. But I've learned to trust my nose, and I smell pungent pathology. Garry Wills, whom I've always respected as a sane voice from the center, catches the same scent.

"The amount of personal meanness is staggering," Wills writes, "even to the casual bystander."

Appalled by the psychotic pitch of the lynch-Clinton rhetoric, veteran Washington columnist Richard Reeves takes his misgivings a little further.

"The mood of the capital right now is poisonous," he writes. "The air is heavy with hazy humidity, fear, loathing, lying, sanctimony and hypocrisy. It's a slimy, desperate place these days, worse than I have ever seen it."

Even Barry Goldwater and William F. Buckley, relics from the days when their party stood for something besides hostility to Democrats, have warned Republicans to take it easy.

"Get off his back and let him be president," growls Goldwater, who will yet make me proud that I supported him in 1964.

How much abuse is justified? I can quarrel with the president from the left or from the right. I think he's let himself be used by some narrow-gauge liberals. I think he's failing, like every president before him, to distance himself sufficiently from the military-industrial high command that still accounts for most of the chronic inequities in the American system.

He's made his share of bad policy, more than his share of tactical blunders. His character, like most characters, seems intricately but not fatally flawed. His legislative achievements—NAFTA, the Brady Bill, the national service act, the omnibus crime bill—are impressive in spite of Republican obstruction. His aspirations are terrific. The administration is crafting legislation to reform welfare, education, campaign spending and the federal bureaucracy, and health care reform is still a priority. He's even reducing the deficit.

This is the first president since Lyndon Johnson who's not only qualified to be president but interested in the job, as opposed to the title. He's the first president who ever stood up to the gun and tobacco lobbies, perhaps the most potent concentrations of selfish, lethal unreason in the entire body politic. He tackled the health insurance colossus solely on behalf of low-income Americans; the Clintons can afford health care, in spite of their legal bills. But it hasn't made him a popular hero.

"I get sick when I think about him," says a registered Democrat in Michigan.

"I wouldn't vote for Clinton for dog-catcher," says another in North Carolina, featured in a story "Democrats run from Clinton."

This is what the president hears with the nation at peace and a resurgent economy growing at a steady three percent, creating disposable income and millions of jobs. Some observers blame it all on the amazing proliferation of talk radio, dominated by right-wing pit bulls (nine are now running for Congress) who encourage callers in their grossest prejudice and cultivate their most irrational fears. But there were always cranks and fanatics to fling sewage at the man in the White House; the weird thing about Bill Clinton is that the stuff all seems to stick.

According to Garry Wills, Clinton "has challenged others at some very deep and obscure level." Several months ago my wife and I had an uneasy dinner with old friends, a couple our age who dismissed the Clintons contemptuously and seemed more amazed than offended when we objected. The interesting thing was that this couple has everything in common with the Clintons: age, class, education, income, community involvement. If they lived in Arkansas instead of Tennessee, they're precisely the kind of people who might have shared investments—hopefully not Whitewater investments—with Bill and Hillary.

Yet they detest the president, and apparently all their friends agree. These are affluent, sophisticated people, anything but ditto-heads. But in the Southern mold they're traditional families, based on an unspoken assumption that the male will lead and provide.

There's no question that Hillary Clinton, the first fully liberated woman to live in the White House, threatens a lot of traditional marriages in and out of the South. But I think it's her husband who really throws them.

The New Woman requires a New Man. The man who can live comfortably with Hillary is not a man the Old School can understand or admire. He represents a loss of status for the males, a loss of security for the females. He represents a future where they don't belong. He's the harbinger of their extinction.

This is my best guess. I think it's supported by another, more dramatic encounter with Old School assumptions. I took a trip to the Galapagos a few years ago with some students, teachers and alumni from my college. The obvious alpha male of this group—the only male over 30, besides me—was a handsome gentleman of 60, the brother of a former director of the CIA. He was an upper-class, boarding-school kind of man, of a generation accustomed to deference.

His leadership faced one obstacle. I'm no leader but I'm a truly defective follower, a kind of passive-aggressive spoiler who has rejected every attempt to lead me since I was five or six. We clashed. In conflict, his natural instinct was to *assert command.* Mine was to seek consensus, to sound out the kids and the women and secure some allies.

Here on this little boat in the mid-Pacific, two types of men locked horns: it was '60s Man vs. '40s Man, Consensus Man vs. Ivy League Alpha Male. My type never expected to be obeyed. Our world didn't condition us that way. We expect to labor and compromise to get what we want, whether it's a good marriage or a ban on semiautomatic weapons.

Bill Clinton is the epitome of '60s Man, or even an exaggeration. Everyone agrees that his Achilles heel is his need to please everyone, consult everyone, keep everyone in the loop. Perfect for a politician, right? But brand new, and alarming, in a president. The presidency was designed for a big old alpha male, which is to say for a constitutional monarch.

A lot of people crave the security of a Great White Father, even if it's just a dotty old actor in makeup or a neutered aristocrat like George Bush. But there aren't going to be any more Big Daddies in the White House. The world has moved on; Bill and Hillary are the proof of that. And all the people who feel left behind will hate them for it.

IV

*N*obody's Business

My wife, a merchant's daughter, accuses me of being deaf to the American Dream—to "the romance of money," as she calls it. But I'm the grandson of two businessmen, one of them successful, and I was his summer chauffeur during my most impressionable years. I've seen "bidness" with its clothes off more often than most newsroom people, who tend to be a little naive about the marketplace. It seems to me that most business writers are even more prone to sycophancy and cheerleading than sportswriters. Along with teachers in business schools, they're way too vulnerable to the philistine's skepticism—"If you know so much about making money, why don't you go out and make some?"

American capitalism suffers from a pituitary problem, an unnatural tendency toward giantism. No one understands the new corporate Frankensteins except the 100 big players who put them together, and maybe their lawyers. The rest of us are just scavengers, and the scavenging gets uglier every year. Wealth is power, and no diehard communist or New Age crystal cultist is more credulous than the capitalist tool who believes that most people will use their power wisely and scrupulously, or that unrestrained greed (i.e., competition) will somehow enrich and ennoble the family of man.

The anonymous carpenter in this story is one of my personal heroes. Much of America's boyish charm—and nearly all of its stupidity and cruelty—derives from its stubborn denial of the most self-evident truths about wealth and class.

Fat Cats and Blind Mice

The Middleton Place, a few miles up the Ashley River from Charleston, is a restored antebellum plantation that stands as a monument to the grandeur of the South Carolina rice aristocracy. Its formal gardens, the oldest landscaped gardens in North America, are impressive in any season and unforgettable when the azaleas are in bloom, as they were when I paid my visit.

Begun in 1741, the gardens reflect the exquisite taste of Henry Middleton (1717–1784), who owned more land than any other man in the 13 colonies at the time of the American Revolution. He also owned, at the peak of his prosperity, more than 800 slaves. "An ardent Revolutionary patriot," Henry served briefly as president of the First Continental Congress. His son Arthur (1742–1787) was one of the signers of the Declaration of Independence. Arthur's son Henry served as governor of South Carolina and Minister to the Court of the Czar under President Monroe, and his grandson Williams signed the Ordinance of Secession that precipitated the Civil War.

A distinguished dynasty that came to an end, at least on the fertile land that nurtured it, when Union troops arrived in February 1865 and burned the Big House to the ground. The ruins remain, to remind visitors of Yankee barbarism. You don't hear much about the Middletons anymore, but they were the American equivalents of European dukes or princes of the blood. From the Benjamin West portraits of old Henry and Arthur and the original furnishings and silver that have been collected in the old guest house—the only building that survived the Yankees—you know that these rice planters lived in a style that most colonists could never have imagined this side of Versailles.

The Middletons, prominent in both the Revolutionary and Confederate causes, qualify as prime American patriots for most of the visitors who take the tour here. The guide's tone when she speaks of them is generally one of reverence. These were gentle-men carrying the torch of civilization in an age of ignorance and savagery. But I found, to my delight, that the official spiel is not the only lecture available to visitors at the Middleton Place.

In several of the outbuildings—the blacksmith and potter's shops, the tanning and weaving sheds—the foundation that runs the place has established craftspersons to demonstrate 18th-century techniques. In the carpenter's shop I found a vigorous gray-haired man in his fifties who was simultaneously planing something that looked like a headboard and delivering a lecture on the Middletons and the history of the United States.

His was not a version of history that the dozen or so tourists in his audience had heard before. It was positively, deliciously subver-sive. Think about what you've seen and heard here, he was telling them. These Middletons, whom you've never heard of, were the absolute lords of the earth. They owned the land, they owned the labor, they owned the banks and mills and transportation. They owned the legislature and the government—hell, they *were* the legislature and the government. (I paraphrase as closely as I can—I didn't take notes.) Every one of these planters sent his sons to law school and then to the capital to make the laws he needed. Every legislator, every magistrate, every sheriff depended on the patron-age of people like the Middletons.

"Their will was the law," the carpenter said. "They left nothing to chance."

When you read about the Revolution and the Civil War you read about patriotism, loyalty, sacrifice, liberty, he explained to his listeners, who were getting restless but not from boredom. Then you learn that the Middletons were in the thick of it, both times. These were the champions of liberty, with 800 slaves? Or was it just business, after all? King George with his taxes and meddling was bad for the Middletons' business; Yankee abolitionists and protec-tive tariffs on European trade goods were bad for business, too. His-tory sanitizes our wars, to make everybody feel better about their motives. But consider the possibility that a lot of poor boys died to protect these Middletons' interests. Consider that not much has changed.

It was all I could do to hold my applause. This was the most con-cise, effective lesson in materialism and economic history I ever heard, delivered in a barn on a carpet of sawdust. Who was this guy? Somehow I doubted that he had spent his whole life planing headboards.

His class dispersed muttering or chuckling uncomfortably, for the most part. I walked out grinning and sat for a few minutes under the Middleton Oak—with a circumference of 37 feet and a limb spread of 145, the 500-year-old live oak is the second most impressive presence at the Middleton Place. For me, the carpenter's speech had the irresistible appeal of anything that's obviously true and obviously oversimplified. But the carpenter had hit the nail on the head. He was pointing at the single greatest political blind spot that afflicts Americans and prevents us from establishing a democracy that lives up to our ideals.

Most American voters not only fail to understand the connection between economics and politics, they fail to acknowledge that one exists. Taught for generations to despise Karl Marx and everything he stood for, they have refused to learn the simple Marxist precept that illuminates history better than anything else political science has devised: An unequal distribution of wealth divides a society into classes, and class interests determine everything else. Economics doesn't effect history, Marx would have said—it *is* history.

Epidemic class blindness is uniquely American. Great Britain has an odious class system, but it's thoroughly acknowledged and factored into the political equation. I have a Laborite friend in Lancastershire who told me he'd never vote for any bloke who'd had his teeth fixed. In the United States there's a pervasive class system, economically determined, that nearly everyone agrees to ignore.

Poor whites are somehow convinced, by appeals to racism and xenophobia, that they have something to gain by voting for their natural class enemies like George Bush and Dan Quayle. They embrace demagogues like Jesse Helms who pander exclusively to the rich and the big corporations. They never seem to ask, why is elective office for sale at prohibitive prices? Why is legislation controlled by industrial lobbies and PACs? Who actually benefits from wars? What happened to the progressive income tax? Why do we have to pay for the S&L bailout?

Sometimes this class blindness, this economic blindness, is simply staggering. At its worst, the American public acts like a quarter of a billion blind mice, mutant mice who circle around the purring candidates every election and deny that these are cats.

"Doesn't feel like a cat to me—maybe some kind of muskrat."

"No, those aren't claws. I think they're cufflinks."

It's pathetic. And the most pathetic development of all is this groundswell of enthusiasm for the presidential candidacy of one Ross Perot. The most shocking statistic to surface, after 12 years of Republican rule, is that the richest one percent of American families, who already owned 90 percent of everything, walked off with three-quarters of all the fresh cash the economy generated during the boom years.

For many Americans, the logical response to this rape is to elect a multi-billionaire—representing the richest one percent of the richest one percent—to set it right.

I honestly feel sorry for anyone who thinks this makes good sense. I can understand disgust with the two-party system and with both parties that operate it, but for Perot to represent himself as the lone wolf outsider is more than disingenuous. It's hilarious. This is one of the men who truly owns and operates our system, who has manipulated it ingeniously to enrich himself and further his purposes. Politicians are just pawns on a chessboard to men like Perot.

Mix Perot and President Bush with a group of America's most influential power brokers and you'd understand, in a flash, who's inside and who's outside. Perot's history as a Nixon courtier and campaign contributor is no secret. Neither is the story of the land he "donated" for an airport that was built, through his lobbying, at the government's expense. The value of Perot's land on every side of the airport was increased a hundredfold—a classic example of the way insiders become billionaires in the United States.

His supporters aren't deterred by any of these inconsistencies, or even by the fact that he has no policies and no positions. They simply like his style. Everyone loves a little bulldog.

The protocol, ever since the Middletons' time, is for major players like Perot to operate in the shadows, lest their egregious affluence offend the less fortunate. But every once in a while there's a Middleton so bursting with vanity that he needs to offer himself to the public in the flesh. He's the one we really have to watch out for.

Even Perot must have been surprised by his enthusiastic reception, though mini-groundswells greeted the presidential aspirations of Donald Trump and Lee Iacocca. There are a lot of mice in this country who love to play with cats. And the voice of the carpenter goes unheard.

I'm always warning young people against the devil in his gray flannel suit. Karoshi is a concept that catches a lot of people by surprise. We'll be hearing a lot more about it as American corporations get leaner and meaner. We need to make the most careful study of business traditions in Japan, in order to proceed in the opposite direction.

Recruiters from Hell

A few days before his death, Japanese advertising executive Toshitsugu Yagi made this entry in his journal: "In the past, slaves were loaded onto slave ships and carried off to the New World. But in some way, aren't our daily commuter trains packed to the brim even more inhuman?"

Yagi died of heart failure at 43, a victim of *karoshi*, the lethal overwork syndrome that kills 10,000 Japanese annually—roughly the same death toll as traffic accidents. The government refuses to compensate the family of a *karoshi* victim unless he was working at least twice his normal hours within a week of his death; Yagi's widow is still trying to collect. Since his promotion a year earlier, he had arrived home after midnight nearly every day, frequently worked all night or slept at a hotel near his office, and worked through all his holidays.

In a video chronicling the deaths of Toshitsugu Yagi and several other terminal victims, a lawyer who litigates *karoshi* cases issued a warning: "We are worried that Japanese firms setting up overseas have begun exporting *karoshi*, through their system of long working hours and few holidays."

America's corporate chieftains admire Japanese productivity and praise the Japanese work ethic. They're "downsizing" their payrolls and calculating their competitive strategies on substantially more work by fewer workers. Imagine a Roman galley trying to improve its speed with fewer slaves at the oars. The captain didn't offer bonuses and incentives. He oiled the bullwhips. That's the mood in many boardrooms, and the specter of *karoshi* is the last thing on their minds.

According to a study by psychiatrist Paul Rosch, who heads the American Institute of Stress, job stress and burnout is a $200 billion-a-year liability for American business. Rosch blames overwork and insecurity for rising rates of alcoholism, suicide and even cancer, which now appears to be stress-related. In another study, 42 percent of working women reported chronic stress related to their jobs, and a third said that quitting was the only way out (but 43 percent said "working harder" was the way to cope with stress).

Sydney Pollack's *The Firm* presented a sort of hyped-up metaphor for the cul-de-sac—"No exit, no ethics, no mercy"—that successful men often encounter in the fast lane. One reporter interviewed upscale white-collar types he met coming out of the theater. Most of them identified with the trapped rats Tom Cruise and Gene Hackman play in the film. They used words like "harassed," "re-indoctrinated," "programmed" and "locked-in."

"If you step off that line, you're dead," said one young manager, enslaved at 33.

The seeds of *karoshi*, native or imported, are taking root in the American heartland. One controversial approach to the work crisis is the new paternalism. In an attempt to ease the stressful conflict between families and careers, some companies are asserting benevolent control over every area of employees' lives. But with layoffs currently proceeding at a rate of 2,300 per business day, American labor has lost its leverage. It's a "Take it or leave it" job market where the needs and feelings of the employee are rarely among the first considerations.

Middle-aged victims of downsizing, fired after years of loyalty and living beyond their means, face dismal prospects indeed. *Karoshi* would have been a kindness for some of these company men and women whose companies said good-bye. But their children, entering the work force at what appears to be the worst possible moment, can learn an invaluable lesson from their parents' miserable fate.

The bad news, kids, is that the workplace is becoming a jungle. The good news is that there are no jobs for you anyway. There's no point in going to college, even, if all you want is a set of credentials for a generic high-paying job. In terms of actual wages, graduates with four-year degrees have been losing ground since 1988. Hardly anyone is hiring, and the "elite" who get through the door are exploited like galley slaves. And it's only by running twice as fast that they can hope to keep up with older workers, desperate to survive, who actually know what they're doing.

For most young people the stagnant economy is, or can be, an unmixed blessing. It may save them from that promising first job that so often, like the first marriage, turns out to be the mother of all poor choices. What looks like a great job to a 23-year-old may look, when he's 30, like a one-way ticket on a slow train to Duluth. But by then he has mortgages and mouths to feed, and a shrinking list of options.

There's a wonderful secret about work, that I learned only recently. I never considered myself a victim of the Protestant work ethic. My doctor never warned me about *karoshi*. I used to work to eat, mostly, and congratulate myself for every minute I could spend shooting baskets or sitting on a riverbank somewhere reading novels.

I still sit on the riverbank sometimes. But now I'm sitting there, most of the time, thinking about work. That happens when you get older. Work gets more important when you stop thinking about sex 24 hours a day, and realize that you'll never climb Mt. McKinley.

It gets much harder to goof off. But the amazing thing is that it's OK. The great secret of middle age is that your work gets to be one of your greatest pleasures. *If*, of course, you've chosen it wisely.

If you're young, never panic. Time is on your side. If a wretched economy keeps you in subsistence-level jobs for a few years, that gives you plenty of time to consider your vocation. Just use common sense. Learn something that will still be valuable in 20 years, something not many people do well. Pick something you can control. Control, in a society of galley slaves, makes you feel like a king.

The catch is that there are powerful forces that don't want you to think this through. A consumer society is a giant treadmill. If there are too many gerbils who refuse to climb on and start running, the slowdown shrinks profits and the treadmill managers face angry stockholders. In their worst-case scenario, college professors start questioning, once again, whether bullmoose capitalism is the perfect recipe for human happiness.

The key to your personal survival is to keep your consumption to a minimum until you know what you want to do with your life. The key to maintaining treadmill speed is to keep everybody consuming compulsively, whether they can afford it or not. The most reliable rodent for the treadmill is the consumer who's always in debt.

The immediate interests of the graduate do not coincide with the immediate interests of these lean, hungry downsized corporations. The corporations have figured that out, and responded with typical cynicism.

They may not have a job for you, but they have a deal for you. Last week there was an appalling AP story about credit-card companies who practically force their cards on college students, and reap big profits from the students' irresponsible spending. One kid at Carolina ran up a $25,000 debt, and campus counselors report that balances up to $10,000 are a common source of undergraduate anxieties.

"It's not a matter of needing them," said a Carolina freshman who has four cards. "They just give them to you."

Some of my friends with children in college have been tearing out their hair—and, after terrible scenes, writing big checks. Their kids, in an ugly preview of real life, will be working all next summer just to pay them back.

The card-dumping ploy is unconscionable, of course, a lot like luring little kids into the bushes with candy. But it's more than that, as I hope I'm making clear. This is the big temptation, the Big Hook. This is the devil trolling for souls, this is Toshitsugu Yagi's commuter slave train stopping to pick up passengers.

A credit card is a ticket that will get you on the train. But the conductor won't tell you the name of the next stop, because the train never stops. You spend, you work, you work overtime, you take whatever jobs they offer to keep up your cash flow. It takes a lot of nerve to jump off the train, because it never slows down either.

This is one of the ways—the main way—that you lose control of your life and your work. It's hard to believe when you're 20, with plastic in your pocket that will take you anywhere. But *karoshi* is one place it can take you, and it may not be the worst place. One way to make sure that you won't end up like Mr. Yagi is to stick your card in its little slot at the top of the instant teller and leave it there.

They say business has no memory. It certainly has no memory of World War II. Several editors thought this piece was over the edge. I didn't think so when I wrote it, and I don't think so now.

The Kindness of Germans

The business pages treated it like the biggest thing to hit the South since Sherman. The front page staged it like *Tristan und Isolde*. Editorialists sang *lieder*.

It was the wooing of Mercedes-Benz, and half the states in the old Confederacy came a-courtin'. It was so big only the sports editor could ignore it, though sport supplies its metaphors. It was the Grand Prix of Groveling, the Olympic Games of Official Obsequiousness, the Americas Cup of Apple Polishing, the Super Bowl of Sucking Up, the Final Four of Fawning.

North Carolina lost in the finals to Alabama, and Tar Heels lined up to second-guess their losing coach. Mercedes turned up its nose at a package worth over $100 million. Was there anything those Germans wanted that Governor Hunt didn't offer?

A few things, as it turns out. One of them was a $45 million agreement to assume the automaker's entire payroll for its first year in Alamance County.

There are no reliable reports that Mercedes asked the governor to round up 100 Alamance virgins to serve as executive sex slaves. And it's only a rumor that the Germans wanted Mebane to turn its Main Street into a kind of Kurfurstendamm theme park, complete with porn theaters and kinky strip shows ("The Festival of the Four Sexes" was one neon enticement I recall from my last visit), to remind them of the raunchy nightlife of West Berlin.

What Mercedes wanted amounted to a little more than concessions and incentives. It amounted to tribute, and it amounted to the hardest bargain any tribute-collector has tried to drive since King Minos of Crete fed Athens' choicest youths and virgins to the Minotaur. If young girls begin to vanish from the streets of Vance, Ala., someone had better read the fine print in the contract Gov. Jim Folsom signed with Mercedes-Benz.

Maybe the Mercedes plant wasn't a prize my state should feel so sick about losing. A Mercedes isn't really a North Carolina kind of product. More than any other car, it's the machine that says, "I can afford this and you can't." I used to get a populist kick out of those necklaces you see on punks in Europe, made of Mercedes hood ornaments. I wouldn't drive a Mercedes if you gave it to me—but go ahead if you feel you have to test me. I'll trade it in for a Land Rover.

German-bashing is tedious because Germans are such easy targets, like California or Buffalo, N.Y. But I met some impressive German businessmen when I went to Berlin in 1989 to see The Wall come down. At the time I gave them full credit for the sensitivity and multilingual diplomacy that seemed so lacking in their American competitors.

By my rules that gives me the right to mention that I've met another kind of German businessman, too. My encounter, nearly 25 years ago, may match pretty well with the recent experiences of several Southern governors and their industrial recruiters.

I broke a rule you should never break, and accepted a job as a favor to a friend. He was a small-time promoter eyeing the big time, and the first sizable fish he landed was a leisurewear convention combining Levi Strauss and a German textile giant that shall go unnamed. Somehow my buddy talked Chet Huntley, just retired as co-anchor for NBC News, into serving as the celebrity "face" for this event. Huntley's script was to be written by me.

Out of respect for Huntley I tried to write the most dignified speech that could possibly be construed as promoting leisurewear. This whole project was way out of my line.

Levi Strauss was no problem. But the Germans, as it turned out, wanted naked, aggressive ad copy. No poetry. My friend the promoter tried to explain that these American journalists had certain scruples, one because he was famous enough to afford them and the other because he was too young to know any better.

This was like a madam in a New Orleans cathouse trying to explain to a roughneck just off the oil rigs, cash in hand, that there are two kinds of whores, those who will do anything and those who still have a little pride.

This kind of businessman, whom I think of as The Eurobigshot, wears expensive clothes perfectly tailored and never makes eye contact. He doesn't even pretend to listen to what you're saying and he keeps looking at your feet as if to make sure you're wearing shoes. He acts as if he's trying to get revenge for the firebombing of Dresden, but he doesn't seem ethnic at all. He seems to have invented himself from the Ralph Lauren and Hugo Boss menswear ads in GQ.

He—three or four of him—was the worst person I ever encountered who wasn't actively trying to maim me. I bailed out in a fury halfway through the project, which cost me some money and a friend. I have no idea what Chet Huntley finally read to the retailers.

Maybe Governor Hunt met this guy, or one of his clones. According to John Ardagh, author of *Germany and the Germans*, Mercedes executives are notorious—even among other Euro-bigshots—for their "smooth conceit" and "sublime arrogance."

A profile of Daimler-Benz AG, Mercedes' parent company, makes interesting reading. A major stockholder is our old friend the Emir of Kuwait. The company lost nearly $600 million in the first half of 1993. It plans to lay off 40,000 workers, 11 percent of its work force, by the end of 1994.

Then there's the indelicate question of history.

Ronald Reagan, The First Man to Forget, probably set a good example when he told us, from an SS cemetery in Bitburg, that there was no one left in Germany who remembered the Nazis. But not everyone dispenses with history as effortlessly as the Gipper.

It's an awkward historical fact that Hitler invariably drove a Mercedes. He rode one into occupied Warsaw, when the Poles were forbidden to show their faces at their windows. Along with the swastika, the Mercedes hood ornament shines front and center in nearly every archive photo of the Führer parading in triumph through another shattered city.

A more sensitive company might have changed its logo after Nuremberg. Is it possible that they sell these cars to Jews and Poles? No one's calling for a boycott on Fuhrer-products, 50 years after the fact. But maybe it's unfortunate that our governors and senators (blood enemies Jim Hunt and Jesse Helms went *together* to New York to charm Mercedes) are obliged to crawl on their bellies to please the company that built the trucks and planes that carried the soldiers who tried to kill them or their fathers in 1943.

A dollar has no memory and a Deutschmark less, the realists will admonish me. The appropriate cliché is "beggars can't be choosers." People who don't generate profits—anyone involved in education, culture, pure research, charity, social service, altruism—have been reduced to begging miserably from people who do. A beggar's bowl should be prominent on the crest and seal of every university. Government, another nonprofit enterprise, is on its knees because wary and selfish taxpayers pull the purse strings tighter every year.

Is this simply the way of the world, or the way of a world that has lost its way? Consider the money spent wooing Mercedes unsuccessfully, and the uncertain advantages for the state that wins. Why not take the same amount of money and offer concessions and interest-free loans to 20 local businesses with the potential to grow big enough to generate jobs?

Is that really bad economics, or is it merely unfashionable and unappetizing to recruiters on expense accounts? To me, it looks like one route back to self-reliance and self-respect—one alternative to the beggar's bowl. An alternative to the kindness of Germans.

I relish a true story that sums up a universe of trashy behavior and exhausted values. This boy's father is an old friend of mine. Of all the moral degenerates our kids might encounter, sexual perverts are probably the easiest to avoid.

Among Thieves

There was a boy from a small town in the Appalachians who went to college in Florida, on a baseball scholarship. After a year of hard work and a brush with fantasy—he struck out George Brett in an exhibition game and made the front page of his hometown paper—the boy decided that he'd earned himself a righteous automobile. On a used-car lot somewhere in the Sunshine State he found what he needed, a vehicle that was described to me as a "kickass" roadster of American make, vintage late '70s, waxed as smooth and shiny as the future must look when you're 20.

His father up in New York loaned him a substantial sum to make the purchase. The boy and his car weren't 20 miles out on their maiden voyage when the transmission more or less disintegrated. He took a bus back to the used car lot to ask the dealer politely for a free tow and a new transmission. The dealer, described as a swarthy individual almost immobilized by fat (life imitates the most obvious fiction), spared the kid just enough time to laugh at him. Apparently it was only the size of the boy that saved him from the classic nape-of-the-neck, seat-of-the-pants exit they call the bum's rush.

He called his father, who booked a flight to Florida to clear up what sounded over the phone like an impossible misunderstanding. When they towed the stricken vehicle to a garage, the mechanic told them that the dying transmission had been loaded up with brake fluid for its brief swan song. But on top of that, he reported, the engine was cracked in two places. If it hadn't been lubricated with an oily substance roughly the consistency of potato salad, it wouldn't have outlived the transmission.

The boy's father confronted the used car-dealer. He told the fat man that he'd been caught red-handed at the oldest and dirtiest tricks in the business. A refund or major free repairs would be necessary if he wanted to avoid the police.

To the father's surprise, the dealer held up the receiver and invited him to dial the station house. As it turns out, the great state of Florida, which in places is beginning to resemble the great state of Lebanon, has an almost nonexistent "lemon law" known humorously as the "50-50" statute—50 seconds or 50 feet. In practice, the used-car business is perpetual open season on the inexperienced and gullible consumer.

The out-of-state father asked the fat man if he regarded the 50-50 law as a license to steal from 20-year-old boys.

"Time your boy grew up," said the fat man. This was the way it worked in the world of men. When the father, furious, asked him if he'd like to step outside and see how things worked in the world of men, the fat man started to call the police.

When he calmed down enough to see that he was in a no-win situation, the father of the victim asked the dealer if he had any concern for his reputation. Did it worry him at all that they were going to alert everyone they knew in the area, and the media, as well, if they could, that he was an unrepentant crook who preyed on boys?

"I'll get by," sneered the fat man.

At the moment, the kid who struck out George Brett is working 30 hours a week to make payments on two automobiles. He was an easy mark because he came from a small place where children are raised to trust adults, and to believe that adults are going to behave better than children. A polite boy from a place like that wouldn't challenge the integrity of any adult, not even a fat used-car salesman in a loud sport shirt. But nothing turns my stomach so much as that line, "Time your boy grew up." It reminds me of a number of arguments I've had about innocence and experience. A childless woman told me once that I shouldn't try to protect my 10-year-old daughter from ugly realities as much as I did, because pretty soon she was going to be living in an ugly world and she'd need all the experience she could get. I really hated that argument. Are we supposed to be inoculating our children with sleaze and deceit so they'll be immune when they're grown?

I wouldn't want my son to accept or even resign himself to a marketplace that operates on 50-50 laws. I wouldn't want him to understand it or move in it with confidence. If I had to choose, I'd rather have a son who gets cheated every time than a son who gets rich by cheating someone else. Used-car fraud is only the low-rent end of a coast-to-coast, basement-to-penthouse phenomenon. At the upscale extreme is Dennis Levine, the 33-year-old investment banker who made at least $12.6 million on Wall Street by illegal insider trading, and hid it in a bank in the Bahamas. The main difference between Dennis Levine and the fat man in Florida is that Levine didn't screw anybody I feel sorry for.

What Levine did may be strictly illegal, but it varies only in degree, as far as I can see, from what everyone is doing on Wall Street. Anyone who owns a dozen shares is trying to outguess the other guy, look into the crystal ball, find out something significant before everyone else knows it. Some people see trends, some hear rumors, some get hot tips. Some, inside major firms like Levine's, actually know in advance about acquisitions, mergers and other major shifts that influence stock prices. But they're not supposed to make any money from that knowledge, even when the whole purpose of their lives and professions is to make money for themselves and others, and when their only worth in their world depends on their success at it. How does a judge decide between a crime and a real strong informed hunch? This is like putting satyrs in charge of your harem and pretending that they're eunuchs, and then mutilating them when temptation overcomes them. If there's any morality on Wall Street, it's a very queer and relative sort of morality, and not a sort I readily comprehend.

Laws are laws, and I love to see the Levines get busted. But I find no real sin in him, and neither do his colleagues. The main concern on the Street now is where the line will be drawn, and how many others will go down with Levine. Size, prestige and conservative image are no guarantee against epidemic sleaze. Just the opposite, apparently. Two-thirds of the firms which do business with the Pentagon are currently under some kind of indictment. E.F. Hutton has hired lovable Bill Cosby to rescue its corporate image from the check-kiting scandal that has spread to 21 states. Don't laugh, please. And 16 banks have been busted in a government crackdown on unreported currency transactions, usually an indication of money-laundering operations.

I'll just nod in passing to the surgeon who was imprisoned for 100 unnecessary operations, including transplants—"Greed, pure greed," said the judge who sentenced him—or the spreading nursing home scandal, where the victims are even more defenseless than 20-year-old baseball players. The list doesn't seem to shock or even interest anyone anymore.

In that climate, where do you want your boy exactly? Have you noticed all the suicides lately—usually bankrupt farmers or unemployed laborers—where the guy kills all his children first? Is that insane selfishness or misplaced philosophy? It's time the boy grew up to what? I wouldn't sooner see my son dead than selling lemons or trading inside, but I'd much rather see him in New Zealand or in a Trappist monastery.

It comes down to a serious philosophical question. Who has prior claim on a child, his parents or the society that he was raised in? Are you doing him a favor by releasing him to a system that disgusts you, and allowing him to learn nasty tricks and absorb false values so that he can make his way? Or is it your duty to protect him as much as you can?

The actor Sterling Hayden, who died last week, won my admiration by sailing away with his children for two years, to get the disease called Southern California out of their blood. More often, the parents who defy the laws and insist on educating their own children entirely are egomaniacs and religious fanatics. Their children usually end up benighted, and sometimes beaten and branded. But at least those parents have the courage of their convictions. I'm just as offended by the consensus out there as any of these alleged crazies. But I've never had the nerve, the energy or the imagination to try to establish a viable alternative for a child. Who are the best parents?

Americans are divided into hundreds of tribes, but businessmen are the dominant tribe. We have to accommodate them. We don't have to ape them slavishly, or adopt their assumptions to court their favor. If United Way hires a CEO whose role model is Donald Trump instead of Mother Teresa, the Aramony scandal is exactly the payback it deserves. Too bad about the needy.

Birds of a Feather

There's a man named William Aramony, now unemployed, who ran the United Way of America pretty much the way Jim Bakker ran the PTL network and Charles Keating ran Lincoln Savings and Loan—like the boss's private cookie jar. Mr. Aramony, soon to be indicted and eventually to join Bakker and Keating in extended penal servitude, appears to have channeled several million dollars of the charity's resources into spinoff organizations that he controlled. In his last three years at UWA, Aramony billed them for $350,000 in personal expenses that included $92,000 for chauffeured limousines, $40,000 for Concorde flights to Europe and $33,000 for airfare to or through Gainesville, Fla., home of "a close female friend."

Apparently the annual compensation of $463,000 that he received as president of UWA was insufficient to maintain Mr. Aramony (is that pronounced Ourmoney?) in the style to which he had become accustomed. This was a familiar story during the unfolding of the S&L scandal, but the skinning of a major charitable institution—*the* major charitable institution—sounded new depths of deceitfulness and greed. The Chorus of the Righteous called for audits of all nonprofit organizations and predicted a sharp drop in charitable contributions by disillusioned Americans.

I was thinking about adding my voice to the Chorus, though rats like Aramony have become so common they're almost boring targets, when I realized that this isn't a new story or a separate story but the continuation of one I've been picking at for years.

Charlotte Observer columnist Allen Norwood pointed me in the right direction, in a separate debate over the $120,000 salary that goes to the president of the United Way of Central Carolinas. The main argument offered for such a salary, Norwood explained, is that a United Way executive needs to be able to deal with Charlotte's corporate big shots as an equal.

Where had I heard this argument before? I remember a long, occasionally acrimonious debate with a pair of close friends. The subject was congressional salaries, and one of their arguments was that you couldn't send your congressman up there on a wretched little salary to live in a wretched little apartment, if you wanted him to be able to hold up his head in the company of CEOs and lobbyists who make $1,000 a day. They'd laugh him out of the clubhouse if they knew he was driving a Yugo and boarding with his sister, and you wouldn't get your money's worth as his constituents. If you wanted to attract good people to Congress, you had to pay them salaries Washington lawyers and businessmen wouldn't despise.

I really hated this argument, which came up again when grassroots environmentalists complained about the corporate salaries paid to the environmental establishment's top executives in Washington. If you wanted to get the kind of people who could stand up to legislators and lobbyists, they were told, you had to pay them a salary these heavyweights would respect.

First of all, why doesn't this philosophy of financial equality apply to journalists? I spent the first decade of my working life talking mainly to professional athletes, entertainers and broadcasting executives. But I don't remember any efforts to raise my salary to a level where those types would respect me more and take me into their confidence.

It's a fine irony—Norwood thought so too—that of all the groups that deal with big shots professionally, only the press has failed to enrich itself through the principle of paycheck respect. And there's evidence that poverty damages our credibility, at least with a certain class of readers. Three or four of the silliest letters I ever received followed my columns on Howard Cosell and Rush Limbaugh, a pair of professional loudmouths so noxious, in their separate ways, that under any rational dictatorship their tongues would have been severed by public decree. In each instance their supporters claimed that I failed to appreciate these trichinous hams only because I was blinded by my envy of their financial success.

This is a painful logic to follow. If we're only credible picking on people who earn less than we do, our criticism would be limited to school teachers, social workers and day laborers, groups that rarely commit great mischief in the world. The rich and powerful would rise above all criticism. Who could we get to interview celebrities on my old TV beat? If paycheck envy had been my principal passion, I'd have been too crippled with covetousness to sharpen my No. 2 pencils.

Paycheck respect and paycheck envy are notions you can reduce to comedy with a small dose of logic. Yet they're invoked, without apology, whenever we discuss compensation for these critical individuals who make our laws, defend our environment, administer our charities.

The top-dollar philosophy rests on several glib assumptions that I contest:

(1) There is some necessary connection between big talents and big salaries, the human-resources equivalent of "you get what you pay for." If this is true today, it certainly wasn't true 25 years ago, when my crowd entered the work force. No study of college graduates in the '60s would show that talent and intellect flow inevitably toward the higher tax brackets; some studies might show the opposite. Business sets the salary standards, and business, like all occupations with a high degree of challenge, has its share of geniuses. But most businessmen will admit that a towering intellect is hardly the first qualification for success in their field; it could be a great liability. Energy and singlemindedness will serve you much better, along with a love of risk (at least a willingness to accept it) and, increasingly it seems, a flexible conscience.

(2) People who choose careers in public service are just as materialistic as everyone else. This is more Reaganite revisionism. I still assume that the impulse to serve and the impulse to acquire are diametrically opposed, and, in their purest forms, define two different breeds of animal. Of course there's some overlap. But not enough. Why do I doubt that William Aramony, before power and temptation turned him into the Emperor of Eleemosynaries, was a missionary ascetic committed to serving the poor, the sick and the handicapped?

(3) Top corporate executives are so nasty and stupid that they respect only money and tune out anyone who appears to come from a lower rung on the socioeconomic ladder. How do they know the guy from the Sierra Club isn't a billionaire's son who works for peanuts because he has a big trust fund? By his shoes? How does salary manifest itself in a person's appearance? How do big shots

know each other? If the corporate establishment operates like a bunch of fraternity boys rushing freshmen, we're in even bigger trouble than I imagined.

I don't believe that any of these things are true. Nonprofit organizations that accept them are digging their own graves. Good causes depend on good people, but somewhere the definition of "good people" was radically transformed.

If you hire someone "good" for whom money is a paramount concern, it stands to reason that you've hired someone who will keep trying to get more. I can't blame the local United Way organizations for withholding their national dues, in the wake of Aramony, and I don't blame the working guy who refuses to take a payroll deduction for a charity that let its president live like the Sultan of Brunei. I'm just sorry if it means that there'll be less money for people who really need it.

Matching corporate salaries in the '90s is not only wrongheaded but hopeless, a wild goose chase that will exhaust the nonprofits' credibility as quickly as their resources. Executive greed picked up so much momentum during the '80s that even a brutal recession hasn't slowed it down. In the '70s the average chief executive earned 35 times as much money as the average worker; in 1990 he earned 120 times as much, with the gap growing steadily. American CEOs outearned their German and English counterparts 2 to 1, Japanese CEOs by 50 percent. The CEO who earns millions presiding over a foundering company, empty factories and laid-off workers is making American business an international joke.

"How do these guys do it?" asks Harvard economist Robert Reich, rhetorically. "Easy. They sit on each other's boards and, after sober deliberation, agree to give one another huge salaries, bonuses and perquisites."

As the figures come in, it becomes clear that all the "prosperity" attributed to the Reagan boom years was outrageously top-heavy, so top-heavy as to be almost a heist, almost a single daring crime of staggering proportions. Led by the corporate warlords, the wealthiest one percent of American families captured three-quarters— $550 out of $740 billion—of all the pretax income the entire population gained between 1977 and 1989. (The richest one percent increased their income 77 percent, to a $560,000 average, while a median family gained four percent and the poor lost ground.)

If that statistic doesn't shock you, no statistic ever will. But no statistic ever started a revolution. What it boils down to is that this country is divided into "us" and "them" in a way that it never was before. "They"—the one percent—hold most of the cards. We can't ignore them, we can't seem to control them, but should we try to emulate them? When we accept their values we accept their superiority, and become their vassals forever.

My own attitude is that those extra bucks are small compensation for some of the things you have to do to be a robber baron. But when we really need some of this money they've accumulated, I think it should be one of ours, not one of theirs, that we send to pry it loose. No matter how carefully we choose our delegates, some of them will defect. Never trust a public servant who wants to talk about his benefits.

You notice that I never suggested raising journalists' salaries to the level of corporate respect. It would be smarter to reduce our few big ones, in D.C./TV-land where we find most of the fraternizing and whoring. A trace of envy—let's say a trace of irritation at seeing fools and scoundrels awash in good fortune and the good things of life—gives a journalist's copy a little edge that's altogether healthy.

Maybe most of us aren't the corporate-caliber kind of men and women who could hope to be president of United Way, and maybe this edge we cultivate is just ignorant pride. On the other hand, maybe it would impress the president of AT&T more than another chauffeur and another tailored suit.

Cigarette manufacturers have raised commercial cynicism, avarice and hypocrisy to the level of pure evil. I hold them responsible—consciously responsible—for the death of my father and many others I miss. But the death of this athlete who seemed the most immortal of all my contemporaries permanently changed my attitude toward my own mortality.

In Memoriam

Quantico National Cemetery, Virginia—Most of us imagine that we've attended a military funeral, but in many cases it was actually TV, a film, an old newsreel. It was JFK or Gen. MacArthur under the flag. The reality erases any doubt about whether you've been there before, with gunsmoke drifting across the fields, the bugler playing taps, the crack team of pallbearers standing straight as flagstaffs in their starched uniforms, eyes at attention, folding the flag from the casket with a precision that is, for some reason, heartbreaking.

It's a memory you won't escape or confuse with a motion picture if you live to be 100, especially if the man under the flag was your friend. Frank and I grew up together. He was the best athlete in the township, maybe the best in the county, and one of the most physically accomplished individuals I've ever known. When I think of his exploits, all the games he won and the teams he dominated, it amazes me that I can never picture him really running, straining and red-faced like the rest of us, though obviously he was running all the time.

It was that easy for Frank. He was semilegendary. Our stupid coach, unmindful of injury to a throwing arm that was major-league caliber by the time Frank was 15, used to let him dominate a Field Day event by throwing a baseball over an elm tree in deep center field, 350 feet from home plate. Little kids would gasp and tired teachers would pause to shake their heads when they saw that whoever finished second was 50 yards short of the prize.

Naturally I thought he was indestructible. He was a big, handsome, charming Irishman who seemed at ease in the world, much more at ease than I ever was, though I don't pretend to know whether he found the rest of his life as easy as hitting a fastball or leading a fast break.

Frank is dead at 48. Since he's gone and there's no appealing this referee's decision, I wish that he had died in something more like a battle, some dangerous activity that was worthy of his unusual abilities. But he received a full-dress military funeral because he was a veteran of the war in Vietman—he came home without a scratch—and because he worked for a veterans' organization. He died when his heart quit on him, virtually without warning, without provocation. Except that he smoked cigarettes. He was too healthy most of his life, too strong and too sure of his strength to fear the damn things as much as he should have.

The other deaths didn't cut as close, but that makes three in a year—old friends, men my age whose hearts have failed them prematurely. None of them were overweight or sedentary, or fit any of the standard profiles for heart disease. The first wave of deaths among my contemporaries struck 25 years ago. It took the Viet Cong, leukemia and a couple of ODs to kill them, and in one case a murderer's knife in Spanish Harlem. This second wave is being killed by little white tubes full of poisonous leaves.

The toll is over half a dozen now, if you count my father, and it would be an understatement to say that I've begun to take it personally. Enough is enough. I live in a tobacco state, I'm aware of the lore, the memories, even the poetry of the tobacco culture, and I respect them. I drove through Caswell County yesterday, up along the Virginia line, and admired the fields of perfect August leaf, each plant and row identical, symmetrical as the vision of a primitive painter. I can understand a farmer with tears in his eyes surveying a field of these delicate plants he exhausted himself to grow. But even nostalgia for the lost innocence of Tobacco Road is becoming an embarrassment, now. For every plant the farmer grows there could be a human being standing there, a person who will never stand in the August sun again.

By magnifying microscopic doubts about the power of their poison, and subsidizing any scientist who entertained the shadow of a doubt, the tobacco industry prolonged the illusion that there was a moral gap between selling cigarettes and selling heroin or cocaine. That illusory gap has closed up tight. The final, EPA-confirmed verdict on "passive" smoke is that cigarette smoke is killing everyone who breathes it, which is like confirming that breathing water will kill you unless you're a fish. The main difference between Philip Morris and Colombian cocaine czar Pablo Escobar is that Escobar courts the ignorant poor, while Philip Morris mows them down. Legality and morality are not, of course, in any way related. What Hitler did to the Jews was strictly legal according to the German laws he created; Mohandas Gandhi, George Washington and Jesus Christ were outlaws.

"This news is the final nail in the tobacco coffin," crowed Fran DuMelle of the American Lung Association, when the EPA panel declared passive smoke a Group A carcinogen and a toxic health hazard. But the industry scarcely blinked; they've heard this coffin-nail stuff before. Far from wrestling with a moral dilemma that might paralyze a fragile conscience, the tobacco companies refuse to acknowledge that any dilemma exists.

As wave after wave of medical evidence washes away its last lines of rational defense, tobacco turns deaf and blind. The Tobacco Institute rolls out its rebut robot, invariably identified as "spokesman Thomas Lauria," to call each new study "politically inspired" and "unsupported by the evidence."

The industry's commitment to denial and disinformation is a wonder to behold. Here on my desk is a volume of essays titled *Clearing the Air*, ostensibly a cross-section of informed opinion on the dangers of passive smoke. The essayists range from Tory parliamentarian Lord "Jock" Bruce-Gardyne to Jody Powell of the Carter White House, and the effect is to calm your fears and leaven your anger with respect for smokers' rights. A brief acknowledgement in the front explains that this book "came to fruition" with the support of Philip Morris Inc., which "in no way influenced the opinions expressed by the authors." I found this volume—a complimentary copy—on the shelf at my public library in Chapel Hill.

It has been suggested that the industry is in denial because of the sheer enormity of its crime. So many, many coffins. French pneumologist Jean Marsac calls cigarettes "the most deadly addiction epidemic of the 20th century." He estimates that in France cigarettes kill 61,000 people annually, the population of Cannes. In the United States they kill 430,000, 53,000 of them nonsmokers. In New York State alone the annual toll has topped 30,000. The body count dwarfs wars, famines, epidemics, tidal waves, volcanic eruptions. The World Health Organization is offering a figure of 7 million deaths a year, worldwide, by 2025. AIDS won't claim half that many lives, according to WHO's most pessimistic predictions, assuming that no cure is ever found.

It isn't reckless rhetoric to call smoking a quiet Holocaust. And it's deceitful to say that it's purely voluntary, a slow suicide of choice for millions of human beings who have no interest in long lives or healthy lungs. No one who's had any contact with cigarettes needs the Surgeon General to tell him that nicotine is the most addictive drug the devil ever conjured. Of the 30,000 New Yorkers who will die from cigarette-related illness in 1992, more than half were addicts at 14.

Free will is a joke if you're talking about cigarettes. The habit gets you when you're an ignorant teenage peer slave who will shave your head, pierce your nipples or risk damn near anything to be part of the group and the scene. Thirty or 40 years later they drop what's left of you in a box, and the pusher replaces you with some kid too green to notice what happened to you.

I wish I could believe that hysterical guilt is driving the tobacco industry to its stonewall denials. Most folks think it's just greed. While fewer cigarettes are sold in the United States, every year, profits have tripled between 1980 and 1988. Though Philip Morris is a conglomerate that sells a lot of other things, like General Foods and Miller Beer, cigarettes accounted for 72 percent of the company's operating profits in 1991—40 percent from Marlboros alone. Tobacco is a $42 billion-a-year business; Wall Street is touting tobacco stocks because the decline in smoking among Americans has been more than offset by a rosy profit picture in the Third World, where the Surgeon General's health warnings have yet to penetrate.

It's hard to imagine a more repugnant moral position, or any place in the whole cynical world of capitalism where profits and decency collide more dramatically. It's hard for me to imagine the people who work for tobacco companies. If you sell cigarettes but you don't smoke because you know better, you're a murderous hypocrite. Does R.J. Reynolds hire only smokers and subsidize their habits, or are employees helpless wage slaves dying slowly of a peer-pressured habit and other people's smoke? All these options sound desperate, and I can't think of any others.

There's no point getting angry at smokers. Most of them are considerate in spite of their crippling affliction. The occasional discourtesy is the discourtesy of an anxious junkie in a methadone clinic. Smokers deserve our prayers more than our curses. Of course any talk of "smokers' rights" is hogwash, where it concerns passive smoke and other people's health. Analogies between smoking and other addicts' habits produce comical logic. We know drinkers sometimes get drunk and stab their wives or drive into school buses, and crack junkies kill convenience-store clerks. But they don't lobby legislatures for the right to kill.

My outrage is directed at the sources of supply, though I don't pretend that anything I write will embarrass them. Nearly everyone associated with cigarettes in the public's mind is dead or dying from the habit, from Edward R. Murrow to Jesse Helms. When one of the virile models for "the Marlboro Man" died last month of lung cancer, Philip Morris denied that he ever worked for them. (But he proved it. Adjacent to the *New York Times* obituary for the Marlboro Man, Walter McLaren, was the obituary of filmmaker Christian Blackwood, also a heavy smoker who died at 50 of lung cancer. A tough day for Thomas Lauria and the Tobacco Institute.)

I happen to believe that our Constitution protects the sale of popular poisons, even lethal ones, as long as they're properly labeled. Cigarette advertising—$3 billion of 100 percent tax-deductible deceit stressing health, fresh air, sex and virility—is an abomination. Ban it. We can't let them lie and lure children. But along with other dangerous, destructive pleasures—among the lowest of the low company that includes marijuana, cocaine, heroin, pornography and prostitution—tobacco should be legal but rigorously controlled, with a large share of its revenues designated for programs that attempt to liberate its victims. People who sell it should sink to the bottom of the social scale with pimps, pushers, pornographers and the rest of the rabble that profits from human weakness.

I'm not sure this tumble would shame them, as long as the profits kept rolling in. But I can't help fishing for some sign of shame. Maybe they see only numbers, and never think of the faces of the people who die. I could send them an album with the faces of my friends. The poet e. e. cummings was mourning Buffalo Bill when he wrote "Jesus he was a handsome man / and what I want to know is / how do you like your blueeyed boy Mister Death."

My friend Frank was a handsome man, too. What I want to know is, how do you like your blue-eyed boy, Mister Lauria?

Mr. Goforth's house stood empty for two years. His real story may never be told. But he was a man who devoted his whole life to his business.

The Great Goforth

We were eating dinner with some friends at a restaurant in Wilmington. A woman who went to school with my wife came over to our table to tell us that our neighbor had committed suicide in Chapel Hill. The only people in the party who hadn't heard of J. P. Goforth were from Austin, Texas. In his prime he cast a long shadow in the state of North Carolina, and he always cast an enormous one in the neighborhood where he managed to live almost invisibly.

Mr. Goforth is gone, but we will still have to deal with the shadow. A man generates a myth, as well as mean-spirited rumors, when he's more successful than his neighbors and then keeps himself apart from them; envy and admiration turn to strange speculations. Goforth's appearances were so rare, toward the end, that they were treated like sightings. The man who lived across the street told the newspaper that he hadn't seen Goforth in two years. It must have been two summers ago that I surprised him, almost before first light, picking up a newspaper at the end of his driveway.

I'm burdened with a hopelessly literary imagination, which means that I'm captive to other people's stories, the ones they tell and the ones they live. When my neighbor killed himself I was one of many, I'm sure, who thought first of the Edward Arlington Robinson poem, "Richard Cory":

> *And he was rich—yes, richer than a king,*
> *And admirably schooled in every grace:*
> *In fine, we thought that he was everything*
> *To make us wish that we were in his place.*

> *So on we worked, and waited for the light,*
> *And went without the meat, and cursed the bread,*
> *And Richard Cory, one calm summer night,*
> *Went home and put a bullet through his head.*

But there are few of us in J.P. Goforth's neighborhood who go without the meat, and the key element in Robinson's poem is surprise. The Goforth tragedy had more chapters to it, gathering clouds, a certain inevitability. Maybe a more relevant story is *The Great Gatsby*. Like Fitzgerald's narrator Nick Carraway, who lived in a humble cottage near Gatsby's mansion, I once found myself surrounded by people who wanted to learn more about my mysterious neighbor. Goforth was building an enormous white beach house, at a cost of several million dollars, on the choicest piece of land on expensive Figure Eight Island, where we were visiting friends. Some of his beach neighbors heard that we lived on his street back home and asked me the obvious questions, like "Who is he, actually?", "How rich is he?" and "Does he give a lot of parties?" I didn't know any of the answers, though I'd passed his house a dozen times a day.

And then there was the famous green light that always burned at the end of Daisy Buchanan's dock, a symbol for Gatsby of Daisy and the world of money and privilege where she lived. Goforth, a farmer's son (like Gatsby) from Statesville, kept all the lights at his long, low house burning day and night—lights along the driveway, along the roof, in the hallways and in all the rooms we could see from the street. Fear of thieves, fear of the dark, who can say? A month after his death, all the lights are still burning.

A suicide casts a curious light on a life that could, for most of its course, have been a feature subject for a business magazine. There was no secret about where James Paul Goforth made his money. I know a half dozen people who live in houses he built, and all of them testify that he built good houses and gave good service to the people who bought them. He built his business and his fortune the old way, with a good reputation, long hours and tireless attention to details. From custom homes in Chapel Hill he expanded into land deals, subdivisions and commercial building throughout central North Carolina, and ultimately into ambitious resort developments like the Landfall project near Wilmington. His properties and assets were valued in the tens of millions of dollars.

It was vintage, B-movie Horatio Alger. The bright farm boy comes up to Chapel Hill, gets his B.A. and a law degree, outfoxes some of the wise guys and becomes one of the biggest developers in the state before he's 40. Goforth appeared to enjoy the fast lane and never deprived himself of its rewards—the big houses and big boats, the private planes and clubs, the fast company.

Then the script began to change, at some point no one seems able to fix. Darker writers took a hand. The Great Goforth, described by most people who knew him as affable and charming, became inaccessible. Details he once thrived upon were neglected, bills went unpaid, key associates left him. There were vague rumors about his health and his finances, and then specific complaints and claims—60 at last count, and 23 lawsuits—from subcontractors and creditors. On Friday the 13th of April, Orange County District Attorney Carl Fox called a press conference to announce that he was asking the state to investigate Goforth's businesses.

The next afternoon they found the developer dead of carbon monoxide poisoning in the garage of the big house at the end of our street. Police noted that the car's engine was running and, of course, that the lights were on everywhere. Goforth was 49.

"The bigger they are, the harder they fall" is a maxim that the smallest people believe in and almost insist upon. Goforth's supporters had good reason to be bitter about the investigation that was theatrically announced before it began, and about *The Chapel Hill Newspaper* story that dignified, in print, an irresponsible street rumor that the developer was suffering from AIDS (a rumor that only the coroner could dismiss, and he did).

His suicide, leaving no note that anyone has found, removed him even further from the ritual respect that the conventional rich receive from the media. Accounts of Goforth's death emphasized the "mystery" that surrounded him and hinted at unsavory transactions. Yet there are people ready to offer a very different picture of J.P. Goforth. I talked to Johnny Morris, his close friend and business associate for 14 years.

"This was a charming guy, likable, a superb salesman," Morris told me. "An average guy, really, with a nice way about him. There was nothing very mysterious. It's just that people never saw him volunteering, chairing committees and all that. He wasn't civic. He liked the real world, the business, the hard decisions. He was totally involved in home building. In his world hundreds of people saw him every day. Only outsiders thought he was a mystery."

The illness that inspired ugly rumors was no mystery either, according to Morris.

"The man had been in pain as long as I knew him, for 20 years at least. It was kidney pain, the worst kind. Some kind of nerve block, adhesions from an appendectomy? They did exploratory surgery at Duke 10 years ago. The pain would come and go, but there were times when he couldn't get out of bed, it was so excruciating. We all knew about it. People would rather gossip than ask a simple question."

Morris speculated that this chronic condition was a small factor, finally, in Goforth's tragedy.

"The housing market changed, you know, it changed for all of us. This is a very, very tough business, with a lot of risk. The market went bad on J.P. just when he most overextended, personally and financially. He was totally involved in the Landfall project down at Wilmington, but his companies up here were so closely held that he had to be both places at once. He lost some of his energy, I think. Then his land, his inventory, began to lose value.

"It just snowballed on him. He kept hoping he could put it back together, make it whole again. He was a fighter who never knew how to go backwards. But other people had been damaged by then, and he knew it. He wanted to make amends."

Your friend could have killed himself, I asked Morris, as a way of making restitution to the people he damaged? (In December Goforth took out a $12.5 million life insurance policy; if the insurance company honors it, it would cover all the claims against his companies.)

"I shouldn't speculate, but he was a courageous guy. As his friend, I have to think that's why he did what he did. Maybe he thought it was the only way to make it whole, make it right again for everybody.

"Of course I know the investigation hurt him awfully bad, having lived his life the way he did. He was a very proud man. To see it in print like that, it pierced him."

What surprised him about the suicide, Morris said, was that he thought that Goforth—like Gatsby—had an infinite capacity for hope.

I asked Morris if Goforth, who owned several homes, ever actually lived in the house at the end of my street.

"Sure, but you have to understand, he worked a lot more than most of us. He worked more than anyone. He didn't have any family to come home to. Evenings, weekends he'd just as soon be up in his office on Columbia Street with the phones, a pencil and a pad of paper. People would come in. That's where he was. It was the same as sitting in our living rooms for you or me."

This was more than I ever expected to learn about my neighbor. I walked by his house again today. The lights were still on, reflected off an acre of glass; the azaleas that were buds when he died have bloomed and faded. At the end of the drive there's a basketball goal in mint condition. It's the one thing he owned that I coveted, because my driveway's too steep for one and all the nets in the neighborhood have been shredded by idiots trying to dunk. I never saw anyone shooting baskets at Goforth's. There were no pickup games, no three-on-threes in that well-lighted driveway.

The death of an unusual person by his own hand is always an enigma, always a subject for sordid speculation and moralizing. Moralizing is my department. This wasn't one of those '80s stories, the Milken-Boesky syndrome of addictive greed and ambition that got out of hand. This man was hooked on the work—the plans, the deals, the structures themselves, the old untainted American Dream of making yourself master of everything you know.

Goforth's dream didn't have any more to do with greed, really, than Gatsby's dream. But a dream that comes true can stretch you out and gut you even faster than the ones that don't, especially if it's the only dream you have. My neighbor loved his work and when his work went sour he had nothing to fall back on. He worked, he lived, without a net. A single dream, whether it's Daisy Buchanan or The American Dream, is never enough.

V

$\mathscr{T}$he Arsenal of Democracy — One Nation under Fire

After wading through vulgarity, venality, mendacity, meanness and cheesy values until his hamstrings are cramping, the weary patholo-gist rounds a blind curve in the American psyche and comes face to face with our one great, bloody, full-blown toad-sucking psy-chosis, the sickness that sets us apart from every other nationality that pretends to practice civilization. Europeans believe in an aver-age American who's never seen a war he couldn't applaud or a deadly weapon he didn't want to own.

In the part of the South where I live, that's not far off the mark. Before I was married I lived alone in the woods by the river. Most of my neighbors were kind and all of them were armed; how kind and how well-armed is suggested by the fact that three of them offered to loan me spare handguns. They couldn't conceive of any-one living alone without firepower.

The White House lawn is littered with bullets, the facade is pockmarked with bullet holes; the homicide center of America is just a few blocks away. Every president, every public figure knows he's a target. The Fifth Horseman of the American Apocalypse looks and acts a lot like Lee Van Cleef in *The Good, the Bad and the Ugly*. The Southern version is more genteel, more like Stonewall Jackson cleaning his Colt revolver by the light of his campfire.

This is a country where an unarmed pacifist will sometimes feel like a rabbit in a snowfield without a hole in sight, watching the shadow of the hawk. Like small nations feel when the American Eagle spreads her wings.

Everything depends on what we teach the children. If we could teach them to figure out these connections for themselves—the fundamental, logical connections described here by Lewis Mumford and W. H. Ferry—I think they could save what's left of the world.

The Beat Goes On

Our children are grown and grandchildren are a mercifully distant prospect, so my only contact with elementary education is the lower-school playground that borders on the running track where I make my daily sacrifice to the angry god of obesity. The kids are a pleasant diversion from ragged breathing, and I pick up occasional pointers on gear, slang and pop culture in pre-adolescent America.

But the other day they scared me. Three or four of us, regulars, were pounding out the quarter-miles in our usual reverie when we were startled by a distinctly martial drumbeat. And down the hill to the edge of the track, led by a girl with a drum, came two dozen elementary students in parade formation, carrying sticks and toy rifles on their shoulders. They split into two companies and pro-ceeded to re-enact some historical battle, perhaps Lexington or Bunker Hill. It was a battle from the age of muzzle-loaders and massed formations firing at point-blank range—the age of patriotic suicide.

A teacher, a woman, was directing the company that seemed to represent the British: "Now kneel . . . aim . . . fire . . . withdraw . . . reload." The battle lines were 10 feet apart. It was chillingly authentic. Of course the kids were loving it. And of course I thought, the only way this exercise might teach them anything is if one day someone substituted real guns and bullets for their sticks and toys.

Even then the survivors, at least the males, would probably for-get the lesson before they graduated from high school. But teachers should know better. I remember something H.G. Wells wrote, before the great wars that killed more than 100 million soldiers and civilians:

"The crazy combative patriotism that plainly threatens to destroy civilization is very largely begotten by the schoolmaster and the schoolmistress in their history lessons. They take the growing mind at a naturally barbaric phase and they inflame and fix its bar-barism."

During the Vietnam War I asked one of the wise men of the peace movement, a kind of renegade Jesuit, if there was any force on earth that could end our love affair with war. "Only education," he replied. "There has to come a time when they beat the drum and no one marches."

I don't think he realized that the drumbeat begins so early, or that fifth-grade teachers are training themselves as sergeant-majors. Logic, memory, history and catastrophe have no perceptible influence on the fatal glamour of civilization's most loathsome perversion. The winter of the Gulf War was the darkest season I ever suffered as a citizen of the United States. The motivation and the propaganda were so transparent, the outcome so depressing, the celebrations so pathetic and the public response so overwhelmingly enthusiastic that I was left with no alibi that any foreigner would accept. So this is my country. I wasn't surprised, in this election year, to hear that their votes against the invasion of Kuwait would be a serious liability for many candidates.

But I was naive enough, still, to twist and groan when the patriots attacked Gov. William Clinton, a presidential candidate—and a Desert Storm supporter—for avoiding service in Vietnam. Vietnam? It's been years since I've read anything but the most half-hearted and perfunctory apologies for that tragic fiasco, a textbook failure of tainted foreign policy by any yardstick you devise. If there was ever an instance when an issue split this nation in two and one side was totally vindicated, beyond any further debate, it was the instance of Vietnam. Ho Chi Minh won the war and Eugene McCarthy won the argument, thank you friends and good night.

Beyond a certain turning point in public awareness—a turning point that arrived too late for thousands already in uniform, or already dead or maimed—nearly every young man with access to accurate information (Bill Clinton, a college graduate and a Rhodes Scholar, presumably had prime access) tried to get out of serving in Vietnam. And all of us, those who failed to get out of it and those who succeeded, should stand together now to declare that there was no honor to be had fighting this war and no dishonor in refusing to fight. This would be a major milestone in the march of civilization—at least one bad war buried without fanfare in a pauper's grave.

But that's never how it works. The male protagonist in Norman Rush's recent novel *Mating* delivers a tirade against his own sex:

"You know men are happy in the army because when they get out they do nothing to keep younger men from joining up, and in fact they themselves join the American Legion to keep their memories of war and killing as fresh as possible and have circle jerks where they call anybody who's for peace commies, and a deep calm drenches the male soul when it feels the persona it inhabits being firmly screwed into a socket in some iron hierarchy or other, best of all a hierarchy legitimately about killing."

Not long ago I might have discounted this outburst as emotional exaggeration, in part because I know so many veterans who don't fit the profile. But the yellow-ribbon war moved me much closer to Rush's persuasion. Pacifism is a beautiful and also a stubborn flower, once it's firmly rooted. I was a confirmed pacifist at 13—the purest example of untutored innocence viewing the Emperor's New Clothes. Later, I compromised and equivocated. I wanted to be open-minded, to respect what appeared to be a consensus, maybe just to get along.

There are compromises that should never survive the age of reason (conscription succeeds by plucking its victims long before that age arrives). Lewis Mumford embarrassed me. In *The Myth of the Machine*, his landmark study of technology and human development, Mumford devotes only 10 pages to war *per se*. Ten are all he needs. He traces warfare back to the lovely pre-Christian tradition of human sacrifice—"the only guess that ties all the components of war together and explains in some degree the hold that this institution has kept throughout history." He explains how "the megamachine," the mobilized nation-state, evolved in a military form long before modern warfare was invented to perpetuate it.

Mumford shows that war was always symbolic, never practical, and that it was always employed to stifle domestic dissent and tighten the rulers' grip on their subjects ("popular hatred of the ruling classes was cleverly diverted into a happy occasion to mutilate or kill foreign enemies"). Though he was writing during the escalation of the war in Vietnam, the calm force of Mumford's argument is only occasionally interrupted by flashes of anger, as when he calls the Vietnamese "an innocent people, uprooted, terrorized, poisoned and roasted alive in a futile attempt to make the power fantasies of the American military industrial-scientific elite 'credible.'"

Once past Mumford, there's no turning back. Only the most out-spoken pacifism suffices, like W.H. Ferry's epilogue to *Conditions of Peace*, a collection of essays published shortly after the Gulf War.

"The war system enters our lives through so many doors that its presence, to say nothing of its dominance, is virtually unnoticed," Ferry writes. "The country is bound together by the system's omnivorous requirements. Simply put, the war system and the American way of life are one and the same phenomenon."

"Patriotism," George Bradford wrote last spring, "is an expression of the defeat of community and the triumph of the state." ("The state is bodies of armed men," said Lenin, no pacifist and no maudlin patriot either.)

These strong words are true, or far more true than any arguments that can be thrown up against them. That so many can be induced to deny them so successfully is a marvel, though no mystery. It's still the human sacrifice that seals the deal.

The best way, maybe the only way to give a flagrant lie the force of truth is to soak it in innocent blood. No one blames the bereaved for trying to link their agony to great causes and noble ideals. For the average Christian, accepting the utter futility of a son killed by friendly fire in Kuwait is as unthinkable as accepting a callous God who allows all this carnage century after century, and probably without granting any afterlife as compensation.

I only blame them when they vote, again and again, for leaders who will make war again and again, instead of leaders who will make every effort to avoid it. How do we break the covenant of the Bloody Shirt?

I'm still crazy enough to believe that warlust is more nurture than nature—to blame the parasite warlords, the media and the schoolmasters instead of some murderous gene we inherited from rogue chimpanzees. It's still possible that we could end the ancient cycle of human sacrifice by reducing the pool of willing victims. The political upheavals of the past 18 months have produced a poignant new argument against the blind patriotism of faithful soldiers.

What we are seeing, more clearly than at any time in the past half-century, is the perishability of the nation-state itself. Afghanistan has been called the Soviet Union's Vietnam. Veterans of that war face the irony that their comrades died for a nation, a flag and a cause that no longer exist. In what had been Yugoslavia, brothers and neighbors could have battled and died under a half-dozen different flags within a month.

Scotland, home of most of my ancestors, is thinking of seceding from Great Britain after 400 years. In Nova Scotia, where I was born, serious people are talking about seceding from Canada and joining the United States. Things change. Things fall apart. The United States is no seamless union. Massachusetts and Mississippi still have little in common besides four S's apiece. I often wonder if it was worth the blood that was shed to hold them together in 1865.

The same vain, covetous old men, in violation of half the Ten Commandments, will send you to your death for a flag, a creed, a party or a set of borders that may be historical trivia long before your natural life would have ended. Don't risk it if you have the slightest doubt. Nations, good and bad, come and go. They're chimera compared with your scared, single life.

I don't condemn hunting, or condescend to hunters, just because I was raised according to different assumptions. But this piece was written in the grip of one of the purest strains of revulsion I ever developed.

Swan Song

Nearly 22 centuries have passed since the Roman dramatist Terence wrote "Nothing human is alien to me"—a bold and generous statement, much quoted and cribbed, that lighted the way for all the humanist philosophy to follow. I doubt that the varieties of human behavior have increased significantly since the days of the Roman republic. But I find it more difficult, with every year that passes, to extend my sympathy as far as Terence recommends.

Much that is nominally human seems alien to me. I don't mean only the horrors, the crimes of deranged ghouls and cannibals like Jeffrey Dahmer who must be tried and executed in public, like ordinary criminals, because the public hungers for the details.

Actually I was thinking of the swans. The worst story in the morning paper isn't always the one that makes you groan or gag. Life invites us to a lavish smorgasbord of horrors. Sometimes there's a story that stays with you, quietly and stubbornly, because it leaves an image you can't manage to erase.

I have this image of 12 dead swans, enormous white birds soiled with blood and clay and piled in the trunk of a Cadillac. Tied together at the throat, I guess, the way game birds appear in those Flemish paintings. White feathers everywhere.

I know my picture is inaccurate. When the wildlife officer arrested Robert G. Shaw, minority leader of the North Carolina state senate, he found one dead swan in the trunk of Shaw's Cadillac. When the senator's hunting party of legislators and lobbyists came up to see what the trouble was—Shaw had no swan-hunting permit—they brought 11 more swans in the same condition. The 12 dead birds were spread around. But I still see them all in a pile, in the trunk of the Cadillac.

It makes a godawful picture. What kind of man goes forth to shoot swans? Perhaps a hypocrite in this case, because Shaw has won several awards for his efforts to protect North Carolina's wildlife. Perhaps a poor role model for lawmakers. The dispute now, since Shaw paid his $65 fine for shooting swans without a permit, is whether the distinguished legislator kicked dirt on the wildlife officer and cursed him.

In the manner of aggrieved big shots, Shaw asked for and received a special hearing at the highest level, with the wildlife commissioner and the secretary of Environment, Health and Natural Resources. The senator, who admits he carried no permit, seems to think that the real issue is why he was the only legislator the officer checked.

But I shouldn't single out Shaw. I don't care about the permit. It's more amazing to me that someone would want to shoot a swan than that it might, in some backward places, still be legal. All North American swans were protected from hunters by the Migratory Bird Treaty Act of 1918. But swan populations increased, naturally, and in recent years several trigger-happy states have applied successfully for limited seasons. North Carolina issued its first 1,000 swan permits in 1984. We now sell 6,000 annually, for a hunting season that runs November 2 to January 31, one swan to a customer.

It shouldn't have been such a revelation for me. I should know by now that if we declare an open season on any living thing—house cats, mules, parakeets—at least one damn fool will show up to claim a permit.

I've never condemned hunting outright, like some of my friends who defend the rights of animals. I'm from the country, I feel affection and respect for a lot of people who like to hunt. And I believe, in my cynicism, that it's a critical safety valve for a lot of marginal people who desperately need to shoot something.

I've tried, generously, to believe that hunters today are still related in some way to the hunters of antiquity, who killed birds and animals for three basic reasons: to feed themselves, to defend themselves and to protect their crops and property from competing species.

The swan-slayer fails to slip easily into any of these justifications. I would like very much to see North Carolina's favorite recipe for roast swan, if someone would be kind enough to send it along. I've found only one swan recipe, written out in rhymed couplets by the 19th-century swankeepers of St. Helen's Hospital in Norwich, England. It recommends a stuffing of ground beef, with half a pint of port and hot currant jelly. The British ornithologist

Sylvia Bruce Wilmore published the recipe with a caveat: "Dressed, the swan has the appearance of a dark colored goose, but it does not taste as good, for although being plumply fleshed and carving well, the meat is leathery and oily."

Please send me, also, any reports of swans attacking children or devastating croplands in North Carolina. Send them postage due.

There's no sentimentality, no anthropomorphic bathos in this particular anger that I'm feeling. That would be hypocritical. I don't credit those swans, just because they were beautiful, with any more sensitivity than the chicken I just ate for lunch. Their death didn't fill me with the sorrow and pity I felt a few weeks ago when I read about the woman whose pet Lab was killed by a bow hunter.

What I felt instead was disgust, and contempt. I can't identify with the swans—I'm trying to identify with the hunter. The swans are of no practical use to us, they do us no harm. They're beautiful, they're wild, they taste like shoes. What do you make of yourself when you shoot one? Does something beautiful always make you want to smash it and blow it full of holes? If this is a disease, is there a name for it? You might as well get drunk and shoot at stained-glass windows. At least you wouldn't get bloodstains in the trunk of your Cadillac.

Considering the intellectual and cultural tradition of our legislature, I'm confident that Shaw and all his friends are familiar with "The Wild Swans at Coole" by W.B. Yeats:

> But now they drift on the still water,
> Mysterious, beautiful;
> Among what rushes will they build,
> By what lake's edge or pool
> Delight men's eyes when I awake some day
> To find they have flown away?

Maybe our lawmakers were just making sure, in their clumsy Carolina way, that these dozen swans would delight no men's eyes but their own. They didn't study enough swan lore to consider that Yeats himself might be among their victims. It has been a persistent conceit, beginning with Pythagoras six centuries before Christ, that the souls of all true poets pass into swans at their deaths. Virgil was known as "The Mantuan Swan," Homer was called "The Swan of Meander," the Welsh poet Henry Vaughan was called "The Swan of Usk." Shakespeare himself, the greatest bard of our language, was styled "The Swan of Avon" by Ben Jonson.

No bird figures more prominently in Western mythology; many of the legends are far more disturbing, if you happen to be a swan hunter. Swans were sacred in Ireland, land of the poets, where killing or even harming a swan violated the strictest taboo. In many districts, the Irish still believe that anyone who kills a swan will die within the year.

The Siberians observe the same taboo, and add the belief that disaster may result just from pointing at a swan, or handling one of its feathers. Many cultures believed that swans embodied human souls. In the Middle Ages the swan was such a potent symbol that the English knights of King Edward I took their vows of chivalry in the presence of two gigantic live swans, who wore gold chains and gilded veils with little bells.

A melancholy descent, from the gilded court of the Plantagenets to the trunk of a Cadillac in Hyde County. A descent that reflects no discredit on the swan.

The moral case against hunters and their cowardice has been made often, and eloquently. Hunters who love to blast away point-blank at a grazing bison, hunters who purchase the lives of decrepit zoo animals and drag them out of their cages to kill them for trophies—these are pitiful cases that indicate profound pathology. A swan-hunter is a different kind of wretch. I wouldn't waste time arguing aesthetics with him, but maybe I can appeal to some remnant of his pride:

Listen to me, blockhead: Is there nothing you can kill that shames you?

Thanks to you and your slack-jawed ancestors, we have even fewer swans than poets. Here's a bit of recycled doggerel that any swan would be ashamed to own:

> *Laws are made by fools like Shaw*
> *But only Zeus can make a swan.*

Remember that 90 percent of gun owners (and many NRA members) supported the Brady Bill. The NRA death lobby, friend to AK-47s and enemy to all gun control, is a coalition of manufacturers and maniacs— Aryan survivalist types who get sexual release from fondling their bullets. One supplies the funding, the other supplies the fear.

William Styron, a Southerner, calls the NRA "one of the most evil organizations to exist in any nation, past or present." Its arguments are incomprehensible, its confidence is unshakable and its resources are inexhaustible. If it doesn't scare you, you're tougher than I am.

High Noon on Franklin Street

Chapel Hill—I drive past it in my car every day, some days three or four times. It's a wayside shrine on Estes Drive that people in our neighborhood have dedicated to the memory of Kristin Lodge-Miller, a young woman who was murdered there in July. A frustrated rapist, 18 years old, executed her with a pistol at point-blank range, in front of several witnesses.

The little shrine changes all the time. At the moment it consists of a dozen arrangements of flowers—some wilted, some artificial, some fresh today—and a child's painting of a blue cross topped with a big red eye, weeping copiously. Ribbons are wrapped around the sapling where the police found her lying in her jogging clothes with the bullethole in her head.

It's just across the street from the lot where the Amity Methodist Church sells its Christmas trees, about a quarter of a mile from my house. I drove past on the morning of the murder, 10 minutes after the shots were fired, while the ambulance was still parked on Estes Drive. My wife and daughter walk the dog along that road. This woman, whom I might have recognized, wasn't just murdered in the neighborhood, in the community where I live. She was murdered in my *world*, in that intimate fragment of creation where my own everyday takes place.

I took it very hard. The whole village of Chapel Hill took it hard. It was a wakeup call, a "Who's next?" crime, one of those crimes that won't vanish with the next wave of statistics. Terror is a new resident in Chapel Hill; when I moved here 10 years ago we had scarcely been introduced to fear.

This is a "Do something" town, a town full of activists, idealists, theorists, experts and cranks. It's not the kind of town where most people are afraid to speak up, or where most people respond to threats by loading up Daddy's deer rifle and locking themselves in their basements.

This appalling murder occurred in the middle of an unprecedented series of shootings here, including a gangland-style "hit" by a triggerman who used to play cops and robbers with my stepsons. It was to be expected, in Chapel Hill, that there would be a popular movement to put some teeth in the village gun laws. A handgun ban seemed like a modest expression of community outrage. What we didn't anticipate was that our intentions would attract an army of out-of-towners bent on scaring us out of it. A Town Council hearing, intended as a survey of local opinion, was dominated by people we've never seen before and rhetoric we've heard a thousand times before.

The NRA circus came to town. If you know Chapel Hill, where it takes a master's degree to get a construction job, you can imagine how poorly this rough act plays here. But fear always finds an audience. When the National Rifle Association pitches its Big Top in your town, you'll see how its presence alters your reality. Like a questionable X-ray, like a rumor of war, it casts a long shadow across your sense of well-being.

Call it a more primitive approach to politics and power. The NRA isn't subtle, or squeamish about crossing the line between persuasion and harassment. A friend of ours, a professor of history, received 28 phone calls in 36 hours after the NRA fingered him as a key supporter of gun control in Chapel Hill. Their pitch, as he described it, is as mechanical and predictable as a cop reading your Miranda rights from the card he carries in his pocket.

But he said they were unfailingly courteous. So it's courteously, and wearily, that we respond once again to arguments that never merited the courtesy of a response. The Second Amendment never guaranteed any individual's right to own firearms. No court has ever struck down a gun control measure as unconstitutional under the Second Amendment. In 1981 the Seventh Circuit Court of Appeals stated succinctly that "possession of handguns by individuals is not part of the right to keep and bear arms."

A conservative Supreme Court saw no reason to review that decision. In 1980, in *Lewis vs. United States*, a Supreme Court majority joined by William Rehnquist ruled that "legislative restrictions on the use of firearms do not trench upon any constitutionally protected liberties."

The NRA's leaders and lawyers know very well that the Second Amendment, of which they quote only half, was intended to protect the rights of states to maintain armed militias, back in the days when invasions, hostile Indians and malignant tyrants in Washington were still legitimate concerns. But NRA foot soldiers have heard this constitutional humbug so many times, some of them have begun to believe it. And not only NRA members. In a national survey in 1986, half the people who responded believed that the Second Amendment guaranteed their right to own a handgun.

Shorn of the Bill of Rights, the NRA position reduces to some astonishing contradictions. Ignoring the fact that 50 to 60 percent of all handgun shootings and murders involve people who know each other (felony murders run only slightly ahead of family murders, 21 to 15 percent in 1989), the gun lobby blames all the carnage on a separate species of congenital "criminals" who are being coddled by the courts. Any cop or schoolteacher could tell them that the kids have the guns long before they have the criminal records.

By now everyone realizes that there are young people on the street whose lack of respect for life, their own or others', seems to place them completely beyond the pale of human sympathy or social theory. But most of them have minimal police records when they pull the trigger that lands them on the evening news. The kid who murdered Kristin Lodge-Miller was a novice who tried to escape on a 10-speed bicycle. Of all the high-profile murderers who made their debuts in North Carolina this year, the only ones who probably belonged in jail were the pair who killed Michael Jordan's father.

I can't actually figure the NRA's solution to juvenile mayhem, unless it's to identify that criminal population—with Rorschach tests?—before it reaches shooting size, and jail them all before they strike. As policy, I guess that's just as sane as arming them all, which is where we're headed now.

Lost in the rhetoric about criminals and self-defense are most of the facts that signify: More than half of handgun deaths are suicides; for every time a law-abiding citizen kills a criminal in self-defense, 118 Americans die in handgun suicides, accidents and murders. For every parent who protects a child with a pistol, there must be 20 children killed by stray bullets (in today's paper—"Stray bullet kills toddler in Gastonia").

But handguns aren't part of the problem, according to the NRA. They're part of the solution. Solutions aren't the NRA's strong suit. To get a feel for this most destructive of all the strains of belligerent ignorance that make Americans special, imagine a conversation between an NRA missionary and the average sane citizen of Chapel Hill.

Citizen: Do you think this is a satisfactory state of affairs, with every punk and junkie over 12 carrying a deadly weapon?
NRA: No.
Citizen: Isn't there something we can do about it?
NRA: Arm yourselves.

According to the history professor, that's exactly the advice his callers offered. Does the gun lobby, with its weak grasp of history, understand that what it advocates is a retreat from civilization itself? Civilization was founded on collective security. Our upward climb began in the Stone Age, when cave families realized that they couldn't breed enough sons or stockpile enough spearheads to protect themselves from every gang of Neanderthals who slouched up the creekbed with blood in their eyes. Villages, cities, nations, empires evolved from collective efforts to survive. Private armies and arsenals were sacrificed, laws were passed to regulate weapons and behavior, public safety was entrusted to militia and police.

On these compromises rested the slow ascent of man. When you declare that laws and lawmen are futile, that no hope lies in that direction, that there's no communal solution to criminal violence, you're taking 10,000 years off the clock and crawling back into your cave with a quiver of arrows.

There's always been a mustang strain of American conservatism that rejects all collective solutions and takes the darkest view of human nature and human potential. In its milder forms it's humorous. The NRA's paranoid politics is that strain carried to the absurd, with terrifying social consequences. It doesn't appeal to all gun owners or even all NRA members, but its influence is so pervasive that even responsible newspapers run irresponsible headlines like "Can gun control work?"

Of course it works, stupid. There were more handgun murders this summer in my community, in Chapel Hill and Durham, than in the entire disarmed nation of Great Britain. But it's a very good question whether gun control can work on the local level, whether one community can create a demilitarized zone in a nation saturated with firearms.

Can the Chapel Hill Town Council stand up to a gun lobby that the Congress of the United States has pampered for 60 years? More than anyone else, the NRA is responsible for the ballistic nightmare that provides its only compelling argument—that the streets are so dangerous an unarmed citizen feels like a rabbit who runs with the wolves.

"There is no reason why all pistols should not be barred to everyone except the police," Justice William O. Douglas argued in 1972. But thanks largely to the proliferation of handguns, there are neighborhoods and whole cities where public safety consists of iron doors, savage dogs and loaded rifles under the bed. Just last Sunday in Durham, just down the road, eight citizens were robbed at gunpoint—seven at the doors of their homes. No one got off a shot in self-defense.

Terror and chaos mean prosperity for the NRA and its arms merchants. A single gun-control ordinance is considered a source of contagion, a place where pernicious sanity might take root and spread.

That's why the out-of-towners are here. But I think they underestimate us. There are many communities where civilization is waning, where it may not survive. I don't think Chapel Hill is one of them, not yet. I think it will be one of the last, not one of the first, to give up the fight.

Fundamentally I'm a hopeful person, and public response to the war in Kuwait—90 percent approval?—depressed me more than anything since the assassinations of 1968. It convinced me that the government's propaganda machine is capable of selling anything military, not only to the people but to the press.

The Yellow Rose of Texas

Terlingua, Texas—In the desert, where waterholes are few and far between, they serve a heterogeneous clientele. At La Kiva, an underground saloon dug into a creekbank on Route 170 between Study Butte and Terlingua, a three-piece band with beards and ponytails was playing border blues for four or five pairs of middle-aged dancers; at the bar, two cowboys and a painter of acrylic sunsets were fighting a losing battle with a devil named mescal; in the corner some weekend hikers from Rice University were drinking pitchers of Lone Star, and just inside the door an elderly couple from Huddersfield, England, were eating barbecued ribs and taking snapshots with their eyes.

In the back room, a party of Chicanos in their Sunday best were celebrating some family or religious occasion and disgorging a steady stream of small, spotless children into the barroom. A vision fetched up at my table, a tiny girl with a yellow balloon. In a pale yellow dress, with a big bow of yellow satin and white lace fastened in her coal-black hair, she was transformed into a walking, giggling yellow ribbon, the prettiest one I ever hope to see.

She wanted to enlist me in a kind of volleyball game with her balloon. The name she gave sounded like "Adelanta." I asked her about the yellow ribbons and she told me that her mother wouldn't let her have a kitten. Her big sister, eight or nine, leaned over and explained that the ribbons were for Uncle Hector, who was "fighting Arabs in the war."

In the doorway, starched matrons beamed at the obvious glamour of this child, who must have charmed many a wandering Anglo before I came along. I volleyed the balloon a few times, tipped over an empty bottle of Tecate, and wished her a kitten when I got up to leave.

Yellow ribbons haven't looked quite the same to me since. I'd never received a clear message from these ubiquitous symbols of grassroots patriotism that marked the winter war, though they were like red flags to some of the people I know. Symbols have never moved me much, pro or con. But west of the Pecos, where there are more mule deer than people, where folks for hundreds of miles around know your family, response to the winter war was not complex: To hell with anyone who might hurt Uncle Hector. Violent solutions aren't uncommon out here, and neither are universal gestures of community support for the victims and survivors.

The truth about the yellow ribbons is that they were an authentic grassroots phenomenon, a manifestation of political innocence and small-town values. Pacifists and intellectuals make a fatal error when they assume that the people in the back room at La Kiva are their rivals in some political struggle that both sides could articulate. In the '60s a minority of antiwar activists, sick with half-digested bits of Mao and Che Guevara, made a catastrophic error when they declared the American enlisted man a class enemy and a moral leper.

Small-town people, who seem to forget almost everything, never forgot that the hippies turned on Uncle Hector. No one in the peace camp made the same mistake this winter, but it didn't matter. The old antagonism remained; the government recognized it and exploited it ruthlessly. As long as you can give Hector his marching orders, you can count on his family and his community to fall into step behind him.

That was the sobering lesson of the winter war, which may not be over—that in this country, at this time, the government can count on majority support for any military adventure it might choose to undertake.

Were there other lessons? In the din of gloating, the nauseating spectacle of puffy noncombatants figuratively dancing on the smoking bodies of the Iraqi dead, I thought for a moment that I heard someone inviting opponents of the war to recant, admit their error, enlist in the new world order. I was probably mistaken, but I thought I heard someone say, "Aren't you sorry you didn't jump on the war wagon when you had a chance?"

Maybe I'm overlooking something, but where was I wrong? I made one mistake that I know of, a mistake I shared with most journalists who wanted to prevent the war. I passed along various inflated figures—some from supporters of the war, most from opponents—for the cost of a ground war, in American lives. These figures came from retired officers, defense department defectors, the usual suspects.

I used them because they seemed to help my argument. I suspect now that they were a deliberate red herring, an effective campaign of disinformation to make the actual war seem clean and painless. If any of these estimates were based on inside information, who could have supplied it except American or Israeli intelligence? The impregnable minefields and chemical terrors, the seasoned ferocity of the Republican Guard, all of this was the usual exaggeration, the myth of a formidable enemy that's supposed to make us feel less embarrassed about the mismatch. It was all a setup, I'm afraid. It was the same game in Panama, in Grenada even, but this time more of us fell for it.

I'll be more skeptical next time, next war. Nevertheless, I always concentrated on the mismatch, because I thought the image of the hulking American Goliath might defuse some of the jingoism that was breaking out, even with such an unattractive actor playing David. The only thing the Gulf War proved to me, so far, is that it was a much worse mismatch than any of us imagined.

Last week the Senate Judiciary Committee—hardly the left-wing hate-America lobby—released its report revealing that the United States is the most violent nation on the face of the earth (or at least the most violent of nations "civilized" enough to keep crime statistics). For murder, rape, assault and robbery there's no one like us anywhere, not by a wide margin. And "the good news," the silver lining that's supposed to rescue our morale, is that our military machine has just annihilated at least 100,000 Iraqis, most of them just poor boys following orders like Uncle Hector, or civilians huddled somewhere just trying to survive.

Even if I subscribed to all the objectives of the Gulf War, real and alleged, decency would compel me to hang my head and observe mourning at a time of so many funerals, so much grief. There's something truly pathetic, something pathologically empty about a society that can achieve euphoria by smashing an insignificant enemy, whatever the moral rating of its leadership. Is it the collapse of order at home, is it our sick and tired economy that leaves Americans with such a desperate need to be reassured, with bombs and missiles, that we're still No. 1?

"The Grenada Syndrome," Garry Wills calls it—these brief "surgical" wars to boost morale—and he predicts that this is just the beginning, if the United States can't find some optimism elsewhere. A nation of violence is the same as a man of violence, a street fighter and barroom terror. He finds himself pitied and ostracized, finally, for seeking respect the only way he knows how.

There's no question that Republicans will use the war as a yardstick for patriotism, to discredit Democrats and unrepentant doves. The party that made Willie Horton famous will stoop to anything, as its dying ex-chairman is currently confessing to anyone who will listen. But even more ominous, in the aftermath of the winter war, are reports that some war-wild Americans are making a scapegoat of the media. This is peculiar, since the press has rarely been tamed and compromised as easily as it was tamed in Saudi Arabia. The Pentagon's strategy for neutralizing Dan Rather was prepared as carefully (and as far in advance) as its strategy for neutralizing the Republican Guard, and it was equally successful.

Most journalists were frustrated captives of a video-designed war that outmaneuvered them, and most TV reporters were shameless cheerleaders for Desert Storm. Cretins impersonating journalists have published some of the most preposterously belligerent, xenophobic, chauvinist drivel I've ever read anywhere. So what was it that offended stateside patriots, I wonder? A handful of good reporters delivering unwelcome background, like Washington's decade-long, illicit affair with the unmentionable Saddam? Or were they outraged by a few scattered observers expressing honest doubts about this war?

If you don't want to hear the facts from trained fact gatherers and you don't care to hear an honest, informed opinion expressed in public, you're living in the wrong country, really. Are more Americans going to turn against their truth-bearers as the truths get harder to swallow?

I'd like to find something positive to say about the war that just ended, besides my obvious relief that Adelanta's Uncle Hector and most of his buddies came home alive. We "won" this war, unlike the war in Vietnam, because we declared a limited objective and achieved it. But in the long run, which country will benefit more? Iraqis, the ones still alive, have been cured of the illusion of military salvation and will probably be relieved of their terrible leadership. As a result of the same war, it looks like the United States is stuck, indefinitely, with the same leadership and the same illusions that got us where we are.

Phil Berrigan and his friends are heroes of mine because they know exactly where the Devil sleeps and because they've got the guts to wake him up and pull his tail. In the cause of peace, no sacrifice is pointless and no protest is futile.

If I Had a Hammer

Here he comes again, disturbing the holiday shopping season, purchasing a moment of our attention with weeks and possibly years of his life. An unwelcome St. Nicholas, this white-haired, kindly old gentleman. In his bag, instead of oranges and ribbon candy, he carries bottles of his blood. Not a jolly old elf, Father Phil, but a stubborn old conscience.

If Philip Berrigan is a saint, it won't be the Catholic Church that canonizes him. It no longer requires his services. But this durable ex-priest, now 70, serves his country as one of the last reliable landmarks in a wilderness of moral uncertainty. We can count on him. Empires crumble, but the old man in the flannel shirt goes on about his business.

I've never met Father Berrigan (I use "Father" out of respect, whether or not he's entitled to it). But there was a memory, long undisturbed, that was tripped when I read that he and three of his disciples had been arrested at Seymour Johnson Air Force Base in Goldsboro—for attacking an F-15E fighter jet with blood and hammers.

The memory dates from 1968, when a group of us were drinking in an apartment in New York. Half of us were young men still eligible for the war in Vietnam. Most of us agreed that the last resort of a clear conscience was a good map of Canada. I had a little status in this group because I'd spent my summers in Canada and could reassure the boys from Boston and Baltimore that Ontario wasn't alarmingly different from Minnesota. Our hostess had more status because two of her uncles, the radical priests Philip and Daniel Berrigan, had just burned some draft records in Baltimore and were fugitives from a federal warrant.

When a man looking for the bathroom started to open a door in the hallway, she jumped up too quickly and asked him to leave that door alone, please, someone was sleeping. Later her boyfriend told me that Father Phil was passing through, and that as long as none of us saw him, none of us would have to commit perjury if we were questioned by the FBI.

For us, novices of conscience, this was a glamorous near-contact with a hero of the peace movement. It made a great impression on me, at an impressionable age when I was changing my mind about everything. Here was a priest, a mature responsible citizen, hunted like a thief by his government—by his own people—because he was right and they were wrong. So you didn't have to be a starving student, with half-formed ideas and nothing to lose, to break the law for peace and peace of mind.

Since 1968, Berrigan has been arrested 100 times and served six years in various jails and prisons. The charge for vandalizing the F-15E is a felony, destruction of government property, punishable by up to 10 years in prison and a $250,000 fine. Held without bond pending trial, he'll spend Christmas in the Robeson County Detention Center—nothing new for Father Phil.

What drives an old man to climb over an eight-foot steel fence at 4:00 a.m., on a cold December night in North Carolina? For one thing, a granite faith that makes most comfortable clergymen, televangelists and Vatican bureaucrats look like time-share salesmen grubbing for commissions. For another, a streak of Irish stubbornness that makes it impossible for Berrigan to resign himself to the wisdom of Plato: "Only the dead have seen the end of war."

We hear the argument that demonstrations like the one at Seymour Johnson have outlived their usefulness, now that the Cold War is over and the nuclear arms race has been defused. It's a shallow argument. Actually this is the one moment in recent history when a vigilant peace movement might make a critical difference.

The real face of American militarism was always masked by anti-communism. Arms sales were dictated by Cold War foreign policy, wars by national interest. Every military decision was a chess move in the match with Moscow. Then suddenly the war machine stood unmasked in its ugliness, scrambling to find a patriotic disguise— and no one wanted to look. The operation in Kuwait was a post-Cold War classic—crooked arms deals gone awry, a dishonest presentation of national interests, managed media, fulsome displays of saber-rattling and flag-waving. It was grotesque, and the polls said most Americans loved every minute of it.

The Pentagon and its suppliers haven't let the fall of communism spoil their sales incentives. In the year beginning October 1, 1991, the U.S. government sold $16 billion worth of weapons to 90 nations, and licensed American companies to sell another $16 billion to 144 foreign governments. Foreign military sales for the fiscal year 1993 may approach $30 billion.

It would take a better flack than David Gergen to explain why every customer is worthy and every sale strategic. We don't rationalize anymore. We just deal, aggressively and promiscuously. So do France, Russia, Britain, Germany and China. If the big guys don't make the wars, at least they guarantee the body counts.

Worldwide, the human race spends more more money on weapons and warfare than it spends on education or health care. Its favorite gun shop is run by Uncle Sam, and this is the shopping season. That's why Phil Berrigan climbs over fences in the middle of the night.

Antiwar activists know that it's now, while there are no enemies worth the name, before another war or international emergency throws America into its traditional patriotic lockstep, that the arms industry is most exposed. It's now, while the president and public opinion are turning against the handgun cult, that people may notice the family resemblance between the companies who sell the little guns and the ones who sell the big guns.

Take away the stars and stripes and it's the same dirty business. I'm surprised that the heavyweights haven't written their own versions of NRA bumper stickers: "Bombs don't annihilate villages, bombardiers do," or "If H-bombs are outlawed, only outlaws will own H-bombs."

Militarism is a religion in its own right. In America, an outlaw with a chest-load of ribbons and medals commands more respect than an outlaw in a clerical collar. There might be something incurably wrong with a society that imprisons pacifist priests and lets Col. Oliver North, now a promising candidate for the U.S. Senate, skate free without spending a night in jail. But pessimism only paralyzes the faint of heart. To Father Berrigan, an F-15E is an effigy of Satan he can engage directly, as Moses engaged the Golden Calf. He can hit it with his hammer.

What else could he do? When I was young and asked embarrassing questions without blushing, I had an older friend who had also turned away from the priesthood, though I don't think he was ever defrocked. I asked him for a simple, bumper-sticker version of his philosophy of life. I was surprised when he answered me seriously.

"Resolve to add nothing to the sum of human cruelty," he said. "That's the first step. And the second step—the serious work—is to reduce it."

What I took personally, the peace movement applies globally. Whether it's a city neighborhood or a civil war in Central Asia, identifying and arming the good guys is a deadly, cynical game no honest person plays with conviction. Disarmament—empty missile silos, empty holsters, empty cartridge chambers—is the only policy that will ever reduce the sum of human cruelty.

The carol says, "God rest ye merry gentlemen, let nothing you dismay." I'm afraid I'm chronically dismayed. But we sit down to dinner with merry gentlemen who send a goose to the Cratchits and an atomic cannon to Sri Lanka. Our commercialized holidays are meaningless, even offensive if they're dedicated to anything less than peace. The Christian messiah is either the Prince of Peace or he's a porcelain doll in a manger scene, an icon of no consequence.

If you were waiting for a Messenger to appear with a sign, there's good news. He already made an appearance, out at Seymour Johnson Air Force Base. And that ringing you heard wasn't jingle bells on a one-horse open sleigh. It was a sturdy hammer on the nose of an F-15E.

Oliver North, multiple felon, convicted gun-runner and perjurer, accused drug-runner, now runs for the U.S. Senate while Phil Berrigan sits in jail for hitting a warplane with a hammer.

In the Lion's Den

Under a government which imprisons any unjustly, the true place for a just man is also a prison . . . the only house in a slave state in which a free man can abide with honor.

—Henry David Thoreau, *Civil Disobedience*

Edenton—I drove into town just at noon. It was a perfect Down East day, not a cloud in the sky. A smart breeze was blowing off Albemarle Sound; the air smelled so promising that merchants and lawyers were pausing on their way to lunch, grabbing a deep breath or two and congratulating themselves for being alive and ambulatory on May 11, 1994.

Edenton is a pretty town any time of year, but this was the old place at its best. Phil Berrigan, John Dear and Bruce Friedrich had to take my word for it. The cells at Chowan County Jail don't come equipped with windows. Except for a 40-minute visit to a county garage, they haven't been outside for three months. Since their arrest last December 7, for a symbolic attack on an F-15E fighter plane at Seymour Johnson Air Force Base, the Catholic peace commandos have seen virtually nothing of the sun or the seasons. As the summer solstice approached, their only clue was the deepening tan on the arms and faces of their visitors.

I was offensively tanned and felt conspicuous. The narrow, windowless cells feel like dungeons because the ceilings are so high, creating the impression that the free world is not only out there but *up there*. Berrigan, Dear and Friedrich didn't grasp the extent of my respect for their sacrifice. I'm clinically claustrophobic, not only about cramped spaces but about any restraint on my movement, or surrendering any power over my body. I couldn't do what they do.

Very few of us could. On or about July 5, they expect to be sentenced to several years in prison for their felony convictions on charges of destroying government property.

Berrigan is 70, an age when a man's time is precious. Dear, a Duke graduate and a Jesuit priest, is 34. Friedrich is 24 and their codefendant Lynn Fredriksson is 30. Those of us who've spent the last of our youth regard their time, too, as more precious than they yet realize. But of all the good people I include in my concerns, the Plowshares activists are the ones for whom I feel the least pity.

You need to see them, in their voluntary captivity, to understand why that isn't rhetoric. "Bring out the activists," the amiable jailer hollered to the turnkey, and turned to me with a wink of conspiracy I was free to interpret. A minute later I was locked in a cell (for the first time in many years) with the prisoners and their friend Earl Crow, a Methodist minister from High Point.

The prisoners looked healthy, sitting there in a row on a narrow bunk with Berrigan in the middle. They were a little pale as you might expect. Phil Berrigan, who's already spent more time in jail than Mohandas Gandhi, looked tired and would probably be some-where else if he followed his doctor's orders. But in sharp contrast to so many of my friends whose lives have taken bad turns lately— if I were a knee-praying man I'd have rug burns—these prisoners of conscience seem to be exactly where they need to be.

"It's a great blessing," said John Dear, a big calm man who could get away with saying that even if you didn't know he was a priest. "I'm a little freer than I was. We're liberated from all the despair out there. We're just ordinary people, but we've been blessed by this action. We took responsibility. It was so concrete. I hit that plane two or three times and made an actual dent in it. I felt it was the best thing I could do for humanity. I feel a deep peace."

A conscience at peace with itself, a thing we rarely see, gener-ates a power cynical journalists may be inadequate to describe. The effect of this conversation in the jail cell was to make me ashamed of my native impulse to turn everything to some shade of irony. It felt like disrespect. These men are in a different place, and I don't mean Chowan County Jail.

A visitor here begins to redefine seriousness. It isn't saccharine or humorless. Through 30 years of civil disobedience Phil Berrigan has perfected the nonviolent expressions he presents to soldiers and policemen; dropping his chin and closing his eyes, he bears a considerable resemblance to the current Pope at prayer. But there's a gruff and rueful side to this strong old man. He almost growled when he recalled his trial in Elizabeth City:

"I've seen 40 of these kangaroo trials, and they're universally bad. But this one was particularly flagrant. With that gag rule, the judge just ignored the Constitution and international law. Do people understand that?"

The Plowshares group chose Seymour Johnson because of the prominent role the F-15Es played in the Gulf War. They never considered the pro-military character of the state of North Carolina, they told me. They couldn't have predicted the hostility of Judge Terrence Boyle, a Catholic conservative nominated for the federal bench by Jesse Helms. But it isn't in their nature, or the nature of their movement, to scheme for advantages.

When they enter the lion's den, they don't expect tame lions. They prepare for teeth and claws. Their preparation intrigued me because it appears to have been so effective.

"It isn't physical training at all," Berrigan said. "It's spiritual preparation—retreats, scripture study, close examination of our faith and our purpose. We studied psychology, politics, the literature of nonviolent resistance. But the key is to build up interdependence and trust. It's in-depth life-sharing. We build a community."

In jail the community continues its discipline. There's private prayer and group prayer, organized Bible study, readings and discussions, daily Communion with Wonder Bread and grape juice, and each afternoon a period of shared silence.

The Edenton prisoners are concerned that Lynn Fredriksson, isolated in the Hertford County Jail 40 miles up the Chowan River, has been cut off from the sustaining community. But they share a great confidence in her strength. They've witnessed as they intended and set an example of principled commitment that even the scandal-crazed media have been obliged to acknowledge, for the most part with puzzled respect.

Their lives send a message, in this pampered country where teenagers are purported to be driven to drugs and suicide by the fear that they'll fail to outearn their parents. But I'm concerned about the reception of the other message, the one Phil Berrigan has been proclaiming since the Johnson administration, the one he carried with him over an eight-foot fence, through a freezing knee-deep stream and across three-quarters of a mile of pavement on his hands and knees, at Seymour Johnson Air Force Base.

It's the unequivocal message that human beings are committing geocide; that war, militarism and violence are all one disease and that it causes all the other diseases—oppression, poverty, starvation, environmental degradation—that are bringing the human adventure to a premature conclusion.

It happens that I share this view, and it's a view that often lures me toward the sin of despair. The North Korean nuclear menace is sweeping the newsmagazines and swelling the columnists with bluster. The Pentagon's Hitler-of-the-Month program, which was so successful during the Reagan and Bush administrations, has resumed with Kim Il Sung. Since the end of the Cold War, the United States has become the Wal-Mart of global arms merchants. We sold weapons to 142 of the world's 180 nations in 1991, and last year we more than doubled our arms exports, for a record gross of $32 billion.

Pacifists wonder if the Clinton administration has repealed the Carter Doctrine that prohibited official aid or encouragement for American arms merchants. Washington is sanctioning reckless gun-running in the Third World, where U.S. companies now hold the largest market share, even while the administration tries to rein in the NRA. Tragicomic embarrassments, like our attempt to buy back 300 Stinger antiaircraft missiles from the Afghanis (terrorists may outbid us), have failed to compromise the policy of protecting Americans' jobs instead of foreigners' lives.

("The chilling effect of such talk is that it doesn't sound crazy when it comes from Berrigan," a *News and Observer* reporter wrote at the time of the activists' arrest. How does it sound when it comes from me?)

Col. Oliver North, multiple felon, convicted gun-runner and perjurer and accused drug-runner, now runs for the U.S. Senate while Phil Berrigan sits in jail for hitting a warplane with a hammer. My own feeble optimism never recovered from Kuwait, when 90 percent of the American people applauded a war so stupid, crooked and obscene that the sad truth will be coming in installments for 50 years.

What I needed—what I drove from Durham to Edenton to request—was an antidote for despair from pacifists who've demonstrated personal resources much richer than my own.

It was a lot to ask.

"We're prey to discouragement," Berrigan admitted. "The public resists the lessons of history—it scarcely acknowledges history.

Americans seem tired of perplexing social issues. It comes from the way we live in this country, I guess.

"Even the church doesn't produce people for this work the way it did during the Vietnam war. The church is a principality and a power, contaminated by the violence of power. But the Catholic church is still a vital entity—extraordinary people emerge from it, into communities of faith like ours.

"Is there a temptation to despair and quit, to fold up our tents and go back to normalcy, to our personal requirements? I suppose. But the consequences of withdrawal are reprehensible. Silence lends assent, doesn't it? Jesus didn't withdraw. I preserve a lot of hope."

The jailer looked in on us, still beaming and accommodating as if he were a little proud of this bunch that brought NBC News to his jail. I'd been locked in for more than an hour with no jitters. I don't doubt that something in that cell was soothing my nerves. When the cell door clicked shut again, Bruce Friedrich addressed the question of hope.

"We have so much hope we can barely stand it," he said. "That's not false idealism. Hope gathers around individuals who support each other and try to serve the human family. I'm learning a lot here, too—I'm sharing an experience common to poor people, and witnessing for them. There's a satisfying irony about being in jail for nonviolence."

I asked John Dear, the Jesuit, if his religious vows—specifically obedience—ever get in the way of his commitment to peace.

"I've had my community's support," he said, and grinned. "But you've divined that our approach to theology is post–Vatican II. Obedience to God comes first. We're trying to *be* the church, a new church that follows Jesus' example.

"From jail I feel hope. This is all about hope, because nonviolence is our only hope. It's the key to the future. As Martin Luther King said, 'It's nonviolence or non-existence.' He was a hopeful man."

The new theology of the peace movement divides the world into life-denying and life-affirming forces, with a single-minded severity that makes sense to me. Tobacco falls among the forces of death and darkness. And here in the realm of King Tobacco, at the mercy of a people who love their guns and smokes, these three unusual men anticipate—with apparent equanimity—years of confinement in one of our overcrowded Southern prisons.

Their talk turns frequently to King, Gandhi, Nelson Mandela and other heroes for whom prison was a gateway to victory. And twice a day, at 7:00 a.m. and 6:00 p.m., they watch the news on TV: The latest pictures from Rwanda and Bosnia, the faces of Kim Il Sung and Oliver North and the face of a prisoner North Carolina put to death with poison gas while he shouted, "I'm human, I'm human."

VI

The Environment — The Shadows Lengthen

I'm a mild-mannered cultural conservative, a sworn enemy of political correctness and all forms of indecent exposure who thinks Ted Turner should be executed for coloring *Casablanca*. I become a snarling wolverine of a radical when it comes to defending the environment. Pacifism and deep ecology are my radical commitments; the hardest thing to teach a political innocent is the way they fit together. Corporations control this country. War, hot or cold, is good for business. Environmental scrupulousness is bad for business, and it rules out war.

It's as simple as that, when you scrape away the crusted pieties of nationalism and capitalism. A corporate shill like Mr. Limbaugh, who's never met a profit motive he didn't like, issues his most dangerous nonsense when he reviles environmentalists as communists and cranks.

A turning point for me was the week I spent in Mexico a few years ago, deliberating the planet's survival with some of its most distinguished scientists and intellectuals. Current technology could still save the earth, they decided, but the political will to mobilize that technology is nowhere to be found. Nothing I've heard since has diminished the pessimism or the outrage that I brought back from Mexico.

"Humanists" have often accused me of preferring animals to human beings. If that's an insult, I can live with it.

Harvest of Innocents

Magdalen Islands, Newfoundland, Canada — From the helicopter, a thousand feet above the ice, it looks as if the globe itself has been painted white from pole to pole and is beginning to crack in the sun. But maybe any simile is cheap. The Gulf of St. Lawrence, frozen for a thousand miles and fissured by its first thaw, looks like nothing you've ever seen in your life unless you're a bush pilot or a sea bird. At first glance the ice is as white as a bedsheet, but in bright sunlight it reveals undertones of green and blue. Remove your sunglasses and the colors change but remain, an evanescent phenomenon like the Northern Lights that tease the eye and defy the camera.

It's a world of pure color with absolutely no shapes, except the curved horizon, on which the eye can fasten. Twenty miles out, the pilot, Rene, banks dramatically and points ahead to the right. At this height they look like maggots on the ice, big brown ones and small white ones harder to make out. As we drop down for the landing more shapes emerge from the glare, and the size of the nursery becomes apparent: several square miles of harp seals, thousands of nursing mothers and bleating pups creating what would pass for a din anywhere more confined than this subarctic vastness.

According to Rene, the nurseries were much larger a few years ago, when he came out on the ice with his father. It was half a day's walk from one end of the herd to the other. He doesn't say what he was doing on the ice with his father, and that's the question we've already learned not to ask.

His other passengers are German journalists who want to interview Canadian scientists, a team that's marking and weighing seals near the landing site. I don't want to interview anyone, so I have the seals to myself. It's like being the only visitor in an open-air maternity ward the size of Disney World. In my bright orange survival suit and snowmobile boots—it's five degrees below zero—I trudge across the ice from pup to pup and pay my respects.

These newborn seals, the whitecoats, are the creatures whose slaughter has provoked international protests, inspired heart-breaking documentaries and UN committees and mobilized animal sympathizers in every civilized country. They are arguably the most appealing infants that occur in nature, so much more attractive than a human at the same stage that only a human's mother would dispute it. The toy designers with their stupid anthropomorphized bears and ponies fall far short of the whitecoat's appeal. Discounting his nasty little digestive system, he's a living crib toy. An hour on the ice with the whitecoats is almost an overdose of cute, like watching two Shirley Temple movies back to back. It takes an antidote of ugly to snap you back. Experienced seal-watchers carry snapshots of Jim and Tammy in their wallets.

They're astonishingly amiable. Some are shy and a few are aggressive, but most of them allow me to pat their wet noses and scratch where their ears ought to be. They love to be rolled over and scratched on their stomachs, and encourage it by clapping their flippers. The scientists discovered one who liked to be pitched and skidded across the ice from man to man, and sulked when they quit the game.

They're amiable and trusting—and absolutely helpless. They can't swim and they propel themselves across the ice at the speed of a fast turtle. Animal absolutists argue that an adult polar bear, hunted with a high-powered rifle, has no more chance than a baby seal. But it takes some skill and effort to get to the bear. By comparison, "hunting" whitecoats is like picking grapes.

Psychologists believe that birth is a major trauma for all of us, but consider the harp seal. He goes directly from the womb, which is 98 degrees Fahrenheit, to the ice where it may be twenty below. His mother nurses him from time to time but usually she's beneath the ice feeding, and in her absence strange monkeys in weather-proof synthetics come to scratch his stomach and take his picture. If he's lucky. In other years, and even this year in other places, stranger monkeys come to hit him on the head with a heavy tomahawk developed in Norway especially for that purpose, and skin him alive. They only wait until he's nursed enough to smooth out the wrinkles in the beautiful white coat he was born with. The pelt is considered prime when he's about two weeks old.

Until 1983, when the protests resulted in a ban on seal products in Europe and the United States, sealers skinned several hundred thousand whitecoats every March. As usual the mystery lies more with the creatures who kill than with the creatures who die. Ten thousand Canadians live in the Magdalen Islands, more than you'd expect in such an inaccessible place, just 100 miles southwest of Newfoundland. Most of them are Acadian French, except for a few Scots on an out island, and most of them, like my pilot Rene, have family connections to the sealing industry. They live in a beautiful place, at least in March when the frozen islands look like ice cubes floating in a green punch, in a cold green sea the color of a Heineken bottle. But it's a hard life. Especially hard since the island girls began to learn in school that a woman has other options in life, other than slaving for a rough man on a cold island. They began to seek their fortunes in Halifax and Montreal, and now there are seven men for every woman in the Magdalens.

This creates tension. In the bar at the Chateau Madelinot, bachelor fishermen stare at Madonna's dreadful new video with an unhealthy hunger. A rather buttoned-up career girl from Chicago has no answer at all when a handsome but fish-soiled young islander accosts her on her way to a Save the Whales film, with Gallic directness: "Allo, I am J.R. Tremblay, I think you like me, no? I take you to a real whale."

Seal Watch '89 doesn't ease the tension—several hundred journalists, photographers and animal advocates from all over Europe and North America, most of the men with well-tended and underworked wives or girl friends, and cameras that cost half a year's wages in the Magdalens. The International Fund for Animal Welfare underwrites Seal Watch, to help replace sealing revenues with tourist money and to create a presence that will discourage fur poachers. A few of the Madelinots are sympathetic to our project; most of them seem mildly amused. (There are humorous elements, like the stern little woman from Dusseldorf who comes seal-watching with a coat that must have cost the lives of half the domestic minks in Germany.) A worrisome number are openly hostile. A sealer with a wet mustache, monumentally drunk, interrupts a lecture on seal migrations to challenge the suave professor. He hunted seals for 17 years, he shouts in a broken English, and there's no fooling him. Most of the seals are gone, he can see that. To him it's some cruel trick perpetrated by environmentalists in New York. "Where are the seals?" His pain is real. No one dares to remind him that 186,000 harp seals were "harvested" every year through 1983.

The fashionable attitude, even among the seal watchers, is that we must respect the culture and traditions of the Magdalen Islanders and speak of the fur ban as if it had been a local tragedy that we must help them through. Everyone seems put out with one passionate animal advocate from Chicago, a classic little old lady in tennis shoes, who keeps reminding us that we can hear rifle shots while we're hugging the whitecoats and taking their pictures. She notes that our hosts always refer carefully to the ban on "commercial" seal hunts, which means that the locals are free to kill as they wish for their "personal" needs. This one woman, who runs an animal rescue mission, asks all the embarrassing questions.

I've been known to fraternize with animal rights extremists. But I'm not a vegetarian, and I consider myself a moderate who will defend hunters and fishermen and point out the illogic of some of the extremist positions. I like the bluff, tactless islanders and admire their sand. I agree that hungry sealers aren't half as culpable, in the eyes of God, as the heedless hypocrites who buy fur coats stripped from slaughtered nurslings. But finally these apologies for indigenous culture don't go too far with me.

These aren't aborigines or subsistence hunters, these French Canadians with their snowmobiles and VCRs. I didn't find seal-burgers on the menu in any of the French restaurants around Cap-aux-Meules harbor. I think they cling to the seal hunt out of stubbornness, the kind of refusal to surrender their prerogatives to outside pressures that sustained segregation in the South for 100 years.

In the final reckoning, you learn respect for life and empathy for other creatures, or you don't. If rich women can learn to wear cloth coats, the Madelinots can learn to coexist with harp seals. If they'd been quicker to learn about their own women, they might have more to choose from.

I wouldn't say that in the Chateau Madelinot. Among my own kind in the village I might hesitate to take sides; out on the ice with the whitecoats I don't hesitate at all. Poor people destroy the natural world out of ignorance and necessity, rich people destroy it out of greed. Between them, like Jack Sprat and his wife, they lick the planet clean. When you consider the whitecoats and the piles of sea otters suffocated in the Valdez oil slick, you flirt with despair. We developed big brains and efficient forepaws, we climbed to the top of the food chain and we let it go to our heads. Is there any possibility of forgiveness for creatures who slaughter infants and eliminate whole species for aphrodisiacs, fur jackets and eye shadow?

Looking at this beautiful, filthy little creature with its head on my knee, wearing an expression at least as trusting as any of the four-legged and two-legged creatures who've rested their heads there, I know that a little old lady in tennis shoes is exactly what I am. The few blameless animals who've survived our excesses deserve a second chance—a second, unmarked planet where only the little old ladies can visit.

There's an organic connection between poetry and the natural environ-
ment. If you care nothing for either, you probably score very poorly on
those personality tests that measure imagination.

Troubled Waters

Twenty-five years ago I would have started this with a couple of
lines from "Sea Fever," though the sea fever that concerns me may
be closer cousin to yellow fever than to the variety which inspired
the poet laureate. Poem and poet alike are in drydock now in the
limbo labeled "sentimental," a limbo where most of the dead giants
of other centuries are dissected and dishonored by the carping
dwarfs of our own.

A pair of sophisticated critics set my teeth on edge, not long
ago, using this "sentimental" as a careless scythe that left almost
nothing standing. There are two kinds of sentimental writing—
the naive kind where the writer doesn't realize he's waxing mawkish, and the kind where the writer has the courage to risk even
mawkishness to say something he feels very deeply. I prefer the
second kind of writer to the ones who avoid sentiment as if it
were something nasty they wouldn't want to step in with their
elegant shoes.

I'm shamelessly sentimental about the sea (it would be less sentimental to say "ocean"). It's true but probably irrelevant that my
mother is descended on her father's side from sea captains—merchant seamen and whaling skippers before them. My first recorded
march to the sea was at Willoughby Spit near Norfolk, when I was
months shy of two years old. According to family legend I marched
fearlessly into the surf like a born mariner (or moron) and was
knocked flat for my innocence, and rescued by my mother from
Poseidon's wrath. In my dreams a great wave still breaks over me
from time to time, often washing me away automobile and all and
compelling me to hold my breath in my sleep. But I survive in the
dream, as I survived in the Virginia surf long ago.

Whatever I learned there, upside down and breathing salt water,
it didn't deter me. I didn't follow my father into the Navy, but it's
my guess that I've spent a lot more time with the ocean—on it, in
it and around it—than the lieutenant commander ever could have.

There were a couple of other times, in Florida and in Brittany, when the waves got the best of me and my mother wasn't there to pull me out. Even a night ferry crossing of the Adriatic, in a tempest that set the chained cars below decks clanking and groaning like hell on holiday, didn't make me quite sick enough to retreat to the safety of my hills.

I haven't seen as much of the ocean in recent years. One of the few disappointments of North Carolina is that a lot of it is more than an hour's drive from the beach. But the ocean, unlike a woman, a favorite city or even a landscape, is a thing you feel justified in taking for granted. After a billion or so years at the same address, "The wind and the water still abide," as Jim Wann sings in *King Mackerel* (the song is called "Timeless").

D. G. Rossetti wrote over 100 years ago:

> *Consider the sea's listless chime*
> *Time's self it is, made audible—*
> *The murmur of the earth's own shell.*
> *Secret continuance sublime*
> *Is the sea's end: our sight may pass*
> *No furlong further. Since time was,*
> *This sound has told the lapse of time.*

Not so sentimental. A Victorian could believe in a sea that was immune to time, timeless because it was time itself—the grandfather clock of creation.

A confidence poetic but alas, premature. No one paid a lot of attention when Jacques Cousteau reported traces of sewage and industrial pollution in the sea ice of remotest Antarctica. What that implied about our offshore waters became clear during the hot summer of 1987. I clipped the news service stories until they became repetitive: mysterious fish kills, strange sores on fish and crabs, unprecedented tides of algae, East Coast beaches littered with dead dolphins; "Scientists say coasts failing as habitats," "Scientists say fish diseases have reached epidemic levels," "'Dead Zone' located off Louisiana coast."

"The river has died to the point where there just ain't anything up here worth fishing for," mourned a veteran Carolina fisherman who works the Pamlico River estuary. "The water won't hold no oxygen. Mother Nature has took as much as she can."

I went up north, to Maine and Massachusetts, and found the same headlines—red tides, polluted oyster beds, condemned fishing grounds, dead zones. The crisis was general on the Atlantic and Gulf Coasts, from Corpus Christi to Bar Harbor. It's probably global. Individual horrors like the dolphin kill were still under investigation, but there was no mystery about underlying causes. An excess of nitrogen and phosphate from sewage and fertilizers is overloading the water with nutrients, reducing its oxygen content until no significant marine life can survive. The water is filthy. Suffocating. Industrial pollution is a big factor, but the major factor is simpler: the ecosystem is overburdened with human beings.

The sea is dying. The grandfather clock is losing time. Even 30 years ago most scientists believed that the oceans were too immense to become our open sewer. No one comprehended the consequences of our reckless multiplication or the careless way we expand our habitat. There are a million species of animals on this planet but only one that presents any threat to the ocean itself.

You can read that elsewhere, and for figures, studies and anecdotes you'll look to Jacques Cousteau or the *Scientific American*. Facts don't seem to create the urgency that's required. It's worth making an appeal to sentiment—to the landlocked imagination. You can't let the suffering sea become an abstraction like foreign wars and starving Africans, a tragedy unfolding far away. Go and see it, touch it, smell it. I spent a weekend at Duck on the Outer Banks. Every time I visit, it seems that a thousand houses have been built since I visited last. I had to stop in the middle of the Audubon Preserve and ignore a No Trespassing sign to walk on a beach that didn't have rooftops poking above the dunes.

But the Atlantic still looks like herself. You can run for miles at the edge of the surf, cut your bare feet to ribbons on the shells, feel as free as you can feel anywhere on earth. A fishing trawler runs aground at night, when a gale wind shifts suddenly on her, and in the morning the seagulls are lined up almost single file from Corolla to Nag's Head, waiting for the catch that will eventually be theirs to divide. You can see the Milky Way the way you remember it, relatively undimmed by light pollution (but only relatively now; the ancients saw the stars twice as clearly as we ever see them, and our grandchildren will see them as a faint muddle in the gray haze overhead). Everything you ever felt about the sea you feel again within 24 hours, whatever the weather.

Sentimental. But universal, I like to think. I hear that there are strange mutants in the cities now who honestly prefer malls, apartments and traffic rhythms to Rossetti's "voices of twin solitudes. . . the one voice of wave and tree." But I don't think of them as people of any consequence, and I try not to think of them at all. Anyone worth saving will respond to the alarm raised by John Merriner, a marine biologist in Beaufort:

"Nature is trying to tell us something. If you can't go in the water, if you can't eat the fish, why go to the coast at all?"

Merriner was suggesting the economic impact, but the impact on me was more profound. I once saw a huge lake, shallow Lake Erie, reduced to a slimy gelatin that deposited unmentionable things on your legs when you walked in the surf. No one would swim there, at one time. When you saw a perfect sunset on Lake Erie, you shuddered to think that those colors were spread out over a vat of corrosive sewage that would singe the fur off a kitten.

It's natural that we're drawn to the water, most unnatural when it repels us. Sea fever is mystical and Freudian. It operates at the deepest level of the collective unconscious. That life came from the sea is something you know in your blood even if you can't accept it with your intellect. To destroy the oceans is to commit a matricide. When we can't go back, when we can't go home, we've cut the umbilical cord and left ourselves orphaned and defenseless. Our common womb will soon be a sewer.

From the primal terror that I feel myself at the very idea of a poisoned, lifeless ocean, I imagine that the impact on the human race would be terminal psychosis. The eventual economic and biological collapse would be nothing but a *coup de grâce*.

The critical moment here is when I imagine I'm seeing a preview of the end of the world—experts swapping theories while continents burn and oceans boil.

Deathwatch for Mother

Morelia, Michoacan, Mexico — It's hard to find the right tone for this report from a conference of scientists and intellectuals who set out to determine whether, and how, the planet itself can be saved from certain destruction. The situation is so desperate and the motivation so sincere that it may deserve a dead serious bulletin-from-the-battlefront treatment, if any assignment ever did. At the same time the mission is so presumptuous, so quixotic that it invites a certain levity at the expense of the 40-odd individuals who were expected—contracted, as far as I could tell—to issue a joint prescription for the survival of life as we know it.

For me, an incurable skeptic, a third choice would be a black-as-midnight satire, a page from Celine: Three dozen poets, cloistered intellectuals and grant-pampered scientists hole up in a luxury hotel in Mexico, surrounded by one of the most polluted and impoverished bioregions in the hemisphere, and presume to raise the earth with their eloquence, even as Jesus raised Lazarus.

The symposium, billed as "Encounter in Morelia: Approaching the End of the Millennium," was organized by the Grupo de los Cien (Group of 100), a committee of Mexican artists and scholars formed to defend their nation's tortured environment. The project was funded by the Rockefeller Foundation and blessed with the full and often visible cooperation of the Mexican government.

The Group of 100, which credits itself with numerous environmental successes, was not well known to most of the participants. The secrecy that surrounded the Encounter in Morelia was unusual, to say the least. No foreign media were invited or even notified until a week before the symposium convened. But the list of participants, which I acquired from a friend, was formidable: Margaret Atwood, Günter Grass, Carlos Fuentes, Gabriel Garcia Marquez, Seamus Heaney, Elie Wiesel, Nadine Gordimer, Octavio Paz, Umberto Eco, Peter Mathiessen and Mario Vargas Llosa among the writers, and at the head of the list of scientists and environmentalists the legendary Jacques-Yves Cousteau.

Day One: At the Camino Real, a huge hotel in Mexico City, the participants seek each other out with the hesitant curiosity of a freshman class on its first day in the dorms. Many of them find old friends from environmental congresses and PEN conventions. It is noted that many of the biggest names are now missing from the list, even Garcia Marquez, who lives in Mexico City. But celebrity has nothing to do with saving the earth; this is still an impressive gathering of intellect and talent.

The air in Mexico City is heavy and gaseous, but breathable. Attractive young women in symbolically green jackets offer bus tours, translations, tourist warnings. I am the only English-language journalist for miles around, and apparently the only member of the press who gets to ride on the bus to Morelia.

The first two hours out of Mexico City offer us a landscape from an impossible future, a land beaten and poisoned and crowded with discouragement. Few of the dwellings are as tall as our bus, or even as tall as the corn. Construction is an ongoing, organic cycle in the Valley of Mexico: A house becomes a ruin, then a pile of rubble, then a building site, then a house and a ruin again, all with the same materials. It takes a keen eye to distinguish one stage from another. People live in piles of bricks. "No mas miseria!" is scrawled across the front of one five-foot-high hovel, where a dark old Indian woman sits in the doorway combing a little girl's hair.

It's a sobering, focusing journey, the best possible preparation for the environmental conscience. But urban blight gives way to mountain scenery, and Morelia is a postcard colonial city founded in 1542—lofty cathedral, ancient aqueduct, center city with cobbled streets. The hotel, the elegant Villa Montana, is styled like the summer home of a Tuscan nobleman. It sits on a hill high above and far away from the life of the city, with the kind of view that costs millions in Los Angeles.

Some of our radicals are troubled by this hotel. But the first antagonism between organizers and participants begins when the visitors see the convention center where the symposium will be conducted. It has been transformed into a giant television studio, complete with a set that no one can believe: a bogus grotto with a bogus Aztec temple in a bogus jungle, a kind of pre–Columbian shrine as a centerpiece, an anomalous fountain and windows opening onto painted scenes of butterflies, flamingos, flying fish. All in the worst taste possible and constructed from some foam synthetic that the environment will never digest.

"Kitsch is not dead in Mexico," says a poet from Argentina.

Instead of the presentations and "informal discussion" that were promised in the press releases, the participants have signed on for a 25-hour TV show.

Day Two: After much muttering, the conference sessions begin. Kirkpatrick Sale, author of *The Conquest of Paradise* and *Human Scale*, speaks for at least a substantial minority when he opens by protesting the cameras and the duplicity.

"TV is the medium of the industrial society that has made a mess of nature," he declares. "It is not the medium of artists or intellectuals. We will proceed, but reluctantly."

Sale's protest introduces a theme that will continue to develop—communication and its impediments. The Encounter at Morelia is handicapped by every conceivable barrier to effective communication. Half the participants are fluent in neither Spanish nor English, the only languages available on the UN-style translator headphones provided. The world's saviors are fighting against incompatible sets of idioms, too: philosophy and the mass media, literature and science, poetry and technology.

"Poetry and ecology make life possible," explains Argentine poet Roberto Juarroz. "Poetry may not be the solution to ecology's problems, but it cleanses human speech and human vision." But at one point in Juarroz' Spanish presentation I find myself listening, inexplicably, to Japanese on my headset. Microphones fail, headsets malfunction, TV feedback renders even the English unintelligible. Equipment failures cause long delays. Even the local papers will begin to make references to the Tower of Babel. It seems at times that the Lord is not planning on an 11th-hour rescue of the earth by these same feisty apes who have defiled it.

"The End of the Millennium or the End of the World?" is the title of the first session. No one shrinks from predicting the Apocalypse. Thomas Lovejoy, a biologist, calls the '90s "the moment of truth" when the critical environmental decisions will be made or be rendered irrelevant. "Extinction," says botanist Peter Raven, when I ask him what he has come to Morelia to stress. "Extinction, particular and general."

"If not the end of the world, the end of a world we want to live in," says Peter Mathiessen. "The end of life and the beginning of survival."

Facts, statistics, terrifying predictions fall like a hard rain that washes away any optimism we might secretly have harbored. Pessimism itself becomes the subject of debate.

"I don't see any political will that will act, that will mobilize in time to save us," admits Petra Kelly, a founder of Germany's Green Party.

"Privately I'm deeply pessimistic," says Sale. Optimists and pragmatists object. But they miss the point about pessimists. It's no good hating them unless you hate them enough to go out and prove they're wrong. In a debate it's optimists that I can't stomach. Look at the world that the Babbitts with their civic pride and silver linings have left us to live in.

For those who've yet to comprehend the implications of environmental politics, the defining moment of the first day is an exchange between Sale and Monika Van Paemel, a Belgian novelist.

"How can we talk about saving the trees when we can't even save all the children?" says Van Paemel.

"If we don't try to save the trees before we can save all the children, we'll never save either," Sale replies with some heat.

This, of course, is the very place where environmentalists and traditional humanist liberals part company. Our survival, according to the ecologists that humanists call radical, depends on understanding that a child, ecologically, is never more important than a tree.

Day Three: Jokes about our police escorts and the "Bower of Babel" give way to a different mood. The event of the morning session is a speech by the Russian physicist Vladimir Chernousenko, who directed the cleanup of Chernobyl. Chernousenko, who was exposed to 650 roentgens of radiation (500 is the maximum you might survive), is suffering from radiation sickness and has been given three to five years to live. His complexion is yellow, his blond hair is as lifeless as a cheap toupee and he gives himself injections. His account of the world's worst nuclear disaster is twice as frightening as anything that has been published or rumored. Chernousenko says that 300,000 Russians are being treated for radiation sickness and that 35 million people may eventually be affected by the blast in 1986. He predicts that there will be at least four more Chernobyls before the end of the decade. He has dedicated the rest of his life to replacing nuclear reactors with safer sources of energy.

Yesterday they served us Apocalypse Future, today it's Apocalypse Now. The participants are unified, in a way, by the sorrow and dismay that Chernousenko has evoked. But the curse of Babel is upon them still. In the evening I attend the first session of the committee that will draft the Declaration of Morelia, a summary of their deliberations and recommendations that will be delivered on Friday to the president of the Republic, Carlos Salinas de Gortari. The declaration is very important to Homero Aridjis, the Mexican novelist and poet who seems to be in charge of this project.

Clearly Aridjis has promised the president that there will be a declaration. But he has naively underestimated the stubborn independence of some of these Northern intellectuals, no matter how much you give them to eat and drink. He has underestimated, also, the language barriers and the ideological distances between some of his guests. The drafting session breaks down completely, into chaos and comedy. Midnight, 1:00 a.m., 2:00 a.m. and nothing is agreed upon. Drinking at dinner has had an effect. Angry people stalk out and late drinkers are recruited to replace them. And I think to myself, I'm getting a sneak preview of the end of the world.

Day Four: Vladimir Chernousenko collapses on the bus. At lunch there's an announcement that he's in intensive care at the Morelia hospital, undergoing tests on his heart. There are 30 or more volunteers to sit up with Chernousenko, who speaks no Spanish or English. Rumors fly. At the Teatro Morelia, where the show takes place, we find a crowd of demonstrators. They're Indians involved in a land dispute with local developers. If these foreigners can save the world, maybe they can do something for the poor people of Michoacan. The demonstrators produce an effigy of a peasant nailed to a cross.

Among the delegates there are activists, like Argentina's irrepressible Miguel Grinberg, who are in their element mixing with the *campesino* demonstrators. Others are visibly confused, as if mothers and babies and peasants with leaflets were too much reality after days of metaphors and eco-romanticism.

At this point, various battle lines have been drawn. No one doubts the figures, the warnings the scientists have issued. Clean air and water are as scarce as gold or diamonds. The rapid and irreversible extinction of thousands of species, plant and animal, is destroying the biodiversity on which all life rests. The oceans are poisoned, the forests and the topsoil (24 billion tons lost annually) are vanishing without hope of replacement. Greenhouse gases are rising, ozone depletion in the atmosphere is accompanied by destructive ozone levels on the ground, even far from cities. Worst of all, the world's human population has doubled in 40 years (2 1/2 to 5 billion) and will soon double again, while food production is falling.

Against such a background of impending catastrophe the end of the Cold War and the liberation of Eastern Europe are minor distractions, as Thomas Lovejoy and Petra Kelly have reminded us. But crisis has not forced a consensus on this group in Morelia, 40 of the best-informed individuals in the world. Political habits die hard. Veterans of the traditional left, inspired here in Mexico by Diego Rivera's wonderful murals depicting the sufferings of the proletariat (our Russian delegates will never again see so many portraits of Lenin), are slow to yield to posthumanist politics that categorically reject Protagoras' "Man is the measure of all things."

Besides the compromises forced on delegates from Catholic countries, there's a politically correct position, of which I had not been fully aware, that further complicates the politics of population control. It holds that industrial nations have no right to impose birth control on the Third World while their own gross consumption is equally lethal to the environment. The word "genocide" comes up. It seems obvious that urgent pressure should be applied to both problems, with no tolerance for the "You go first" position that has plagued arms control. But it isn't obvious to everyone.

Finally, as the fourth day in Morelia reveals, there is a rift between theorists and people who are waiting to hear answers and solutions. Sessions titled "The Ecological Imagination" and "The Conquest of Paradise" have produced a parade of fine metaphors and distributed the blame for the tragedy of the human race and its ruined home—narcissism, anal fixation and the death wish (psychiatrist Fernando Cesarman), alpha males (eco-feminism), the suppression of aboriginal peoples and their spiritual bond with the earth, science and technology, the violent nature-hating Western civilization itself.

"I think intellectuals and scientists have a habit of generalization and self-accusation," says Miroslav Holub, a Czech poet. "This is just a new romanticism. Maybe it's corporations, not civilization, that should take the blame. Be specific."

Day Five: The last sessions of the symposium are conducted with Holub's objections on the table. Peter Mathiessen warns against "sentimentalization" and introduces Lester Brown of the World Watch Institute, whose bimonthly magazine may be the best single source for information about the environment. Brown, a recent recipient of one of the MacArthur Foundation's "genius" awards, is prepared to be specific. He outlines his model for "an environmentally stable global economy," he explains the technology for alternate sources of clean energy—sun and wind—to replace fossil fuels and nuclear reactors. He points to countries like Japan and Thailand that have successfully stabilized their populations. He even outlines funding, from "environmental taxes on environmental sins."

"We can turn the environment around with existing technology," Brown insists. "It is doable. But there isn't much time. And it all depends on a revolution in reproductive behavior."

Mathiessen concludes the conference with a call to the delegates "to put aside the things that divide us, and concentrate on the things that unite us." The cameras nod off and the lights go out, forever we hope, on the styrofoam Bower of Babel. But unity is as uncertain as the final draft of the Declaration of Morelia. The committee, which has suffered a 90 percent turnover in its membership, is still meeting and quarreling long into the night. The sticking points are rumored to be population, nuclear energy (the Mexican government is committed to a nuclear plant at Laguna Verde) and whether the statement should be long and specific or short and poetic.

Day Six: We return in the bus to Mexico City, where the dreaded inversion has now occurred. The sky is full of clouds that are not clouds or even half-clouds, but some horrible chemical cousins to clouds. It's a sky of apocalypse. The committee is still drafting on the bus, at the Camino Real, and, at the 11th hour, at Homero Aridjis' home in Mexico City.

At the presidential palace we face each other around a rectangle of four long tables. The president's chair is empty. Then applause erupts, and I think, they applaud the president every time he enters the room? But the applause, which becomes a standing ovation, is for Vladimir Chernousenko. Pale, stooped and trembling but grinning from ear to ear, he makes his entrance on the arm of a beautiful Mexican actress to whom, in his few days outside the hospital, he has become attached. Chernousenko is very sick but his heart, he says, has passed muster.

Every cause benefits from an authentic hero. The entrance of President Salinas is anticlimactic. He is a short, bald, shrewd-looking man with a mustache and small black penetrating eyes—hunter's eyes. His unsuccessful opponents call him "The Atomic Ant." I don't know why presidents always make me feel like Hunter Thompson. I guess I have a problem with authority. I'm directly opposite Salinas and I catch him staring at me. I stare back until he quits, a weird victory.

The presidential reception goes well. The Declaration of Morelia is finally produced—even the president has to wait for it—and it is stronger and more specific than many of us thought it would be, although the language on population is a little lame. Chernousenko makes a passionate speech against nuclear plants, warning that "we could bring the world to extinction by the beginning of the next millennium." Mathiessen rises, as he promised us he would, to make a last plea for a sane population policy—"or the human animal will devour the earth."

Promises are made, and congratulations are passed around. We file out, I shake the president's hand in the reception line ("An honor, sir") and tell myself, maybe this is a good man who will do something, who knows. Then I step into the cool night air of Mexico City, the largest and most polluted city on earth. I take a deep breath of the night air and it isn't air, it's just a little more useful to me, trying to breathe, than it would be to a fish. Two days later, at home in Chapel Hill, I can still smell and taste it.

There is no credo more insidious or suicidal than Protagoras' "Man is the measure of all things."

The River of No Return

As you read this, I'm in a canoe somewhere in the Okefenokee Swamp in south Georgia. If I don't roll off a sleeping platform and make a great feast for the blackwater alligators, in six weeks I'll be back on the water in the Sawtooth Mountains of central Idaho, rafting down the Salmon River Canyon—the River of No Return.

Blackwater, whitewater, I'm usually game. Readers have noticed, over the years, that I come up with a suspicious number of datelines from places that are hard to get to, underpopulated, more notable for creatures than for creature comforts. I've heard suggestions that I'm caught in some kind of Grizzly Adams fantasy and suffering a protracted adolescence. But I'm not sensitive about it.

I know what I'm doing. I'm not an indoors person; I never spent an eight-hour day in an office that I didn't regret and resent. I take these trips because I know that the best of what's outdoors—the real and relevant world, as I see it—is vanishing even faster than my physical ability to experience it firsthand.

I don't want to miss anything. I read Aldo Leopold's account of his 1922 canoe trip through the Colorado Delta—a unique, spectacular wilderness that no longer exists—and I feel physical pain, personal loss.

"Relegating grizzlies to Alaska is about like relegating happiness to heaven," Leopold wrote. "One may never get there."

I don't deny that I've been influenced by a more intrepid traveler. When I finally met Peter Mathiessen in Mexico last summer, I experienced, almost for the first time in my life, a trace of that thing they call envy. Not for anything Mathiessen has or is, though many have envied his prose, but for where he's been. For the places he has seen that I will never see. I've read his books, but books are just a taste, a tease almost. Walking with Mathiessen along the wharf at Lake Patzcuaro, talking about some crazy writer we both knew, I shamed my Luddite soul by wishing that humans were more like computers, capable of looting and storing each other's memories.

Mathiessen has traveled to some of the most inaccessible places on earth—the high Himalayas, the Amazon rain forest, the game savannas of Africa, Lake Baikal in Central Asia, every wild corner of the United States—and taken a kind of inventory, with a naturalist's eye and poet's sensibility.

In order to bear witness, he has ignored Aldo Leopold's injunction:

"It is the part of wisdom never to revisit a wilderness," Leopold wrote in A Sand County Almanac, "for the more golden the lily, the more certain that someone has gilded it. To return not only spoils a trip, but tarnishes a memory. It is only in the mind that shining adventure remains forever bright."

Leopold never revisited the Colorado Delta. Mathiessen has returned many times to the scenes of earlier adventures, invariably to record and mourn the vanishing game herds, the clearcut forests, the rivers dammed and polluted, the reckless waste of resources, the earth sown with poisons. His latest book, African Silences, chronicles the decline of the forest elephant in the Congo Basin and the disappearance of almost all wild animals in overpopulated West Africa. His most pessimistic book, Indian Country, sounded an alarm—largely ignored—over the insane destruction and contamination of American wilderness (much of it owned, claimed or held sacred by Indians) by timber and energy corporations, with the full cooperation of the federal government.

Like Mathiessen, I ignore Leopold and go back sometimes, to the places I've loved the most. In the Pacific Northwest, even on Washington's awesome Olympic Peninsula, forests and everything that was in them seem to vanish overnight, replaced by timber-company signs that announce a mature forest in 2102. In the Chisos Mountains of West Texas' Big Bend Country, the view south into Mexico from Casa Grande had shrunk 60 miles since I was there last, according to a ranger. He blamed air pollution from California. Last spring we saw no antelope and no coyotes along the Rio Grande.

Even worse than the decline you can see for yourself is the bad news from the wire services, lethal little items like postcards from the nursing home where your friend is failing fast. My volunteer clipping service, Mrs. Louise Weiss of Friendship, Maine, never misses an environmental alarm or defeat. Is it possible that they're planning to build *six* hazardous waste dumps along the Rio Grande, four upstream and two downstream from Big Bend National Park?

The news from the Northwest isn't good either. In a ruling billed as "a victory for the timber industry," the U.S. Supreme Court just gave the green light for logging in 16 new areas of old-growth forest that were protected as the habitat of the spotted owl. At the West-inghouse Corporation's nuclear weapons plant in Hanford, Wash., scene of the most widespread radioactive contamination this side of Chernobyl, the federal government's cleanup program is failing miserably, according to local watchdogs.

Sometimes the alarm comes even before you visit the place. The current issue of *National Geographic* includes a feature that exam-ines the effects of a phosphate-mining operation, a paper compa-ny's sludge dump and developers' defective septic fields on the deli-cate ecology of the Okefenokee. In Idaho last week, there was a red alert over radioactive contamination from a nuclear fuel reprocess-ing plant at the National Engineering Laboratory.

It breaks my heart. It breaks my heart because I see clearly that in 50 years people will read Mathiessen as Mathiessen read Leopold—and as Leopold read John Muir and Muir read John James Audubon—as a witness to lost wilderness so pristine and vast that it sounds like science fiction. Only there will be no more names in the succession.

My Earth Day message is the same as last year and the year before—the situation is critical and the hour is late. If it sounds more desperate, that's because the message has been encountering so much resistance. At the conference in Mexico where I met Peter Mathiessen, scientists and ecologists assured us that the earth can be saved, with existing technology and expertise. It can be saved without economic catastrophe and in the little time remaining, they agreed. And then they agreed that they could see no political will to make the correct choices that have to be made.

The primary reason that the earth is dying is that there are far too many people living on it. There were 200 million human beings in the year 0 A.D. and there will be 6.3 billion in the year 2000. This is a cycle of planetary extinction—familiar throughout the universe, for all we know—that may play itself out no matter what we do here in the United States. But as the most powerful country in the world, as the leading consumer of the earth's resources and especially its energy, as the automobile-enslaved polluter that produces 20 percent of all the greenhouse gases that are raising the earth's temperatures, the United States is naturally expected to provide leadership in this environmental endgame that has become a race for survival.

Our government's response has never been more bitterly disappointing. The Reagan administration's decision to withhold funding from Third World family-planning programs may have been the most craven, short-sighted piece of bad policy since the Munich Pact, but the Bush people are falling over themselves to top it. Their refusal to sign a treaty reducing carbon-monoxide emissions ("U.S. lone dissenter, stance may detail global warming treaty") is a humiliating scandal. Their new definition of "wetland" that would open 30 million acres of wetlands to developers was denounced as "The Mother of all environmental hooliganism" by the North Carolina Wildlife Federation, hardly a radical fringe group.

The ex officio White House Council on Competitiveness, chaired by Dan Quayle, apparently exists to help businessmen evade environmental restrictions, even those still enforced by emasculated government agencies. Worst of all, the White House appears to be using the recession and the unemployment crisis as a club to win environmental concessions for big business. Since January, the administration has weakened the Clean Air Act to please the auto industry, backed down on hazardous waste regulations and sided with industry in disputes over strip-mining laws and clear-cutting in national forests.

It's an unqualified sellout, at the worst possible moment. And at the same time Washington's environmental establishment, plagued by fund-raising problems and top-heavy organizations (Jay Hair, president of the National Wildlife Federation, is alleged to earn $250,000 a year) has been rendered so ineffective that it stood mute last week while the Senate voted to release a million acres of Montana's virgin pine forests to the timber industry's chainsaws.

If Mother Nature has any friends at all in Washington, they're not the kind she needs. In an angry article in the *New York Times*, political scientist Stephen Meyer of MIT ridiculed the new right-wing rhetoric of "environment-bashing," which he calls "a political gimmick of special interests."

"The 'jobs issue' is being used cynically and deceptively by special interests to manipulate public opinion," Meyer argued. "They insist that the development of public lands will create jobs. But logging, mining and drilling rates are set to make quick profits, not establish a sustainable local industry. New jobs at one site merely cancel lost jobs at the last one. Employment in these localities just goes from boom to bust in a few years."

Bizarre demagogues like radio's Rush Limbaugh stir up right-wing rabble with tirades that compare environmentalists to terrorists and communists. But mainstream comment is sometimes just as astonishing. This Krauthammer individual, whom I do not admire, dishonored *Time's* Essay section with a Neanderthal manifesto he called "Saving nature, but only for man." His reasoning, some of the worst I ever encountered in print, was drawn from an ancient, poisoned well: Protagoras' primitive maxim that "Man is the measure of all things."

If we have learned just one useful thing in the last 25 centuries, it's that old Protagoras was dead wrong. Only human beings—except for Krauthammer—have evolved enough to grasp the irony: In the eyes of a slug, if slugs have eyes, slugs are the measure of all things.

Anthropocentric thinking dies hard; biocentric thinking, survival thinking, is being born too slowly. But it's too easy to blame human arrogance and give up the fight with a fatalistic shrug. Let's be honest. In this country it's our corporations that are killing us.

Corporations—good ones, bad ones, indifferent ones—control the government, the media, the universities, the national mythology and the terms of discourse. They rarely take the long view that sane environmental policy requires, and their aggregate will is a dangerous one. The unspeakable proliferation of hazardous and radioactive waste was the result of unnecessary technologies to develop unnecessary weapons to kill unnecessary enemies. In the past year, 8.4 billion precious tax dollars were committed to the SDI "Star Wars" boondoggle, a defense-industry goldmine that aims to protect the U.S. from imaginary enemies with Klingon-level technology.

It has been proven repeatedly that people will do anything, under certain circumstances, to make money, save money or protect an investment. Whenever I doubt it, I take out my clipping on the company that knowingly distributed defective artificial heart valves. Or I contemplate the tobacco industry.

There is very little we can do to defend ourselves or our

environment from this belligerent and often malignant will, a will misguided by the belief that unrestrained acquisitiveness is the primary law of nature. Even Thomas Berry, whose language is more theological than confrontational, set the conflict clearly in *The Dream of the Earth*:

"These are the two radical positions—the industrial and the eco-logical—that confront each other, with survival at stake: survival of the human at an acceptable level of fulfillment on a planet capable of providing the psychic as well as the physical nourishment that is needed."

"But we are so few," a Bolivian ecologist named Margarita Marino de Botero said one night, on the mountain in Mexico, when some of her friends in the movement seemed momentarily intoxicated by the power of their own ideas.

We are few. In this country it would be a start, but only a start, if we could turn out this government that functions as an active enemy of the earth and replace it with one more independent of the military-industrial conspiracy. But that won't bring back trees, resurrect animals, evaporate poisons that are gathering under the earth. Every minute of inaction is a defeat. Some good people are so frustrated that they believe the only choice, at this point, is between civil disobedience and despair.

Since Earth Day last year I've read *Confessions of an Eco-Warrior* by Earth First! founder Dave Foreman, the notorious tree-spiking "ecoteur." I confess that I find no sin in this man or his creed, which is that the earth is the one thing worth dying to defend. Foreman is a warrior, a scholar and a philosopher, worth a thousand silk-stocking eco-executives or Secretaries of the Interior.

Young people face a choice between Foreman's philosophy and its opposite, epitomized in the sad, symbolically powerful story of Wallace Stegner's father. As his son tells it, the elder Stegner was a quintessential American, a rambling, gambling man who believed that the world was his oyster, if he could just pry open the shell. In a dozen crazy speculations in oil, timber, minerals, wheat and real estate, he despoiled a dozen beautiful places and never made a nickel, finally dying "broke and friendless in a fleabag hotel, having done more human and environmental damage than he could have repaired in a second lifetime."

Everything depends on what the young people choose.

A Green conscience doesn't grow from intellectual, theoretical convictions. It's personal, and its's physical.

Fire in the Lake

I wasn't boasting, exactly. It was no great feat of strength or daring. The lake is less than a mile wide, the water was lukewarm, the surface was as flat as a windowpane. The starlight was exceptional. I could see the far shore all the way across, and I swam at an old man's pace: breaststroke, backstroke, sidestroke, anything but the powerful crawl the artists imagine in their engravings of Leander challenging the Hellespont.

But at breakfast I needed to tell someone about it, to make it official. I'd swum across the lake and back, starting after 1:00 a.m. I'm not sure what reaction I expected. A lifted eyebrow, maybe, implying that I'd had too much to drink. Some of the patronizing humor with which our women dismiss most of our childish physical excesses. Maybe just a trace of respect, some recognition that there was life left in my aging imagination, at least.

I wasn't prepared for the alarm that bordered on hostility. The consensus was that I must have been very angry at someone, maybe my wife, and taking an irresponsible risk out of spite. Death wish hypotheses were offered. Disapproval was unanimous.

I was hurt, but there was no point in arguing about it. We do these things alone and maybe it's better to keep them to ourselves. When I went into the water I intended to paddle around the boathouse, cool off and tire myself a little so I could sleep. Once I was out there on the lake, sleeping became irrelevant. In a cloudless, moonless sky hundreds of miles from the nearest city, the stars were so bright that the lake returned a mirror reflection of the universe. From something below the surface—from fish, microorganisms, I have no idea—there were more reflections still. The light was all around me. It was like swimming through the stars.

I was an incidental ingredient in an astonishing celestial soup. It was a more subtle and more hypnotic effect than any moonlight I can remember. I have nothing in common with someone who could shake his head in admiration, towel off and go to bed. I kept my glasses on so I wouldn't miss anything, and set out for the far shore, a narrow band of black sandwiched between fields of stars. A huge goggled creature swimming silently. I didn't think there was anything lurking in the depths that was big enough to mistake me for a lure.

Epiphany is a gaudy word. But these journeys that are more than physical journeys don't present themselves often, and only poets find them in parking lots and apartment kitchens. Most of us need a master hand to set the stage. Until I was 30 I spent nearly every summer of my life at one or the other of these northern lakes. Their rocky beaches and wooded islands represent summer to me still; I love the South, but tropical summers with a little life sustained by air conditioning are worse than no summers at all. So here in Maine on one lucky night in August, while the Southerners and the Manhattan Islanders were sleeping soundly, the stage manager gave me summer back exactly the way I thought I remembered it, right down to the weird night chorus of the loons.

It's not surprising that I paddled around half the night with a spooky grin on my face. But I'm sure I tackled that lake with twice the passion because I spent the whole summer reading about the poisoned lakes and filthy beaches, the dead forests and the clouds of smoke and ozone that hide the stars. You have to do a lot of traveling now to get to a solitary place where the air and the water are relatively pristine. It takes a lot of money just to get there, and a lot more to buy or even rent the right to stay there. Already, poor people in the cities have no clean place to go. On the crowded Atlantic beaches where their parents found a refuge from the stifling ghettoes, their children build sand castles with hypodermics for flagpoles.

There are thousands of lakes between Maine and Minnesota, and across southern Canada. When you travel that country—by air, especially—you can't imagine that we'll ever run out of lakes. But hundreds have already been destroyed by reckless development, urban pollution and acid rain. The body count increases every year. Unlike most members of my family for a couple of generations, I've never owned a summer place in the lake country or even a lake boat to pull behind my car. I have no stake. But I've just been to the far shore, and you come back from the far shore with a religious conviction that there's no other issue worth addressing, no battle worth anyone's time and effort until this battle to protect what Jesse Helms calls "the envarmint" has been fought to the last man. The other stuff is just distraction. When there are no more starlit lakes clean enough to tempt a swimming fool like me, it really doesn't matter who holds the wealth and the power, who's neglected or abused, whose faith or ideology prevails. It'll be nothing but a sordid endgame, with doomed idiots quarreling on a sinking ship.

There's no further point in calling on the government to intervene, or even turning out the vote for Democrats and candidates with "strong" environmental records. Governments are managed by the flow of money. Lobbyists who defend the nuclear power industry and the acid-rain offenders will always spend far more money than any public interest group can raise or commit. If the battle is supposed to be fought on the floor of Congress, the battle has been lost.

It's going to come down to basic cultural perceptions, and it's going to come down to us and them. I know we're surrounded by spiritual mutants who see no difference between a lake and its picture on a postcard. If you doubted that there are prominent businessmen who will do absolutely anything to make a profit, read about the indicted management of a company that deliberately sold defective pacemakers to heart patients. They'll literally cut your heart out. I even believe that people who create ugliness— junk architecture, mutilated landscapes—actively hate beauty and attack it. People who create filth are offended by its absence.

But I don't think these groups form a majority, not yet. Beautiful places defend themselves, as I see it, by producing a better class of people. All my cousins spent their summers on those lakes, and my family has yet to produce a stripminer, a clear-cutter, a junk-mail architect or developer, a polluter or anyone who works for one.

I think there's a connection. And I think it's time for a roll call. If it turns out that we outnumber them, we should have recourse to the majority's most powerful weapon. Not the vote, which in this perverted democracy has been neutralized by money. I'm talking about a full-force cultural taboo. Why should people who poison us for profit enjoy a higher social status than child molesters, who in this country are stigmatized by such a powerful taboo that it's almost impossible for the accused to obtain justice? Taboos have long teeth and long lives. Taboos against incest and homosexuality, instituted by the ancient Hebrews to maximize their breeding potential, have governed half the planet for three thousand years.

In these latter days, defending the habitat is no longer a less urgent priority than defending the young or the genetic integrity of the species.

Taboo means ostracism, it means creating a fear of mobs and vigilantes. Men who are responsible for dumping medical wastes should wonder whether their children will come home safe from school. It's too late for contributions to the Sierra Club. Tar and feathers will be more cost-effective. No frontier justice could be purer or more poetic than the Solo Swimmer's Acid Test for enemies of the earth: if the night riders took one manufacturer or waste-disposal contractor and made him swim 20 yards in a 100 percent solution of the soup they caught him dumping, it would send a louder message than a billion dollars in fines.

What's the metaphor, what's the image that will make it clear? Our boat is sinking, most of us are bailing like crazy, but there are people aboard who sell the bailing cans and auction off pieces of the sail. We still haven't thrown them overboard, and that's beyond my comprehension.

VII

$\mathcal{G}$ame Galled, on Account of Darkness

I've always been curious about people who lived without sports, without playing or watching any of America's games, or talking about them. Some of them seemed human enough, but there weren't any in my family. When we were kids there was a whiff of the locker room in every breath we drew. My first serious ambition, as soon as I knew I'd never be the next Ted Williams or the next Jim Brown—or even better than my little brother—was to make myself the best sportswriter since Grantland Rice.

When I was a young neurotic in New York, running out of optimism, sports all but kept me alive. I loved nearly all of them. Baseball, basketball, tennis and football filled the calendar year with possibilities. I'm old enough to remember when people took boxing seriously. If you spoke the language of the sports page, it admitted you to a community that transcended every barrier of class and race and income—a clubhouse where you could hide from reality. It was my shelter, my sanctuary, my only certainty.

Now it's my constant sorrow. Now our games mirror the real world all too accurately; they seem to soak up the worst the world has to offer. The players, the owners, the fans, even the writers seem tragically diminished. Are things falling apart as rapidly as they appear to be, or was I in denial about the corruption that was there all along—an aging little boy clinging to his last dream, who finally woke up? Take your pick. But what I see happening to my games, and most painfully to my baseball, has just about broken my heart.

This sorrowful survey was written in 1988, when I thought the news on the sports page was as bad as it could get. I was wrong. New Olympic doping scandals—the Chinese, the Germans—seem to surface every week.

One Hand Clapping

A serious love affair doesn't end all at once, with doors slamming and no looking back. It dies slowly, illusion by illusion. And usually there's a final straw.

My infatuation with sports, a source of amusement for friends with more highbrow pretensions, was bred into me by a father and grandfathers who considered sports as essential as a brush-cut for any child who intended to present himself as a male. I learned a lot of games and played every one of them as long as my body was willing, succumbing only recently to a rash of back miseries and ankle injuries. I earned my living as a sportswriter, at one time, and as a fan (I prefer connoisseur, fan sounds uncritical) I was often in a class by myself. I can't think of anyone who's spent more time and money to see the best athletes do what they do best.

For over 35 years I've turned to the sports page first, regardless of the wars, scandals and natural disasters that were raging on Page One. I recommended it for the troubled generations behind me, assuring doubtful fathers that no boy who cared passionately about the World Series and the ACC Tournament would ever get into real trouble.

But the sports page has become a place where you wouldn't want to take your boy. A bad neighborhood, really, an embarrassment. A slum. You think of Hogarth's "Gin Street" when you look at the criminals, junkies and derelicts who have taken over the columns where we read eulogies of Lou Gehrig and Red Grange. From this weeks's sports page alone we have "Seattle cornerback charged with punching a woman in the face, while being treated for a drug problem"; "Nets' guard arrested for cocaine possession"; "Hawks center suspended for substance abuse"; "All-Pros who failed NFL drug tests reinstated"; "Boxer Dokes jailed for assault on girl friend"; "'He shakes. He pushes, he swings,' says heavyweight champ's wife. 'I've become very, very much afraid'"; "Olympic drug scandal widens. Silver medal weightlifter disqualifed."

Enough? And those stories were only from the bottom, from the edges of the sports page. At the top was Ben Johnson, the world's fastest human. Or is he? And who is? Is an athlete, swollen with drugs that are currently illegal, of a different species entirely from the other athletes swollen with drugs that may be undetectable, or legal because the regulators don't know about them yet? In their secret laboratories the witch doctors of sports forge ahead, building better springs for the better mousetrap.

Johnson's disqualification, after the buildup and the drama of his race with Carl Lewis, is a kind of final straw for me. I don't single out Johnson for any special contempt; in these Games where national prestige is supposed to be at stake, the athletes themselves are more like experimental machines that teams of experts prepare for competition. Think of NASCAR, with the wily pit crews tinkering and often cheating for tiny advantages. Johnson's pit crew put in one quart of STP too many. Johnson himself, a half-literate, inarticulate emigrant from Jamaica, is little more than a promising chassis upon which the Canadian Dr. Frankensteins built a perfect sprinting machine.

It doesn't matter who's guilty, or most guilty. It was painful to see the perversion of the sprints—the purest, least esoteric of athletic contests and always the one most certain to capture the public's imagination. Who will argue about the world's fastest human when runners have been dismissed as laboratory freaks—like the weightlifters, who've aroused so much suspicion at the Seoul games that a senior member of the Olympic committee has asked to have their sport removed from the Olympic menu?

What's left? The 100- and 200-meter dash events were about the only things on the menu I couldn't resist. Win-at-all-costs has turned the Olympic Games into the International Pharmaceutical Exposition. Between performance-enhancing drugs and the recreational varieties, a kid picking up his first sports page will see a ward full of junkies where I saw immortals. But in the postmortem on the Johnson affair I picked up a new concept that explains a lot about the athletes of the '80s. One of the side effects of steroids that Johnson exhibited is called "roid rage"—an irrational urge to damage yourself and others.

Reading about cornerbacks and prizefighters punching women, and college football teams decimated by indictments for rape, riot and aggravated assault, I naturally wondered why big muscles seemed to go with bad manners and bad blood. In my day the sports world was graced with a lot of gentle giants. "Roid rage" explains it all. It even explains the hitherto incomprehensible motion pictures of Sylvester Stallone. The vest-popping little steroid stallion isn't really enacting sado-patriotic fantasies under the auspices of the CIA. He's just showing us how he feels.

I never cared much for the Olympics, where politics, hypocrisy and belligerent nationalism are added to all the other sicknesses that afflict big-time televised sports. Now the Games are becoming a weird hybrid. How does it happen that a professional tennis player like Chris Evert, who's been a millionaire for 15 years, is competing for gold medals alongside 13-year-old gymnasts? There are no amateur tennis players? Or is it just that the best ones turn pro so young? Why not let Michael Jordan play for the Soviets, or Wade Boggs play third base for our baseball team? What's the difference? Let Michael Tyson box for a gold medal instead of $15 million. He'd show them "roid rage."

Haphazard solutions to the amateur problem have already cost the Olympics most of their credibility. There's no going back to the phony purity the Games affected during the reign of Avery Brundage, and nowhere to go but open competition in all sports. Which will lead to unconvincing, almost unconnected little professional tournaments, like the tennis farce in Seoul, in a number of major sports. They're talking about letting in the National Basketball Association, which by then will include Soviet players, in 1992. But by then the pharmacists may be peddling their wares in open booths around the Olympic stadium, with posters of medal-winners who swear by each product for sale.

The Olympics were always a little ugly underneath the glitter and the soaring anthems. But they were the last vestige of the prehistoric, pre-television era when sports were governed by some considerations besides money. It's regrettable, when people have so little that they can believe in, that this was the year of the loaded urine sample at the Olympic Games, and the year when something worse than "roid rage" drove representatives of the host country's team to assault a referee. The networks won't have any trouble hyping the next Olympics for decent ratings, any more than they have trouble hyping the Super Bowl, which hasn't produced an interesting game in years. But they won't be able to sell it to the old-timers like me, who are spectators not out of any fanaticism attached to hometowns or alma maters, but just for the quality, for the love of the games we know played well.

It's sad when a man in his forties loses his faith. I'll always watch the World Series and the Final Four, but maybe more out of habit than conviction. There are cynics who say that sports were never more innocent, that the public was just more naive. I dispute that. But sports are a kind of religion, and religion, like love, is based on cherished myths and illusions. I'm about out of illusions. To all the warnings that we've lost control of our lives, add this modest warning: we've even lost control of our games.

Use

If you set out to select the single lowest moment in the entire American adventure, there would be a lot of interesting nominations. But the hyping of the Dream Team is mine.

Operation Desert Slam

They aren't reminding anyone now. But a few months ago Michael Jordan was expressing serious reservations about playing in the Olympic Games, and taking a predictable pounding from the sports-page patriots. And a couple of years ago—time flies—Gen. Colin Powell, Chairman of the Joint Chiefs of Staff, was expressing serious reservations about a military operation in Kuwait, exposing himself to the taunts of lap-top Green Berets who fight on the op-ed page.

Jordan and Powell were both concerned, among other things, about the embarrassment factor. America's top soldier knew what none of the rest of us knew at the time, that the Iraqi army couldn't take 24 hours of the mechanized blitzkrieg Washington had in mind; he doubted that the push-button massacre would enhance his government's image inside or outside the United States. America's best basketball player, its crowned Emperor of the Air, may have wondered how 70-point humiliations of plucky teams of Third World peasants could reflect much credit on Jordan, the NBA or the USA. "Why do they need me?" said Michael.

Both of them overestimated the role of shame in the evolving American psyche. We are becoming disciples of Hyperbolus, of whom Plutarch said, "Having no regard for honor, he was also insensible to shame." (Quote courtesy Annie Dillard, *The Living*.)

As individuals we still find shame in flagrant mismatches. We censure large men who kick over wheelchairs or beat their wives and children. When it comes to geopolitics, these scruples disappear. Dancing on the graves of 100,000 Iraqis or sending the Marines to Grenada, we're just as happy if the victim is puny. The punier the victim, the fewer the American casualties to spoil the celebration. In the yellow-ribbon euphoria that followed the liberation of Kuwait, my instruments detected no trace of the embarrassment Gen. Powell anticipated. If the Hitler of Arabia couldn't give the GIs a 20-minute workout, so much the merrier.

We recognize no chivalry, no sportsmanship among nations. International games are no different, I'm afraid. Our pathological pursuit of Number One-hood, in everything from fast food to nuclear fission, poisons any competition we undertake. Our NBA Olympic Team—Operation Desert Slam—has become the most embarrassing excess of all.

Its games are unwatchable, of course. They aren't really games at all, since nothing—not the roof collapsing and squashing half the players as they sat feigning interest—could prevent the United States from winning. I had a glimpse of one game, I think the semifinal of the Tournament of the Americas, during a break in a Wimbledon doubles match. It was 6-0 USA. I switched back to tennis, watched two games and flipped to the basketball game again. It was 35-11. The NBA players were obviously trying to hold down the score, overpassing and refusing easy shots, substituting freely, resting on defense. There was nothing they could do. Cuba, a "strong" team by Olympic standards, lost by 79 points. The average margin in the qualifying tournament was America by 51 points.

I remember bloodthirsty fans of the old New York Yankees who never tired of watching their heroes humiliate the helpless St. Louis Browns, who cheered every pitch when Whitey Ford shut out Kansas City 11-0. I thought they were sick people. I don't think they'd be sick enough to stomach this. Team USA appeals to a sports fan who loves to feed live rats to his python.

When the Soviet Union provoked this awful retribution by beating our collegians in 1988, American patriots focused on the goal, the gold medal, and forgot about the games themselves. It's silliness to speculate about how "great" a team might be when there's no competition to test it. What's the point, where's the virtue in Patrick Ewing slam-dunking over a cowering midget, or Michael Jordan faking some thick-ankled graduate student out of his jock? What does it prove? Would anyone pay to see Roger Clemens strike me out with a 95-mile-per-hour fastball?

Aesthetically and psychologically, these games are horrible. We damage our children's character if we ask them to root for Goliath while he smashes David to a pulp. Any kid with a trace of spirit or courage knows that it's sick to celebrate bullies and revile underdogs. We force them to choose between their natural decency and the red, white and blue.

Is there any possible justification? Christian Laettner, the lone collegian chosen to play with the legends of the NBA (some say he was chosen because his famous arrogance would protect him from an ego-shrinking ordeal), said he didn't think the other college players, reduced to a scrimmage squad for Jordan and Company, resented missing their chance to play in the Olympics. "They know the gold is the main thing," said Laettner.

One nation under gold. Since the public's main source of information about the Olympic Games is the TV network that loses a fortune if they can't convince us to watch, enthusiasts tend to forget how drastically Olympic gold has been devalued. The 1988 Olympics were dominated by urine samples and technicians in lab coats. "Olympic drug scandal widens; silver medal weightlifter disqualified" was one headline I've saved. Sprinter Ben Johnson, "the world's fastest human," turned out to be a triumph of steroid technology, and got caught. The impression, after weeks of disqualifications, suspicions and accusations, was that undoped athletes were the exception at Seoul. I referred to the Games, in a disgusted postmortem, as the International Pharmaceutical Exposition.

I also suggested, in the spirit of satirical exaggeration, that the professional tennis tournament they added for the Seoul games left us open for anything in Barcelona—Wade Boggs playing baseball, Mike Tyson hammering Mongolians, even Michael Jordan taking the court against Angola. I was kidding.

Tyson wasn't available for the Games this year, but it's been ugly enough without him. Last fall the president of the United States Olympic Committee, Robert Helmick, was busted by his peers for taking payoffs from representatives of sports that were trying to get into the Olympics—bowling and golf, specifically (why not senior citizens in the medal chase?). Helmick, an attorney, called the payoffs consultants' fees and admitted an "apparent" conflict of interest.

He was selling influence, selling chances. It was disgusting. The lily-white patricians of the Avery Brundage era would have hanged him without a trial. But there's very little left of their "Olympic ideal." NBC Sports and its heavy-duty corporate sponsors have taken over the Games, athletes and all, so completely that it's hard to tell whether the Games are a commercial, a TV show or a promotional video. Reebok, a sports-shoe manufacturer, had America's two highest-rated decathletes spending more time in the commercial studio than on the practice fields, and one of them failed to make the team.

The gold that drives the Olympics is no longer the pittance they melt into medals. The NBA millionaires will be wearing as much gold around their necks when they arrive as when they leave. Check out some of those chains. Team USA, unbeatable and unwatchable, is only the most conspicuous of 100 dreams of avarice that feed the Olympic flame.

The chemical carnival started early this Olympiad, with the discovery that the U.S. shotputter Jim Doehring is not only a recently reinstated self-doper, but a convicted drug dealer as well. Without the fawning approval of most of the media, I doubt that the Olympic establishment would still be able to sell the nation that it's heir to "a higher meaning" and a noble tradition.

The Olympic Games are a sacred cow that became a sick cow, infected with every strain of chauvinism, materialism, expediency and mendacity that the "Olympic spirit" was supposed to purge from the company of nations. History may remember them as a noble experiment that failed. They seemed to inflame the aggressive nationalism they were supposed to defuse. They were the hottest theater of the Cold War, and warm-ups for real wars. They had their moments, like Jesse Owens' glorious triumph over Nazi science in Berlin. But they carried their sputtering torch during that single century when more people slaughtered each other than ever before in history.

If team sports were eliminated and all nations and flag-bearing entities were strictly excluded, I might vote to keep the Olympic Games going, commercials and all. Just for the athletes. In the meantime—even though Larry Bird is my favorite player and I acknowledge Magic Johnson and Michael Jordan as the greatest who ever played the game—I have my own impossible dream attached to America's Dream Team. I hope they lose. I hope someone whips their gold-plated butts. Secretly, you hope so too. I believe in you.

Some people saw Jim Valvano as a hustler. I saw him as a victim of the most flagrant and tenacious hypocrisy in sports, the big lie that allows greedy universities to exploit professional athletes by pretending that they're just larger-than-average undergraduates with special problems. Even the former head of the NCAA says, "Pay them, for Christ's sake." But don't hold your breath.

Paths of Glory

Once upon a time there were three coaches, upon whom fortune smiled. The oldest coach was so successful that he became a national institution. A huge blue arena was built as a monument to his achievement, and powerful men traveled great distances to sit at his feet. In the fullness of his years, he enjoyed his greatest triumph, and celebrated at the White House with the president of the United States.

The second coach achieved equal success, even more rapidly than the first, and a giant corporation rewarded him with an enormous pot of gold, more money than any coach had ever seen.

The third coach was blessed with great charm as well as coaching ability. He won the highest prize when he was still a young man, and all the riches and power that went with it. But then fortune turned her back on this coach. He was accused of misdemeanors. The press hounded him and the public turned against him; his reputation was tarnished and he lost his job. His friends said he was run out of town. Then he was diagnosed with a dreadful disease and died, still young, just 10 years after his most famous victory.

Down here where I live, there's no need to attach any names to these brief biographies. Basketball rules in North Carolina, and coaches speak with the authority of archbishops. Now that our local universities have won three national championships in a row (and five of the last 12), it would take a pretty feisty partisan from Indiana or Kentucky to deny that North Carolina's Triangle, the cradle of Michael Jordan, is the center of the basketball universe.

But it was just at the moment of our greatest glory, while President Clinton embraced Carolina's Dean Smith and the Nike sneaker tycoons embraced Duke's Mike Krzyzewski, that the Triangle was forced to pause and observe the horrible public death of the third coach, Jim Valvano.

Maybe the pause will count for something, for some overdue self-examination. I didn't know Jim Valvano, actually. I met him twice and liked him. Most people liked him. What happened to his career wasn't fair. What happened to his life wasn't fair.

He was saying just that in his interviews, toward the end—"Hey, who ever said life was fair?" But we can't just walk away from it like that, as if it had been the death of a man whose brakes failed or whose next-door neighbor went trigger-happy. As if fate just rolled the dice and they came up snake-eyes for the Italian wise guy.

How about some guilty consciences? If you never acknowledged that Valvano got a raw deal until you heard that he had cancer, you should hang your head. If you had a hand in running him out of Raleigh, maybe you should apologize to his family. There's a certain editor, now retired, who should have been the first to apologize. I hope he found the strength.

A lot of people still don't get it. A columnist in Texas wrote that Valvano "came to exemplify much of what has gone wrong with big-time college athletics. He got greedy."

That's not fair. Jim Valvano was the product and the victim of a corrupt system that he finally failed to understand, at least in the form that has evolved here in the basketball capital of America. He was a professional basketball coach who was hired to compete successfully against the high-powered programs at UNC and Duke. When he succeeded beyond N.C. State's gaudiest expectations, he became the Prince of the City in Raleigh.

His employers turned out to be adoring fans who would give him anything he wanted. He took what he thought he needed. He never grasped the pathological side of the Tar Heel basketball frenzy—the dogged hypocrisy, the desperate hunger to pretend that these transient mercenaries in size 16 shoes are still "scholar-athletes" descended from the teams that Daddy played on back in the '30s and '40s.

According to some of the best Southern writers, it's a powerful capacity for denial, more than anything else, that sets Southerners apart from their countrymen. The South is the place where ministers of God stood in the pulpit and conferred the blessings of Jesus Christ on Jim Crow. It's where agrarian dreamers still contend that the antebellum South was a balmy Eden of enlightened gentleman farmers and cheerful darkies singing in the fields.

With such a rich legacy of denial, it's almost comprehensible that people could talk about a basketball program's "graduation rates" and "academic standards" without expecting anyone to laugh. Jim Valvano was from up north, where they barely pay lip service to basketball's Big Lie. He didn't understand that some people down here cherish their illusions as much as they cherish their championships. He gave them victories. He recruited Chris Washburn, with a 470 on his SATs and the willpower of a six-year-old. When a network news crew came to film some Wolfpack players in class, Valvano neglected to warn his scholars, and the truant players were filmed clowning with their girl friends in a parking lot.

Some of the "fans" who were married to the Big Lie turned out to be sportswriters, editors, politicians. Valvano failed to respond to the urgent needs of their denial. They cut his heart out. I was in Seattle when I read about the "scandal" at N.C. State. But to this date there has been no scandal. None of the NCAA violations—minor ones—involved the coach in any way. *Personal Fouls*, the book by Peter Golenbock that proved so damaging to Valvano, was one of the most careless, malicious, unreliable manuscripts ever compiled by an individual who had the temerity to call himself a journalist. It contained hundreds of errors no editor had ever attempted to correct.

Personal Fouls was a cut-rate generic expose that could have described almost any successful program in Division I. But there were only a few coaches with profiles high enough to sell the book. Coach Valvano, charismatic and careless, was the perfect guy to take the fall.

It might make us all proud if we could bury this great millstone of hypocrisy along with the coach who was crushed by it. But it's the coaches who profit most from the myth of the student athlete, and they're not about to let it die. The worst hypocrites of all become the darlings of the NCAA, that shameless pack of pimps that runs a prosperous whorehouse and pretends to be the vice squad. I guess Dean Smith is so eminent now that he can just run his program and let other people feed the fools what they want to hear. But the fellow over at Duke is saying things that make me grind my molars to stumps.

Never mind that Mike Krzyzewski has the meanest rabid-rodent courtside sneer this side of Gene Keady. The man can coach, as they say, as if that makes up for anything. But lend an ear to his latest sermon in the *New York Times*:

"I believe college sports, as an extension of what we do and learn in the classroom, is an invaluable facet of higher education."

What is he talking about, this pompous little guy who teaches a dozen itinerant gland cases how to set picks? Why wasn't a Duke education and the bonding, sharing experience of playing on a national championship team enough to keep Billy McCaffrey in Durham? Did Vanderbilt offer him a better choice of electives in European history? Players transfer from Duke, which has one of the best academic reputations in Division I, for the same reason they transfer everywhere. For more playing time, which is critical to any professional player who's trying to showcase himself for the NBA.

Playing time is the main thing that matters to these kids, the same as it matters to the Boston Celtics. If you can deny that, you've got a denial problem I couldn't dent with a diamond drill. An actual "scholar-athlete"—a quality player who masters serious courses and works toward a serious post-graduate profession in spite of his coach's ridiculous demands on his time and energy—occurs only accidentally among these boy professionals, and about as frequently as a homosexual or a Buddhist or a munchkin like Muggsy Bogues.

And the teaching, character-building, citizen-molding function of the coach, as described by Krzyzewski? I seem to recall a player named Christian Laettner, who had something to do with Duke's success. After four years of character-building under Coach K, it took Laettner about a week to establish himself as the most immature, obnoxious player in the NBA.

Krzyzewski is a fountain of self-righteous nonsense. But I used to give him the benefit of the doubt. What if he believed this stuff? There were people who believed that David Koresh was Christ.

The multi-million-dollar shoe deal ought to silence most of Coach K's defenders. A million-dollar bonus and a 15-year contract worth $6 million to switch his kids from Adidas to Nike sneakers? Remember when Valvano was denounced for his greed?

I'm sure there's some major difference between Krzyzewski's bonus and a simple bribe, but so far it hasn't been explained to my satisfaction. And then immediately we read about Krzyzewski's $250,000 donation to the athletic building fund, "in honor of Duke's student body."

That's what we call "a Hill and Knowlton bequest," an image-repairing ploy by an individual who knows he's been caught red-handed. Like Mike Milken's famous burst of post-indictment charity. But it only makes things worse. Krzyzewski is always calling himself a teacher. How many of his colleagues on the Duke faculty are making bequests that amount to $400,000 before taxes? It would be like signing over half of everything a professor grossed between tenure and retirement.

The sneaker scandal exposes the atrocious double standard in force at the NCAA, which trashed Jim Valvano because some of his players sold their sneakers for pizza money. It shows the cynical, venal side of this myth of the student athlete. Maybe there's a doomed idealistic side, too. But this is the side that says the coach can collect millions because he's a professional and his team gets nothing because they're college students.

Somewhere there must be an ex-Duke player who really needs his share of this treasure. You explain to me why he shouldn't have it. His coach is always talking about sharing.

Tell us about "the true purpose of college sports," Coach K. Tell us why you were a role model while Jim Valvano was a hustler. At least the phonies won't have Jimmy V to kick around anymore. He was a good guy, and gifted. Wouldn't it be nice to think that he's coaching in a league where the hypocrites don't always win in the end.

No wonder they lied to us about our boyhood heroes. Maybe sports heroes were a bad idea in the first place. How could we market trading cards with pictures of teachers and social workers?

The Last Wolverine

When the book comes out this fall—the definitive biography of Ty Cobb, from Algonquin Books of Chapel Hill—a reviewer somewhere will write, "It's like digging him up and driving a stake through his heart."

It's like that. I just finished reading the manuscript, by veteran sportswriter Al Stump, and my only concern is that the stake isn't sharp enough to do the job. With the possible exception of Adolf Hitler, Ty Cobb must be the most frightening human being I've ever encountered in a biography. And some comparisons favor the Führer.

Hitler, by all accounts, was unfailingly kind to his dogs. Cobb loved to kick hunting dogs as much as he loved to spike third basemen.

Tommy Hitchcock, the great polo player, played a chukker or two with the great baseball player and was nauseated by the way Cobb would "whip the hide off his ponies." But he treated animals better than he treated most people. This was a man with an incredible history of _beating_ people. Not defeating them, mind you, but thrashing them. His victims included his wives, his children, his teammates, opponents, fans, umpires, policemen, and dozens of unfortunate waiters, cab drivers, bartenders and desk clerks.

Cobb boasted that he beat a man to death in Detroit, a mugger who fled when the ballplayer pulled his pistol. His courage was rarely questioned. He took on anyone, including professional prize-fighters. But he seemed to specialize in women and black people. A violent racist, he beat up blacks just for touching his body.

Detroit teammates once pulled him off a black laundrywoman he was trying to strangle. She was luckier than his son, Ty Cobb, Jr. When the boy flunked out of Princeton, his father showed up at his rooming house with a bullwhip and beat him raw and bloody.

Cobb was a human wolverine. Armed and dangerous, a law unto himself, he was unquestionably insane. If he had been less gifted at playing baseball and making money—he was a genius at both—he might have spent most of his life in prisons and asylums.

Instead he was an intimate of presidents, tycoons and movie stars, and the idol of generations of innocent American boys. One who grew up on his exploits was Joe DiMaggio; years after both of them had retired, Cobb limped into Toots Shor's saloon and DiMaggio whispered, "Here comes God."

I was another believer. I was a strange 10-year-old, better at memorizing statistics than hitting fastballs, and I used to recite Cobb's astonishing statistics to anyone who would listen. I even liked to say his name, "Tyrus Raymond Cobb," for its virile rhythms. I tore that famous picture out of *The Sporting News*, the one where he's sliding with his face in full profile, like an eagle in a baseball cap, and taped it over my bed.

I made a shrine for a psycho. Someone should have told me. Did my dad, a baseball nut of DiMaggio's generation, understand that Ty Cobb was a sociopath?

Boys have to grow up. But it's rotten luck to learn this whole story 40 years later, when I'm down to my last few illusions about baseball. This was the year they eliminated commissioners and pennant races; the new president of the National League, replacing Bill White the old first baseman, is Len Coleman, the old Wall Street banker and marketing consultant.

How do you defend a society where Ty Cobb could pass for a hero, or even pass for normal? There are grave doubts that he was even honest. Accused of throwing a game for gamblers, Cobb—who played poker at the White House with Warren G. Harding—enlisted the support of several U.S. senators and bullied and lawyered the commissioner of baseball into submission.

If you're a purist who thought John McEnroe was a national embarrassment, if you seethe every time they reinstate the coke-head pitcher Steve Howe, consider Ty Cobb. He survived and prospered, with his image relatively untarnished, through six decades of psychotic belligerence and criminal assault.

Cobb found the crack in the American psyche where athletic competition confuses itself with warfare, and he pushed until it was just wide enough to let him through. It's no coincidence that Gen. Douglas MacArthur was his biggest fan.

His sickness was a distorted reflection of our own. You can make

a case that he influenced the outcome of more major league baseball games than any player who ever lived. The question is whether
that achievement means anything at all, considering the pathology
of the athlete and the human cost he incurred.

At 10, I would have waffled on that one. It's clear to me now
that the answer is "No."

I never went along with the conscientious objectors of the playground, who preach that competition itself is a disease. For individuals of ordinary temperament, athletic competition is probably a
healthy outlet for aggression. Muscular Christians tell us that
courage, character, discipline and self-esteem can be found on a
playing field, and in ordinary cases I think they're right.

The problem isn't that competition is a disease, but that it
attracts and rewards the diseased. Winning at any price is a principle that puts a premium on the marginally deranged. Their worst
behavior is not only excused but rewarded, and reinforced.

Ty Cobb was the extreme. It appears that he went completely
around the bend at 18, when his mother killed his father in a
shooting that was never fully explained. But he shared some classic
symptoms with other famous psychos of sports. He collected every
book ever written about his idol, Napoleon Bonaparte. "He knew
how to win against the odds," Cobb told Al Stump.

When his minor-league roommate beat him to the bathtub after
a ballgame, Cobb, 17 years old, pitched a fit and snarled "I've got
to be first at everything—all the time."

That wouldn't sound psychotic to Pete Rose, the most aggressive
ballplayer of his time and the man who finally broke Cobb's 50-
year-old record for career base hits. If Cobb was a sociopath, Rose is
only a louse, and a creep. Rickey Henderson, who now owns the
stolen-base record Cobb held for half a century, is merely a jerk.
Leo Durocher, no sweetheart himself, was probably voicing the
convictions of most ballplayers when he said, of Mel Ott, "Nice
guys finish last."

I could fill pages with the names of successful athletes who are
certified creeps, bullies, woman-beaters, megalomaniacs and
unpunished criminals. But Ty Cobb's most direct descendants, the
true heirs to his mantle of meanness and menace, are some of our
so-called "college coaches"—these glorified gym teachers who
cover their trophy rooms with pictures of General Patton.

Among the most weird and pathetic cases were the late Woody

Hayes, who ended his career by punching a kid on the other team, and Jackie Sherrill, who motivated football players by castrating a bull on the practice field. But watch the faces on TV, through just one season of football and basketball, and you know half these coaches would sacrifice their first-born child for six more seconds on the clock.

Pathology is rampant. I've even heard people defend Bobby Knight of Indiana, a festering head case who kicked his own son on national TV and will someday shoot a referee right between the stripes. Swollen with self-importance and sneaker payoffs, insulated from reality, crazy coaches threaten boycotts and concoct wild things about civil rights and minority opportunities when the NCAA tries to limit their scholarships. They're grown men, arrested in adolescent hostility, who threaten to kill each other when 20-year-old athletes disappoint them.

I remember writing, years ago, that coaches are people who come unglued under the unnatural pressure of living as if something utterly trivial—winning games—were a matter of life and death. But these celebrated outpatients live in a world we made and maintain for them, a world where no one ever questions the importance of winning these games.

If Bobby Knight thought he was the only person in the world who gave a damn whether he won more college basketball games than Dean Smith or Adolph Rupp, would he lighten up and start treating players and sportswriters like human beings? It's a long shot, I'm afraid. Coaches with perspective are eliminated at the high school level. If you'd rather be loved than feared, if you'd rather be a loser with friends than a winner with sycophants, if you walk away from the gym with a smile win or lose, I'll bet my pension you never coach in Division I.

If Knight, Rose and the other winners harbor enough self-doubt to wonder how things turn out for guys who will kill to win, they'll read Stump's *Cobb*, or at least see the movie, starring Tommy Lee Jones.

They called Cobb "The Georgia Peach." He was so famous that when some wag hung the same nickname on Josef Stalin, everybody in the United States got the joke. In Cobb's papers Stump found fan letters from Mark Twain, Thomas Edison, Theodore Roosevelt, William Randolph Hearst and Ernest Hemingway.

But after he retired he was unable, with millions of dollars from

Coca-Cola investments, to buy his way back into the game. He played 24 years in the American League and left without a single friend. Eventually he alienated everyone, including his children and his family. He terrified nurses and servants, so he lived his last years absolutely alone in a big house south of San Francisco. He died at 74 of cancer, heart disease, diabetes and alcohol. Except for a couple of old teammates who forgave him, baseball ignored his funeral.

Baseball—1871–1994. They ought to designate an abandoned cornfield somewhere, where old bleacher fans can crawl off and die.

Field of Nightmares

The restructuring of baseball is the end of Western Civilization as we know it.

—Bob Ryan, *Boston Globe*

For each of us who takes the game personally there's a personal final straw, a shock that confirms a vision of baseball's future too drained of life and meaning to sustain the faith. The restructuring of the schedule to add "wild cards" and ever more rounds of post-season playoffs showed that major league owners no longer understand the difference between their ancient game and the degraded, revenue-driven spectacles of professional football, basketball and hockey. The threat of a season-ending player strike, canceling the World Series as even Hitler and Tojo never could, showed that baseball is managed with no concern for the integrity of the game or the passionate cult that defends it.

A strike will result in millions of apostates, many of them fourth- and fifth-generation fans who made the pilgrimage to Cooperstown with their grandfathers. They've been wearing out *Field of Dreams* on their VCRs and praying for a miracle. I don't believe in miracles. But I believe in symbols, and for me the final indignity was the merchandising of The Yankee Clipper.

Madison Sports and Entertainment, a sports memorabilia outfit with interests in roller derbies and riverboat gambling, is paying Joe DiMaggio a modest $3.8 million to limber up his signing arm and autograph 1,941 baseball bats (1941 was the year of his record 56-game hitting streak). This dubious feat will take Joe, 78, about 20 hours to complete. That's $190,000 an hour, more money for a single hour's foolishness than DiMaggio received for his entire prewar career as the Yankees' center fielder, seven seasons including the wonder year of 1941.

Most of the bats will become the property of a cable shopping network, guaranteeing a dignified showcase for the last baseball player whose legend was built on dignity and class. Is there a sentimental columnist in America who isn't quoting Paul Simon's "Mrs. Robinson"? ("Where have you gone, Joe DiMaggio, a nation turns its lonely eyes to you . . .")

Gone to the home shopping network, coo coo ca choo. I have no quarrel with Joe, who's conducted his life like an archdeacon compared with most of the stars who succeeded him. Like a lot of Americans of the Depression generation, he's known to be a miser. But lonely eyes were still turned in his direction because there was no place else to look.

The memorabilia and trading-card racket is getting sick and obsessive; at card shows, bored stars charge kids $10 to ask questions, and there are more card magazines than baseball magazines at the drugstore. The kindest thing I could say about baseball's fanatical collectors is that they must look backward because it's the only view they can endure.

The sports pages are evenly divided between the antics of imbecile owners and infantile athletes. The commissioner, who was hired to restrain them both and punish their excesses, has been conveniently eliminated from baseball's equation. I was amused to read that Duke University's athletic director, Tom Butters, was lobbying for the job.

"It's time to bring some common sense to the game," said Butters. But the commisssioner's job is vacant because no one with any pride or common sense would touch it with a fungo bat. My guess is that Butters hasn't been reading the sports pages lately. Another guess is that he could have the job any time, with a higher salary than the last poor chump, if he'd submit to a simple operation that my tomcat shook off in a day or two. But no commissioner with a full set of accessories will last a year with George Steinbrenner and Jerry Reinsdorf. If they name a commissioner at all, put your money on Ed McMahon or Ronald Reagan, Jr.

Scan the roster of baseball's 28 owners and ownership groups. The percentage of bastards and buffoons is so high it must be a divine judgment against baseball fans for our hubris, for the arrogant way we always looked down on the trash sports with their six rounds of playoffs. Is this a true cross-section of the class of megarich Americans who can afford a major league baseball team? Where are there other rich ladies like Cincinnati's Marge Schott, a neo-Nazi with the personal graces of a fishwife who called her ballplayers "niggers" and "monkeys" and provoked mutinies when her St. Bernards soiled the infield during batting practice?

The Yankees' George Steinbrenner is an ex-convict (for illegal contributions to Richard Nixon, the one crime comparable to genocide or child rape) with a history of shady deals and shadier associations that would have landed a poorer man in a maximum-security facility. It was Steinbrenner's strange affair with the late Billy Martin, an extended series of firings and rehirings that resembled a lover's quarrel among dimwits, that broke the sweet spell of the '70s and showed us how quickly the game could descend from the sublime to the ridiculous.

Blackmail was Steinbrenner's latest diversion. His threat to move the Yankees to New Jersey had Governor Cuomo and the entire state of New York scrambling to appease him. A reporter discovered that the Yankees, a business worth a quarter of a billion dollars, already pay less in taxes than the neighborhood orphanage.

Schott and Steinbrenner are so disgusting the other owners had to pretend to punish them to keep the press and politicians at bay. They get the headlines. But don't overlook lower-profile swine like Jerry Reinsdorf of the Chicago White Sox, who methodically harassed and humiliated Carlton Fisk, the last of the old-time work-ethic ballplayers, and dumped him without apology at mid-season after 25 years in the game.

And even these subhumans aren't the worst thing that's happening to baseball. They've all been known to spend real money to keep their teams competitive. Compare them with the owners of the San Diego Padres, who auctioned off $12 million worth of marquee players just to cut their payroll in half.

Whatever you've read about Connie Mack or Harry Frazee, the man who sold Babe Ruth, there's no precedent for a team to dump all its best players in the middle of a pennant race. No commissioner could have approved the Padres' fire sale, which virtually nullified the National League season. San Diego became a minor league team, and games with the Padres should have been declared exhibitions.

So what's left, and why care? Baseball management in the '90s is epitomized by the new owner of the Houston Astros, who heard a rumor that he was hiring Davey Lopes to replace his manager and asked, "Who's Davey Lopes?" If he doesn't know, of course, he doesn't know a second baseman from a second mortgage. When

Kansas City owner Ewing Kauffman died this summer, the eulogy said "First of all he was a baseball fan." Kauffman may be the last owner ever buried with those words.

Under such owners, the players might have become stoic gladiators, suffering much for the sake of the fans, the home city and the game's sacred trust. Instead, overpaid and insecure, married to their price tags and shuffled around like faceless pawns in the board game of baseball's new economics, they've become petulant children who need camp counselors to keep them from harming fans, reporters and each other.

The antics of the desperate New York Mets resembled nothing so much as the nasty, dangerous pranks little summer campers begin to play on each other when it rains all week. When Vince Coleman nearly blinded a little girl with a cherry bomb, when Bret Saberhagen threw firecrackers at reporters and sprayed them with Clorox from his Supersoaker squirt gun, the appropriate punishment was to withhold their candy-bar money or sentence them to a week without Jello desserts. But they're 30-year-old men who play baseball for a half a million dollars a month.

It isn't the salary scale that will turn me against baseball players, not when 20-year-old drug punks with tattoos make tens of millions selling "songs" about sex and slaughter to fatherless eighth graders. It's the mounting evidence that there's a new generation of players with no knowledge of the game and no respect for their own profession.

Like most of the owners, they seem to be in it for the quick buck. With fewer American kids (and most ominously, fewer black kids) playing and learning baseball, teams fill out their rosters with all-purpose super-athletes who've discovered that baseball is more lucrative and less dangerous than football. Bo Jackson was a treat, for all of us who revere pure talent. But we began to recoil when talented Deion Sanders said, "I'm a baseball player, not a baseball fan." When half the black players on one team were unable to identify Jackie Robinson, we began to comprehend the gulf that's opening between the people who love the game and the people who play it.

It surprises me when I meet "purists" who are still griping about the designated hitter. That's like complaining about the wine in first class while the crew is lowering the lifeboats. What about the stale air in the new domed stadiums, zombie crowds watching themselves do The Wave on scoreboard TV screens, horrible mascots who look like cartoon road kill, Disney World ballparks with shopping malls, video arcades and built-in motels?

I went to a game in Seattle and saw major leaguers play dome baseball on stained, dog-eared artificial turf that looked like the tortured felt on a very old pool table. That's the elegant setting that frames the exploits of Ken Griffey, Jr., who might be the best young player since Willie Mays.

No one who loved the game could ever have cursed it with artificial turf. One night on TV I watched a lame single take an Astroturf bounce over the center fielder's head and ricochet like a pinball while runners raced around the bases. I realized this was nothing like baseball I was watching. It was sillyball, something halfway between bumper pool and indoor soccer.

Rubber fields—so why not rubber balls as well? The Baltimore Orioles' TV announcers were discussing the amazing run production in the American League, the .400 hitter, the 40 others hitting over .300, the bloated earned-run averages and the fact that Roger Clemens, for the first time in his life, couldn't seem to get anybody out. Jim Palmer, the Hall of Fame pitcher and a dangerously indiscreet individual who'd better watch his back, said in effect, "Come on guys, everybody knows they loaded the ball last winter." Palmer might have thrown a cherry bomb in the broadcasting booth, for all the scurrying his partners executed to make sure everyone knew he was kidding.

Well, of course they put a rabbit in the ball. Don't believe me, check the figures for yourself. Boosters called 1993 a great season, with all the hitting and scoring, but you could probably achieve the same effect by making pitchers strap 30-pound weights inside their bloomers. Already there's a gentlemen's agreement between the umpires and batters to ignore the top half of the strike zone.

They show no respect, the hustlers who run the game now. Neither do some of the pigs they target with their sales pitches, the corporations that buy up all the good box seats we see vacant during pennant races, while real fans stay home or sit up with the pigeons. Not to mention the big shots with gold chains who use their luxury skyboxes for Neronian orgies, like the public striptease that scandalized Dallas. Baseball has come a long way—in the wrong direction—from the small-town, blue-collar game we all grew up on.

If they pay the bills, do they have the right? Who owns the game? Baseball was never just another business, another case of "roll out the merchandise and let the buyer beware." Since 1922, when the Supreme Court exempted baseball from federal antitrust laws, the game has enjoyed a special status not unlike a precious natural resource or a national park.

It has also enjoyed a monopoly. The rationale for a protected monopoly was destroyed by television revenues, which attracted the high rollers who dishonor and disfigure the game. No one believes these vultures still deserve a special break from Congress. But no one is comfortable with the possibilities if the antitrust exemption is lifted. Would outlaw leagues spring up everywhere and disperse the talent among 100 franchises?

The truth is that each of us who loves baseball thinks he owns it, and thinks he knows what's good for it. Some sports encourage mob psychology, but baseball speaks to the individual. You bring what you know and what you think you know and project them against the games you see on the field.

Each of us is the commissioner. I'm no exception. Among baptized believers, I rank myself as a moderate. I admire the lyrical auguries of the poet Donald Hall and even the soaring epiphanies of a baseball dervish like W.P. Kinsella. I loved Kinsella's novel *Shoeless Joe*, and I cried like every other man during the scene in *Field of Dreams*—Hollywoood's adaptation—when Kevin Costner plays catch with the ghost of his father. But a little of this goes a long way, for me.

I try to steer away from the mysticism and intellectualization that abound in baseball circles. I don't see the symmetries of the universe in the rhythms of the game. I don't harbor a lot of illusions or deify a lot of heroes. I appreciated Robert Smith's recent book, *Baseball in the Afternoon*, because it communicates so much affection for the game without whitewashing any of its icons.

This old-timer's account, beginning before World War I, makes it clear that the godlike commissioner Kenesaw Mountain Landis was a petty and often ruthless tyrant. It reminds us that the immortals Ty Cobb and Tris Speaker—Christ and John The Baptist when I was a boy—were probably gamblers and game-fixers who should have been banned for life like Shoeless Joe and Pete Rose.

I try not to ask too much or make too much of the game. I don't expect ballplayers to be idealists and role models, or owners to be magnanimous Dutch uncles and aunts. But they'd better remember who *we* are—and here I take the liberty of speaking for everyone who doesn't write in to dissociate himself from my generalizations.

Above all we want—we need—an honest game. An honest ball, an honest strike zone, honest competition, honest-to-God grass and air. It's not the spectacle, it's not even hometown loyalty that comes first to a baseball fan. It's preserving, with the maximum of verisimilitude, the game our fathers taught us. It's keeping the faith.

Baseball used to be our only refuge from chaos and unreason. I still cringe when an umpire makes a terrible call, even when the call goes against a team I hate. Baseball fans are fatalists and stoics. We don't want a second chance, some cheap wild card resurrection. We want a pennant race—a meaningful, *final* resolution. We despise those ragbag NFL and NBA seasons where they play hundreds of pointless games just to eliminate the worst four teams. We despise carnival gimmicks and mascots.

If they forget who we are, it won't be long before there are no fans at the games—just *crowds*, and crowds are fickle. I don't think baseball can compete with more kinetic sports if it comes to seducing the masses.

But I've put the whole burden for saving the game on organized baseball, which is probably unfair. Baseball is a family. If it's a dysfunctional family, its fans have to share the blame.

I saw some big league games this year—I saw Barry Bonds homer at Candlestick and Clemens labor at Fenway. But my best moments with baseball, the moments when I felt the most optimistic, were far from the TV cameras and skyboxes. One was a June night at Boshamer Stadium in Chapel Hill, during the last innings of one of the last games of the Carolina Invitational.

I was sitting talking baseball with the grandfather of Danny Hubbs, an All-American relief pitcher for Southern Cal. The old man had come all the way from Oregon to see his grandson pitch, but the boy hadn't been out of the bullpen all weekend. When they finally waved Hubbs in to save this game against Carolina, the grandfather seemed more anxious than relieved.

But suddenly it all came together: Hubbs was throwing one perfect strike after another past the Tar Heels, the old man was beaming and talking a blue streak, bats and June bugs were diving, 100 diehard fans were muttering appreciatively on a warm spring night under the lights, and W.P. Kinsella should have been there.

I also remember a hot morning at the nationally renowned Durham Athletic Park when there wasn't a professional ballplayer in sight, just 100 or so long shots trying to impress a pair of scouts from the Atlanta Braves. I stood over in the bullpen by the scout with the speed gun, who called out the numbers as the pitching prospects aired out their best fastballs.

One was a guy 63 years old, whose arm had held up maybe better than his sense of reality. He told me later that he didn't trust the speed gun. But he threw one pitch that was clocked at 72 mph, with genuine movement on it, too.

Then there was Jeff Bock from Barton College, a baseball thoroughbred. Bock is the son of former Durham Bulls general manager Pete Bock and the grandson of Claude "Buck" Weaver, a long-ago Bulls pitcher whose ashes were raked into the pitcher's mound at DAP. The big right-hander was throwing over 90 mph with ease. The scouts were nodding and scribbling. Two weeks later Bock was pitching in a rookie league for the Braves.

But the pitcher I remember best was a 15-year-old left-hander from High Point. I don't think he was clocked over 80, but he had a breaking pitch, a sweet changeup and the smooth mechanics that are very hard to teach. His T-shirt was stenciled "If it is to be—it's up to me."

I talked to the little lefty's father, a youth-league coach who turned out to know a lot of baseball. I thought about all the baseball knowledge and energy that goes into these Rotisserie fantasy leagues, and into sabermetrics and the statistical arcana of the Bill James school of baseball. I'm not one to criticize. I've always been nuts about the numbers. But maybe some of us have worked our way so far out on the branches of this game that we're forgetting about the roots, forgetting that if the roots die it all falls down.

I think a lot of these collectors and statisticians are almost unaware that it all starts with a game that little kids play, if someone buys them a ball and a glove. If baseball is dying from the ground up, maybe it's because there aren't enough baseball lovers who can find the time to coach, or even play catch with their sons.

Legends of the Fall

It was a chill wind from somewhere in Canada, out of a deep blue sky with a thumbnail moon for its navel. Acorns and hickory nuts rattled off roofs and decks, rang like spent bullets off truck hoods and mailboxes until my neighborhood sounded like a combat zone in a war between goblins and squirrels.

A few leaves had turned yellow, a few were falling surreptitiously amidst the acorn cannonade. There was one last flawless red rose, and on the neighbors' vine one bunch of unwithered Concord grapes. The heat had given up its hold on the Carolinas, maybe for good this time, on the last day of September. It was perfect weather.

Series weather.

I used to have a routine for the World Series. I'd find a motel in New England, next to a mountain lake or a river, and hole up there for a week in October, in a clutter of record books and pizza boxes.

TV reception had to be perfect, or I'd change rooms or motels. Sometimes my best friend joined me. A game would end and we'd walk out into the five o'clock sunshine and those blinding red and yellow maple leaves and play catch in the yard by the swimming pool. I was working on a knuckleball. My old yellow fielder's glove was a Don Hoak model, which I could never figure because Don like all other third basemen was right-handed.

I've attended a score of World Series games, and I covered one classic Series from the press box. But I remember those motel Series just as clearly—Brooks Robinson, Lou Brock, Bob Gibson, Narragansett beer, roadhouse fish fries, foggy mountain mornings, woodsmoke, whitetail deer in the headlights. I can't recall when the world as a package ever pleased me more.

How much have they hurt me, these alien bastards who are killing baseball? Absent friends seem to understand. I've been getting letters of consolation, written with the delicacy and compassion we reserve for a death in the family. Dave writes from Baton Rouge, "There is a world still out here, if *sans* baseball."

I hurt a lot, I guess. But the pain didn't come all at once this silent autumn, the first October without baseball since my grandfather was 15 and the World Series was an ancient tradition of exactly one year's standing.

There was an omen. It was seven or eight years ago in Hillsdale, New York, up in the Berkshire Mountains where I went to college. There's a great French restaurant in Hillsdale; after a major league dinner crowned with a couple of Armagnacs I took a walk down the highway in the moonlight. Just across the road from the restaurant was a baseball diamond. The three-quarters moon was so bright you could have hit fungoes. The grass was freshly mown. I took off my shoes and socks at the right field line and walked barefoot across the outfield toward the pitcher's mound.

Before I reached the shortstop's position, I realized this was a ghost diamond. Weeds were spreading across the infield dirt, clogging up the baselines, climbing the pitcher's mound. It was late summer, so no one had played here all year.

It was a nice ballfield, too—level, at least 350 feet deep to center field, with a tall chicken-wire backstop and a section of bleachers behind third. Home plate was still in place. If small-town kids didn't play here—didn't flock here—then they didn't play the game anymore. And if they didn't play it anymore, in 20 years baseball would be another rootless professional exhibition like hockey or jai-alai.

It was profoundly depressing, this hard evidence that baseball was succumbing to root-rot. I didn't expect the whole organism to start dying so soon. Even while I was walking barefoot in Hillsdale, major league owners were entering into collusion to destroy free agency, a documented conspiracy that Ken Burns' *Baseball* characterizes—correctly, in my opinion—as a criminal betrayal of the game far worse than the Black Sox scandal of 1919.

When they conspired to ignore free agents, for a period of at least three years, the owners were agreeing not to compete for league championships. The enormity of that "fix" had been obscured by 1993, when the baseball commissioner had been eliminated and the competitive climate so blighted by greed and indifference that the San Diego Padres sold off their best players in the middle of a pennant race.

No one made a move to restrain them. Maybe it was the trade of Fred McGriff to the Braves, confirming that the Padres retained no remote interest in winning anything but salary arbitrations. Maybe it was a World Series game that ended 15-14, after many reversals, and somehow was not at all a great game or even a good game but instead a silly scramble like a slow-pitch softball game where nearly every pitch results in a triple. But I was numb with pessimism long before 1993 was in the record books.

When they carved up the leagues into little NFL subdivisions and introduced NFL wild cards, I shrugged. When they loaded the ball so that $4-million pitchers looked like sore-armed bushers and 160-pound shortstops began to hit like Mickey Mantle, I wasn't sucked into caring or protesting. (I didn't even cry when Dwight Gooden—a god at 20, a junkie at 30—failed another drug test.)

The players' strike was no surprise. Baseball people warned me in March. The cancellation of the playoffs and the World Series was the inevitable finale for this farce. It was only after the season was dead and buried, in the deafening silence of October, that I got this big lump in my throat.

The PBS broadcasts of *Baseball*, Ken Burns' 18-hour history of the game, were scheduled to coincide with September's pennant fever. Instead they became a voice in a vacuum.

As a baseball co-religionist I'm forever grateful to Burns for gathering all those wonderful images in one place. I know I'll visit them again. But the film revealed eccentric choices. It was an insider treatment that fell short of the insider's morbid passion for the facts. For the faithful it was a painful overdose of nostalgia, almost like rubbing salt in our wounds. For casual fans and the uninitiated it was an exercise in overkill and skewed perspective.

I thought it was fine to give the Negro leagues equal time, reminding us that American kids collected pictures of white ballplayers who would have been standing in soup lines if Satchel Paige and Buck Leonard had been allowed to compete for their jobs. Racism is America's original sin, and certainly baseball's. No doubt Jackie Robinson, like Joe Louis, commanded respect that transcended sports and helped to end the reign of Jim Crow.

To present baseball as a paradigm of the American experience is, nevertheless, to create an acute problem of scale. Branch Rickey wasn't Abraham Lincoln and Jackie Robinson wasn't Martin Luther King. The 1975 Series wasn't Chickamauga. Burns probably deserved the dig from "Saturday Night Live," which substituted candlepin bowling for baseball: "Saigon fell, Nixon was pardoned, and Lew Noodus converted the impossible 4-6 split."

Baseball's just a game, a game venerated by an inbred cult that forgets most Americans can't define "designated hitter," just as a Catholic might forget that the pope is a medieval curiosity to any-one outside the church. Burns could have avoided embarrassment by hiring one irreverent infidel to remind him. But I loved his independence from the baseball establishment, his explicit con-tempt for the owners and particularly for George Steinbrenner, "the man who destroyed the Yankees."

Steinbrenner, like Jackie Robinson, cast a shadow too long for the game to contain. His grotesquely deformed personality, exag-gerated by the tiny theater of baseball, taught America life lessons about tycoons and their egos that may have inoculated us against H. Ross Perot.

Burns scored well on attitude, not so well on timing. *Baseball*, intended as a celebration, ended up sounding like a eulogy. It pro-duced unintentional irony when Donald Hall and Roger Angell, eloquent deacons of the church of baseball, called the game "America's family heirloom" and spoke of its "everlasting life." Was it Angell or Thomas Boswell who said "It's something in my life I can count on, and I know it will never let me down"? After a month of the strike, Boswell wrote "We want the strike settled *in theory*. But in reality, we're sick of baseball."

I felt sorry for some of the older guys in the film. Even at 50 we begin to lose our landmarks—old houses, old trees, old friends are falling. Vistas shrink, possibilities wither. It's the strangest season of my life. To survive we develop new capacities for denial, like the kind that sustain Republicans and fundamentalists, or we suc-cumb to an abysmal form of resignation.

Once I thought baseball would provide my continuity, too. But for several years I've sensed that a great loss was imminent. My grandfather was 50 years older than his last hero, Carl Yastrzemski; I can't imagine that I'll ever idolize a left-handed hitter born this winter.

Ken Burns couldn't read the writing on the wall. That was left to Pat Jordan, in the *New York Times Magazine*. Jordan profiled acting commissioner Bud Selig and four other owners. They ranged from outrageously mean and insensitive to merely dense and pathetic; the best of them, labor lawyer Peter Angelos of the Baltimore Orioles, knows less baseball than my mother.

It was another chilling glimpse of the bloated creatures who sprawl at the top of America's food chain. Baseball—like the movies, like our newspapers and magazines—has fallen into the hands of rich, vulgar people who neither love nor understand it. There's no future for baseball or any of these other institutions unless the people who love them can ransom them back.

VIII

$\mathscr{U}$gly Americans — A Pathologist's Portfolio

In the worst of times, there are many things about the United States of America that are attractive and edifying. I've heard that some newspapers, responding to readers' complaints about depressing headlines and negative editorials, have hired "happy face" columnists to tell good news and toss bouquets to good citizens. That's a job for a guy in a clown suit, or a beauty queen dressed like Little Bo Peep, riding in a golf cart through the mall. It's no job for a journalist. Boosters don't need our help to go on boosting. But the bad guys the press doesn't bite will go unbitten.

At least one out of 14 strangers would be happy to murder you if the price was right. That's a lot of potential hit men, between 15 and 20 million. We've got serious problems in River City, Marian. The Invasion of the Body Snatchers must have been a documentary.

The Ugly Americans

Washington, D.C. — It was a night like any other night in the Murder Capital of America. Crossing the city from Chevy Chase to Alexandria we heard sirens and saw packs of police cars and ambulances with their lights flashing, racing to save someone or clean up after someone whose rescue came too late. The morning paper described the carnage at the Orbit Lounge on Alabama Avenue, where an impatient customer in a slow weapon-check queue stepped out of line and mowed down his fellow music-lovers with a handgun. A 19-year-old boy died at D.C. General and six other victims were hospitalized with big holes in their bodies.

"This is really a nice club," said the Orbit's owner, Daisy Poindexter, "but the young people are tearing up everything. These young people are so bad now."

An older man who used to work as a disc jockey at the Orbit told the *Washington Post* reporter that he's too scared to go there now, the kids are so bad: "If there's a confrontation, they're going to pull out something and you're going to pull out something because we're all packing guns. Who wants to go to jail at age 40?"

The deceased, William Dent, was the 157th homicide victim in Washington this year, keeping D.C. on a pace to tie or break its record for homicides set in 1990. A total of 640 people have been shot to death in Washington since January 1, 1990, two-thirds of them with handguns. Meanwhile, over on Capitol Hill, the National Rifle Association's gun lobby (surely the craziest bunch of evil bastards ever to fatten themselves on a national psychosis) was flexing its muscle in an 11th-hour attempt to defeat the Brady Bill with its modest seven-day waiting period for handgun sales.

The next night we ate at an Ethiopian restaurant in the Adams-Morgan district; a few blocks away and a few hours later, hundreds of young Hispanics in the Mount Pleasant neighborhood started torching cars, looting businesses and stoning policemen. After two days of rioting, 13 cops had been injured and a burned-out city bus sat smoldering at curbside like a hapless Iraqi tank. Asked about her chances of reducing violence and cutting the murder rate that is regularly described as "skyrocketing," Mayor Sharon Pratt Dixon said, "Not great."

When I wrote a previous column from one of America's domestic war zones, a reader reminded me that the war is everywhere, and I took it to heart. North Carolina's murder rate was up 12 percent in 1990, two percentage points above the national average, and violent crime was up 13 percent; Durham, where my wife and I work, reported a 19.4 percent increase in serious crimes.

"We're in the top 20 most dangerous states," said a ranking law enforcement official, "and we'll probably be in the top 10 by the end of the decade."

But the slaughter in Washington provides a wonderful showcase, a compelling advertisement for America to seduce the foreign diplomats who slip fearfully through the capital's burning streets in locked cabs and sealed limousines. What do they think of a government that polices the Persian Gulf more effectively than it polices its own neighborhood?

Mayor Dixon campaigned on a promise to bring the city's homicide epidemic under control in six months. After four months in office she tries not to mention it, and the metro page headline in the *Post* reads "Mayor's vow to stem the tide gives way to grim reality." The rapid education of Sharon Dixon signals—must signal—the end of the era of criminal make-believe in the nation's political rhetoric, an era epitomized by "drug czar" William Bennett claiming victory in his paneled office on The Hill while teenage drug dealers committed Capone-style massacres not half a mile away.

The get-tough fantasy—more cops, more prisons, death penalties, harsher sentences, phony wars on drugs—has been such a spectacular failure that no credible person could still sell it or buy it (that doesn't mean no one will). There's nothing left in that bag of illusions. There's no money left to waste on it, either. No money at all, unless we take it from the last few social programs that hold the American underclass one rung above Third-World, Bangladeshi poverty. That would be like spending a fortune to kill mosquitoes while refusing to drain, or even acknowledge, the swamps where they breed. That's what the get-tough fantasy has been like, actually, all along.

Where does that leave us, when tough talk and tough posturing have become a bad joke? There's only one experiment that might provide even temporary relief from our .38-caliber cannibalism, and that would be the criminalization of all handguns—we should set up metal detectors in the street, if necessary—and the legalization of drugs.

I'd try it in a heartbeat. The government will be forced to try it eventually. But we place too much responsibility on the government. In a monarchy or dictatorship, the people are often the innocent victims of their leaders; in a democracy, there's always a sneaking suspicion that the majority gets precisely the government they deserve. And there's demoralizing new evidence that the average American deserves very little.

I sensed a spreading sickness during the Gulf War, when every clergyman I respect and every reputable religious denomination came out foursquare against the war—and 90 percent of their parishioners ignored them. (I can't speak for all faiths, but any Christian clergyman who chooses our current series of designer wars over his faith and his conscience is unfit to say the name "Jesus" aloud, and secretly knows it.) Now it's confirmed in a new book called *The Day America Told the Truth*, the result of a confidential survey of 5,700 Americans: In spite of all the lip service to God, Jesus and heaven that turns up in standard polls, most Americans pay no attention to the nagging voice of religion. In this survey only one of five had ever consulted a clergyman, and only one in eight believes that all Ten Commandments still apply. America's awkward shotgun marriage between God and Mammon is souring in the ugliest way.

And it gets much worse, in this report compiled from lengthy questionnaires people filled out in 50 locations around the country. The prevailing impression we get from the Orbit Lounge incident and a thousand like it is that there are people in the streets with no discernible human feelings—no empathy, no guilt, no conscience. The new survey, which probably includes very few criminals, drug addicts or mental patients, seems to confirm this abysmal indifference to the deaths or sufferings of others. *Seven percent* of these people admitted that they'd murder a perfect stranger for a cool $10 million.

The next time you're in a crowd of 50 people, reflect on the fact that three or four of them would murder you in cold blood if the price was right. And of course the price is morally irrelevant. These are cheerful volunteers for eternal damnation.

If you'd consider first-degree murder, there's no reason to be squeamish about lying, cheating, stealing or committing adultery, and the survey indicates that most Americans aren't. Asked what they'd most like to change about their lives, two-thirds said they'd like to be thinner and wealthier.

"Most Americans are very confused about their personal morals right now," the book concludes, with hilarious generosity. Why mince words? Surveys come and go, but what this one tells us is that the long-suffering little guy the cartoonists label John Q. Public is a vicious, amoral swine.

If religious morality has vanished as a force in most Americans' lives, where do young people turn for their values? Their parents are failing them. "People just don't pay attention to their kids," says the owner of the Orbit Lounge. Divorce and two-career marriages have taken a terrible toll; our gruesome diet of headlines about crack babies, Fetal Alcohol Syndrome, neglect and physical and sexual abuse of children indicates that there are few societies where the sacrament of parenthood is more widely profaned.

Can kids find their way by instinct? No help there. Bird dogs have more constructive natural instincts than human beings. Learn from each other? Worst choice of all. Multiply a troubled teenager by three and you seem to get a pack of assassins. The starving public schools are impotent, morally neutral. That leaves television—sex, violence, gossip and poisonous advertising that says, "You can have it all." Not to mention sitcoms that manage, with style alone, to so thoroughly trivialize love, death, loss, betrayal and all the major milestones in human lives that you wonder how anyone in their audiences could summon up an honest emotion. Fifteen percent of the survey subjects said they preferred TV to sex.

What about the media, the noble free press? I think kids ignore us, but the survey indicates that their parents despise us. As usual the press was ranked dead last among American institutions, way below fictional TV characters as "a moral authority" in these people's lives. I despair of the press myself. But I doubt that people in this poll are disgusted, like me, at the obsequious way the press makes love to power. I suspect they're furious with that dutiful remnant of the free press that sometimes—rarely—tells them honestly what they are and what they're creating.

America is a tough audience for a preacher, now that war has been established as the most effective national mood elevator since Elavil. In such a moral vacuum, it's little wonder that so many of our children end up in prison—at least one in four black males, at last count. Little wonder that the streets of Long Beach, California, are so dangerous that many of the city's 45,000 Cambodian refugees are moving out, complaining that Long Beach is no better than home—home of the Khmer Rouge and *The Killing Fields*.

Without ethics—without right and wrong—a free country is merely licentious, and obscene. Nothing could be more obscene than a nation of defiant convicts and furious jailers, a reality evident nowhere more clearly than here in the Carolinas. We can't build enough prisons. "Build them and they will come," we say down here. When is it late in the game? When the one sure legacy of a free society, besides horrendous debt and pollution, is miles of high walls with guard towers and millions of windows with bars.

History doesn't offer a patriot much consolation. J. Edgar Hoover was the ugliest American of all, and maybe the most powerful. The devil sent him to test our moral courage and nearly everyone failed the test, especially three presidents.

A Nation of Finks

If I had died in Vietnam in 1967, like my friend Brooks, I would have died believing that all sex was safe sex, that typewriters were forever and that presidents of the United States respected the law and their marriage vows. I'd have died believing that civil rights were a national priority, that Richard Nixon and Ronald Reagan were tired California jokes with no future in national politics and that the martyred president John F. Kennedy had better sexual manners, and morals, than the average neighborhood gangster.

Back then every one of us believed that Grace Kelly, revered even by the septic tabloids, was a fairytale princess with the upright morals of a Catholic matron. The things we've learned, Brooks, that we never wanted to know. Revisionist histories, kiss-and-tell memoirs and psychosexual biographies have soiled every reputation and dispelled every illusion that sustained us Americans when we were young and dumb.

It's natural to recoil, to shut our ears against the latest whisper. Usually we can afford to ignore it; sometimes we can't. Sometimes, like the Russians squirming under Stalin's long shadow, like the French wrestling with the ugly secrets of their collaboration with the Nazis, we're obliged to confront the worst things we know if we ever expect to put them behind us.

It's more than just a miserable irony to discover that Walt Disney, who has become an international symbol of American culture and the American imagination, was a key stool pigeon for the FBI in its war on the Hollywood "Reds." It was never disputed that Disney, a Red-baiting union-breaker and a ruthless opportunist, was a right-wing force in his industry. But Marc Eliot's unauthorized biography—*Walt Disney: Hollywood's Dark Prince*—promises to supply another essential piece of a dismal portrait of postwar America that's emerging gradually from the secret files of the Cold War.

It's a portrait we're going to have to look at, when it's complete.

It's a portrait of our time—of our lives. My brother gave me a tape of William S. Burroughs reading a numbing epitaph for America ("The last and greatest betrayal of the last and greatest of human dreams") titled "A Thanksgiving Prayer." Burroughs may not be the single most reliable witness to our common experience. But I can't forget one of the lines in his prayer: "Thanks for a nation of finks."

Walt Disney, designated "full Special Agent in Charge Contact," was a kind of commissioned officer in the Bureau's mercenary army of informers and spies—the legion of finks. Disney's dirty little history of snooping and snitching is a tale worth telling because of the man who put him up to it, the master he served faithfully for 30 years.

We've learned only recently that J. Edgar Hoover was a bizarre homosexual, a closet drag queen, a kind of Lavrenti Beria in fishnet stockings. This information is especially disturbing if we recall that homosexual smears and homosexual blackmail were among Hoover's favorite power plays. The targets of his smears included Adlai Stevenson and the Nixon team of John Ehrlichman and H.R. Haldeman. "Homosexuals are the worst security risks of all," said Hoover, applying his eye shadow.

Twenty years after his death Hoover has become a laughingstock, the butt of cheap gay jokes on late-night TV. But he was no laughingstock when he ruled Washington, by blackmail and intimidation, for almost 50 years. He was the dark at the top of the stairs. No other American of any era has been such a fountainhead of evil, dishonesty and dishonorable behavior. If Walt Disney was the Dark Prince of Hollywood, J. Edgar Hoover was the Emperor of Hell.

Hoover was the big worm in the American apple. He was the power behind every political figure you despised, if you're even a moderate progressive, and he was the force that destroyed, or attempted to destroy, every political figure you admired. Disney, with his image as the whimsical "Uncle Walt" of children's entertainment, is especially distasteful in his role as an FBI informer. But he was by no means the most prominent of Hoover's snitches.

Ronald Reagan, who carried the code name "Source T-10," was a president of the Screen Actors Guild who specialized in spying on his union brothers for the FBI. Gerald Ford was a special

Hoover protégé; he served as the FBI's mole on the Warren Commission, and carried out Hoover's vendetta, culminating in an unsuccessful impeachment proceeding, against Justice William O. Douglas. Joe McCarthy was considered by insiders to be Hoover's creature entirely. Richard Nixon, who earned his witchhunter's stripes prosecuting Alger Hiss, had been in Hoover's pocket since he first arrived in Washington. According to biographer Curt Gentry, Hoover bragged to his aides that he had "created" Nixon.

J. Edgar Hoover, lipstick and all, is a chapter of American history no one can afford to ignore. There's every indication that he would have been Joseph Stalin, if he had been born in Moscow instead of in Washington, D.C. He demonstrated as early as 1919, in the FBI's infamous "Red raids," that he cared nothing for the American Constitution or the civil rights of American citizens, if those citizens appeared to be radicals or "Reds."

His vanity and his paranoia were boundless. "The FBI Story," the TV show with Efrem Zimbalist that we all watched when we were kids, was virtually produced by Hoover as a mirror for his ego. When an enemy appeared on his horizon, he moved to destroy him with a ferocity that Stalin would have envied. There was never a hint of scruples. Political hardball wasn't really an American sport until Hoover invented it. When he heard that a major magazine was preparing an unflattering series on the FBI, he went into his files for photographs of the publisher's wife having sex with her chauffeur in Rock Creek Park, and mailed them to newspapers all over the country. The series never ran.

Maybe it was the democratic system that saved us from even more of J. Edgar Hoover. His bulldog face on campaign posters would have frightened children, and his secret homosexuality may have kept him from reaching for the Oval Office itself. But Curt Gentry documents a deal that he made with Thomas E. Dewey in 1948—in return for the FBI's help in defeating Truman, Dewey would have named Hoover attorney general and then Supreme Court justice, with elevation to chief justice after a decent interval.

That was a close election in 1948. Instead of our dictator, Hoover became our secret-keeper, our arm-twister, our dream-buster, our silent censor and enforcer. Most of all, he became an acid test of character for several generations of Americans in public life. It's very depressing to admit that those who failed the test most miserably were the ones who rose to the highest levels of power.

Those who resisted him invariably suffered for it. Of his enemies, only Harry Truman called his bluff and survived.

"All congressmen and Senators are afraid of him," Truman wrote to his wife in 1947. "I'm not and he knows it. If I can prevent it there'll be no NKVD or Gestapo in this country. Edgar Hoover's organization would make a good start toward a citizen spy system."

History shows that Truman was unable to prevent the spreading network of informers and wiretaps that Hoover used to feed McCarthy and HUAC, the notorious House Un-American Activities Committee. Hoover tested the moral courage of America much as the Gestapo tested the Europeans. The Good Germans among us protected themselves and looked the other way. The most ambitious, as always, transformed themselves into active agents of evil. But the penalty was somewhat less dreadful for an American who resisted. It was career damage for the most part, in the worst cases a few months in prison—never death or deportation.

Was Burroughs right about us, then? Is there a special flaw in the national character that accounts for so many willing snitches, ratfinks, scabs, stoolies, Judases among us? What makes us so cooperative with Big Brother when He appears?

It's a question that fascinates me. I grew up believing profoundly in that old male taboo against informing on your mates. It was about as powerful as the taboo against incest, in my adolescent brain. Maybe I got it from the labor songs of Woody Guthrie and Pete Seeger, or a biography of Eugene Debs I read in the ninth grade. But it played a major role in some of my first significant decisions.

I remember confronting a girl I was dating, a tall athlete from Smith named Anne, when I heard that she'd turned in her own roommate for an honor code violation. I was stunned. We weren't really intimate—this was 1962—but we had shared a lot of intense conversation and I thought I knew her. I told her that only one guy at my school had ever done such a thing, and that he was a campus pariah known as Slippery Abes.

Institutions—schools, companies, governments—are always asking us to show our loyalty by doing their dirty work, I told her. But the loyalty they're talking about is always one-sided. Your conscience knows. Honor means obeying the rules if you believe in them, facing the music if you're caught breaking them, *never* shifting the blame to anyone else, *never* informing. Be responsible for yourself, I told her, not for somebody's goddamn system.

I was in a passion. It was our last date. But I still believe almost every word of my tirade, 30 years later. I'm sick with shame for Walt Disney, for Reagan, for all of them. Sure there's a gullibility factor, a real fear of the Red menace that was once epidemic. But isn't it always the opportunists who commit the worst indecencies? Maybe it's those me-first myths of manifest personal destiny that make Americans so prone to betray each other for profit.

The snitches knew what they were doing. Hoover, however he dressed when he was alone, was a shrewd, remorseless infighter who knew that very few people have the guts to do the right thing instead of the safe thing. After his death in 1972, his private secretary destroyed his dreaded personal files—25 filing cabinets, by some reports. In them, presumably, was the whole story of the generation of finks that this monster created. It's not a charming story, but is has a better moral than *Snow White*. Too bad future generations won't have more of it to read to their children.

*I see now that my conclusion in this piece was a little premature. It was-
n't the collapse of civilization I was witnessing, but the death of small
towns. They can no longer support the deep-rooted, flower-conscious
middle class that used to be the backbone of American civilization.*

Ghost Gardens

The Iranian army is using 12-year-old soldiers, "Allah's martyrs," as
human mine detectors in its war against Iraq; Texans cheered and
threw candy and shouted "Trick or treat" at the gates of Huntsville
prison while the state executed "the Candy Man," Ronald Clark
O'Bryan, by lethal injection. If the poor devil heard them, they
must have given him the first certain sense of superiority he ever
felt in his life.

But it isn't always the circus elements, the wide-screen effects,
that provide the most accurate index for the collapse of civilization. Things crumble quietly. A survey noted that the most popular
new names for America's infant daughters were all taken from
soap-opera characters. George Gallup took a poll of Americans to
determine which man and woman they admired most in the whole
wide world, and he came up with Ronald Reagan and Margaret
Thatcher. And depression ambushed this observer during a futile
Easter-week search for perennials.

The only way I can cushion this is by admitting that it happened
up North, which leaves us free to imagine that it's a Yankee disease
that may spread very slowly or not at all. The pathology isn't
entirely clear to me. But I was stunned by the degree of devastation, the sense of village and countryside abandoned, that's con-
veyed by a thing as small as the absence of flowers in their yards.

I arrived on Easter Sunday, near the end of April, leaving the
Carolinas already half-exhausted from their reckless excess of dog-
wood and redbud. I'd last seen New York's hill country in January,
and I found the weather and the landscape virtually unchanged.
The latest and coldest spring on record, they told me. I offered a
silent prayer of appreciation for the Southland, which I was fortunate enough to find when I still had a few good years to stretch my
weary muscles in the sun. But at midweek the rain stopped, the sun
came out and the temperature climbed 35 degrees. And nothing—

or almost nothing—happened. I realized why it had taken me so long to spy a daffodil, why I drove through three villages before I found a crocus. It wasn't just the winter weather. They aren't there anymore.

I'm no gardener myself, but my religious relationship to the seasons was always connected to my faith in the perennials — crocuses, daffodils, tulips, poppies, peonies, irises, lilies-of-the-valley and a dozen others I can't name. The houses of my childhood, my parents' and grandparents' houses and the houses of their neighbors, were all old houses on old properties. Every bed and border held bulbs that they had planted when they were young, or even inherited from earlier owners. When I was young and married, we rented old houses from old women, and the best thing about those houses was watching the unpredictable flower gardens through the spring and summer.

It has more than a casual hold on me. There are a couple of abandoned houses out in the country, in advanced stages of decay, where I go just to see the few daffodils and irises that still come up among the wildflowers, in the tall grass. I never knew the people who lived there, or whether they were still alive. But someone civilized was there. With perennials you can have ghost gardens.

It's natural that I'd notice. Those are old villages up there, and I swear that when I was a kid the yards were full of flowers—around the porches, along the hedges, behind garages. Where are they now? I haven't researched the life spans of the different varieties, but I know from my mother's garden that some of them last decades. Do the young people just fail to replace them, or does it take dogs and children and unchecked rodents to dig them up? There are broken toys and pieces of rusted machinery along the hedges now, and the hedges are ragged. New houses sit on raw new lots as naked as the day they were prefabricated. Big old houses have been carved up into apartments, and the people who live in them must have manured the old flower beds with lye. I checked some of them carefully, on foot. Not a leaf.

I'm interested in anyone's theory. Is this really the generation of nuclear paranoiacs, living on borrowed time, unwilling to send down roots literally or figuratively, afraid to make themselves comfortable on a piece of land? Is it a generation so dazzled by its color television that it lives indoors, and never misses a few colors on the lawn? For some reason they don't plant, or even tend the perennials they inherit. And it's more than flowers. I've seen orchards and vineyards, devoutly tended for 50 years, axed and uprooted by new landowners and replaced by swing sets that rusted in a season.

Perennials are a potent symbol. I've never been a passionate advocate of private property. In my utopian days I visualized a communal arrangement where we'd all walk barefoot through something like Duke Gardens. But if there's one acceptable way to take possession of a piece of property, it's to plant it and tend it and make it more than it was before. If you've ever been to England, you've seen how householders in a land-poor country force every square inch to blossom. Our flowers may be the only aesthetic improvement over untended Nature that we've ever managed. Which makes them the essence of civilization. The most civilized man I ever met was a gardener, a man with no formal education, an hereditary retainer who presided over acres of roses and perennials that belonged to a Scottish marquess. Ford Madox Ford, in his last book, predicted eccentrically but accurately that any civilization that abandoned its gardens was lost.

When we stole all this land from the Indians, civilization was what we were selling and boasting, and their primitive, subsistence agriculture was one of the excuses we used when we grabbed. Now some of the Americans who believe themselves most civilized live in apartments and townhouses and condominiums, blind and deaf to the land. I could never understand that anyone might live by choice where he couldn't have at least an acre of green to plant as he saw fit. But to have that acre and ignore it, to fail even to maintain a few flowers that require almost no maintenance, is to break a covenant that goes back to Thomas Jefferson and Johnny Appleseed. When our houses sit there on our land like bunkers on a battlefield, like checkers on a checkerboard, it's time to give all of it back to the Sioux.

In the news business I've had a fair amount of contact with policemen, most of it positive. Cops are the mine canaries of an endangered society. When they start selling drugs, committing suicide, committing felonious assault and generally deteriorating as a social subtype, there isn't a lot of mileage left in the status quo.

Urban My Lais

St. Petersburg, Florida — My mother and I misplaced a rented car, temporarily. It sounds pathetic, but it could happen to you, in a strange city on a hot day. They all look the same; after you've driven a couple of hundred cars your memory plays tricks sometimes.

The police officer who found it for us—it took him about 10 minutes—was the kind of uniformed patrolman you used to see in Bing Crosby movies, long before *West Side Story* and anticop dramas like *Serpico* and *Prince of the City*. He was courteous, comforting, even charming, and humorous without making us feel like complete imbeciles. He projected that reassuring combination of confidence and amiability that makes actors rich and politicians dangerous.

Of course Mother and I don't look much like the kind of people who come to Florida to ambush policemen and steal their squad cars. But most of my exchanges with police officers, over the years, have been almost as successful as this rescue by the model cop in St. Petersburg. I think that's true for most people who live inside the law and *look* as if they do, and this is a good time for us to remember all the cops who were there when we needed them. I bring it up, of course, because the savage Tonton Macoute–style beating of a black LA motorist by a gang of werewolves with badges has put the police on the defensive. The amateur videotape of this atrocity silenced a lot of optimists who would have rejected any report of such an incident ("not in America") if they hadn't seen it with their own eyes.

We have no right to assume that there are a lot of policemen who would have participated in the attempted murder of Rodney King. But we have every right to ask, How many?

The man with the videocamera, George Holliday, is an American hero 100 times the magnitude of Schwarzkopf of Arabia, if he shocks this country out of its habitual denial and the civic and patriotic boosterism that passes for public concern. In our media, selected nations, usually socialist or critical of American foreign policy, are routinely stigmatized as "police states" and charged with "human rights violations." But what about the human rights of Rodney King? If American self-righteousness isn't an incurable disease, those horrific video images should be some of the strongest medicine we've ever taken.

Much of this country's denial is the product of honest ignorance. The United States is by and large a comfortable, indulgent place for middle-class white people. I've seen police stupidity, belligerence and incompetence; I've never seen anything approaching police brutality. With luck I never will.

But there are law-abiding American citizens who see it almost every day. They live in a police state, and they take it for granted that their children will, too. The racism and sadism of a minority of police officers—and no few police administrators—aren't really the source of their misfortune, and they know it.

The rogue cop and his victim are both casualties of a conscious government policy to abandon a whole class of Americans, as well as the cities where most of them live.

Much was made of the black Marine recruits, during the war in the Gulf, who told reporters in Buffalo that they'd feel much safer in Kuwait than they ever felt at home. "Fight here, fight there," said one 18-year-old, "It's all the same to me." Most newspapers played up the black Desert Storm veteran who was gunned down in the street in front of his home in Detroit a week after he left Saudi Arabia (it turned out that he was murdered by a faithless girlfriend and her brother). But apparently it takes combat footage to convince most people that the cities are a war zone. George Holliday gave them combat footage. Perhaps CNN, as a follow-up, would provide us with a documentary tour of the South Bronx, where huge areas look just like Kuwait City after they called off the bombs. Only the Bechtel Corporation isn't moving into the Bronx to rebuild it overnight and better than new.

In the Bronx, in Detroit, in LA and East St. Louis there are vast dead zones of architectural and biological devastation, America's Lebanons, patrolled by packs of murderers, scavengers and dealers in deadly chemicals. It's a world after the Apocalypse, like the one in *The Road Warrior*, where survivors band together for protection, where no one but a superhero has the guts to be a loner. I found an article on the rapid growth of youth gangs, whose membership, in America's 45 largest cities alone, is now estimated at over 120,000. Since 1984 the average age of members has dropped from 15 to 13 1/2. The phenomenon has nothing to do with moral decay or anti-social behavior, the article made very clear. The kids join for protection—and for family. In most cases, a gang is the only place where these kids can find either.

In the dead zones, the first law is the Law of the Jungle, the law of combat survival—everyone is presumed to be armed and dangerous, and whoever shoots first lives longest.

Deliberate neglect has created outposts of hell, a few miles as the crow flies from luxury condominiums, million-dollar homes and manicured golf courses. No other nation suffers from such a sickening case of contrasts. Anyone can drive across the tracks and see the dead zones for himself, if he has more courage than good sense.

But in fact a middle-class American never sees the dead zones up close—unless he joins the police force. Police atrocities like the beating of Rodney King emerge from the same paranoid nightmare that produced the massacre at My Lai. There's no way to excuse the police officers, as there was no way to excuse Lt. Calley and his platoon. And LA police chief Daryl Gates should lose his job if he said half the insensitive things they attribute to him. But it wasn't the weak moral fiber of American soldiers that My Lai exposed, it was the moral and political blindness of the leaders who left them to their own devices in Vietnam. By the same logic, a national movement to reform police forces is a completely inadequate and irrelevant response to the shock that George Holliday's videotape produced.

America forgets about the deadly messes its policies create until the guys who are supposed to contain them begin to buckle under the strain. LA is a war zone, no less than My Lai. Extreme conditions produce extreme behavior in all types, and the worst types tend to step forward. Some instances of police overreaction are so extreme they defy explanation. Three years ago in Tampa, a gardener named David Bailey heard a noise in his yard. Thieves had been stealing his gardening tools, so he stepped outside and fired a shot to scare them away. Two police officers, who had come to question his son, immediately riddled Bailey with 18 bullets. His body was found with holes in the soles of his feet.

The officers who killed Bailey might have been out of their minds—or scared out of their wits. Much like the troops in Vietnam, they're in a place where they don't belong, where the enemy and the innocent bystander look just alike. Denizens of the dead zones don't come labeled Good and Bad, Armed and Unarmed, and one mistake can be fatal if you're a cop. Last year 63 officers were killed in the line of duty.

Added to police paranoia is the frustration of seeing most of the people they arrest go free. Fewer than 10 percent of the people arrested for serious crimes ever serve serious time in prison. Risking life and limb to apprehend the same criminal he previously arrested in March, June and September, a cop can get peculiar. It's hard to tell who's on the edge or over the edge, about to change from a public guardian into a deadly predator.

Like the trial of Lt. Calley, the Rodney King incident forces Americans to ask themselves a simple question: Who are we? Some of the answers are getting ugly. We're a nation of unimaginable personal wealth where one of every eight children is hungry and one of four is undernourished; in the dead zones thousands of children are born with AIDS, Fetal Alcohol Syndrome and cocaine addiction. "We're putting kids into graves instead of kindergarten," said a Florida children's advocate, Jack Levine.

We're a nation where nervous police forces, apparently strained to the breaking point, struggle to hold the lids on ghettoes spilling over with illegal drugs, legal firearms, homeless families, derelicts and disease. Federal money is always available for new weapons but never for low-cost housing or social services. The most successful politicians never talk about rescuing the children of the poor. They ask for more prisons, longer sentences, more executions, more cops.

Genocide is a strong word that's applied too casually in political rhetoric, too often. But it's a word that describes America's policy toward its poor, and their cities, as well as it described our policies in Southeast Asia. It's no less lethal for being passive and bumbling. President Bush is so hopelessly out of touch with the realities of the poor that his responses would be hilarious, if they weren't tragic. "Lend, spend, invest," he urged his fellow Americans, if they hope to end the recession. With what? The rent money, or the next windfall from the numbers runners?

There are no surefire formulas for reviving the dead zones. But money is necessary, and the Republicans with their ridiculous trickle-down theories have multiplied the agonies of the poor. Killer cops are one symptom of a general systemic failure, a failure of good will and common sense. We don't need better cops—we need better national priorities, so cops can get back to helping befuddled tourists and their mothers. We're losing this war on every front. Do you need a picture? George Holliday has some pictures you won't forget.

Even if you got past the age of drug abuse relatively unscathed, drugs are bound to hurt you in the long run—as a parent, a crime victim or a tax-payer. Chances are you won't be hurt as bad as Patrick Donahoe. I can't seem to shake the image of this two-year-old with his throat cut.

The Tomato Field

You may have noticed that 1988 A.D. is not a year that began well. The papers were full of mass murders—family affairs as usual. "A loner," neighbors said. "Kept his distance." And at the bottom of every column, one of those two-paragraph horrors that appear in clusters when a bad moon is full:

"Frozen Woman's Head Is Missing."

"Indian Man with World's Longest Mustache Found Beheaded."

"Girls, 9 and 4, Found Strangled in Burning House."

"Girl, 19, Shot 26 Times—Father Sought."

At 7:00 a.m., January 1, in front of the Love People One Disco in New York, two New Year's Eve revelers quarreled over who stepped on whose shoes. One man produced an Uzi 9mm machine gun and blasted the other man's legs out from under him.

Inauspicious. But a friend saw the dark mood I was in and counseled me against beginning the year with this column. "Write against your mood," an old tired columnist warned me long ago. Choose a cheerful subject when you're cheerful and you'll manufacture saccharine three times out of four. Choose misery when you're miserable and the result is often bathos and self-pity. It's like the best advice for drinkers: drink when you're tired, drink when you're irritable or frustrated, but never drink when you're really depressed. There's no such thing as "drowning your sorrows." Sorrows are fish.

So I waited a couple of weeks, a month almost. I feel a little better. But not about Patrick Donahoe, Jr. The Associated Press took just four paragraphs to tell Patrick's story. The longer I hold on to the clipping, datelined Accomac, Va., the more my imagination fleshes it out. The thing's gaining weight, it's getting heavy. It's a novella already and it will be a feature film if I don't get rid of it now.

The bare facts would have more impact delivered in a baritone, in a radio style like Paul Harvey's. Print is a limited medium. Patrick Donahoe, Sr., 25, was out for a drive with Patrick Jr., age two. Headed nowhere in particular, apparently, and in no hurry to get there. Donahoe picked up a hitchhiker, Dean Edward Crowell, a young man his own age.

They got on well, at first. They drank some beer, they smoked some marijuana. At some point one of them produced a quantity of cocaine, which added its momentum to the occasion. I don't know the time frame here, or how Patrick Jr. amused himself while the men were making friends. But at some point it began to go sour. Knives came out. In a tomato field somewhere along the Eastern Shore, Donahoe Sr. and Crowell tried to kill each other.

Crowell was the winner by a wide margin, leaving Donahoe for dead with 22 stab wounds. There was only one witness, and he was two, but that was one witness too many for Crowell. He stabbed the boy six times and cut his throat.

With 22 holes in him, Donahoe crawled out of the tomato field and more than a mile down the road to a farmhouse for help. He survived, and so did his son. Crowell, who drove away with a double murder on whatever passed for his conscience, was eventually convicted of malicious wounding and grand larceny, and sentenced to 45 years in prison. In court he argued self-defense and insisted that the stabbing of Patrick Jr.—all seven wounds—was "a mistake."

Talk about your heart of darkness. The story haunts me. It would mean less if Patrick were merely one of thousands of innocents martyred annually by crazy parents and carnivorous loners. Their deaths, the deaths of the New Year's massacres, have become a grisly cliché. But this little boy lived. What did he see? Try a nonjudgmental, infant's-eye view. Think of the expressions on the faces of two-year-olds when they look at something they've never seen before. Patrick will be growing up, and people will be watching Patrick. The scar will be there to remind anyone who might forget who he is.

Presumably, Patrick still lives with his father. I wouldn't care to bet that 22 stab wounds have converted Patrick Sr. to Jesus Christ and Diet Coke. We miss the point if we marvel that things like Dean Edward Crowell are out there thumbing rides. The Donahoes didn't pick up the devil on a back road in Accomack County. Crowell had no special history of violence. Up to the point where he panicked and cut the child's throat, there's no evidence that he was any more deranged than Donahoe.

The devil was already in the car. Donahoe and Crowell both belong to a growing underclass of individuals whose lives make no sense at all outside the context of narcotics. I hear that a journalist is researching a book that will blame the stock market crash in part on cocaine, focusing on the drug habits of a few key players. But down in the tomato field, at the level where Donahoe and Crowell fought for their lives, the players are losing more than their money, and society is losing more than economic stability. These people marry, work and raise children, after a fashion, but mainly they commit crimes.

Bloodless statistics lose stature next to a story like Patrick's. But there's a new one that may change the entire philosophy of law enforcement. Urine tests of 2000 men arrested for felonies in 12 cities showed that 70 percent were using illegal drugs. Over half had taken them within 48 hours. Tests for hard drugs (excluding marijuana) ran as high as 74 percent positive in Washington, D.C. Preliminary data in a similar screen of women indicated an even higher percentage of drug dependency.

Drug dealers weren't included in the sample, and few of the subjects had narcotics arrests on their records. The scandal is that law enforcement officials, as recently as 1984, had estimated that only 20 percent of serious street crimes were connected to drugs. Cause-and-effect is still open to argument, but the new study suggests that in this country drug use and criminal activity are almost insepara-ble. Late and lame as usual, a Justice Department official has declared, "If we are going to do something about the crime rate, we are going to have to confront the drug problem."

During the Administration's brief and half-sincere War On Drugs, an unnatural alliance was formed between some of us who were horrified by the civil-rights implications of drug tests for unac-cused job-seekers, and another group that dismissed the whole issue of drug abuse as a red herring. As usual, Washington had taken a moronic, inappropriate approach to the problem. But the problem, far from imaginary, was even bigger than Reagan rhetoric had dared to suggest. While upscale magazines were declaring drugs "out" for trendsetters, like long skirts or last year's rock group, the same drugs were turning the economy's permanent losers into a permanent criminal class. And the most pathetic delusion, common among Republicans, is that drugs can be sealed off in the trailer parks and housing projects, where the middle-class kids will never find them. Drugs are a bond, a common language that bridges class barriers. If, for instance, you're interested in a truly integrated extracurricular activity, check out the lunch-hour drug market in most high-school parking lots.

When we think of children as the innocent victims of calamity or pure evil, our images are from Auschwitz, Hiroshima, the Ethiopian famines. Drugs are going to destroy more children—and more adults—than all of that. The pictures of children dying of AIDS because their mothers used needles are effective enough, but their tragedies came quietly, from within. I submit the picture of Patrick Donahoe, Jr., the world's oldest toddler, with the ugly scar on his throat. I never put much stock in the John Birch Society, but they got a lot of mileage and a lot of political passion out of the martyr they designated as the first American victim of communism. The War On Drugs might amount to something if the Patrick Donahoe Society could stay half as angry about what happened to Pat.

IX

*S*ex and Gender — Hitting below the Belt

In some ways I'm more puritanical than you'd expect, for an American who reached manhood in the Age of Aquarius. My kids have noticed it. I come from the old school that believes you should do it as much as you like but almost never talk about it, certainly never with anyone except your lover or your shrink. I think Calvin Klein, Madonna, Howard Stern, Karen Finley and all 57 syndicated talk-show hosts and their guests should be turned loose naked on a monkey island at the zoo, to rut and root and gawk at each other until they drop dead or lose interest, whichever comes first. But sex is a great thing to write about because readers can sense your sincerity, your lack of detachment. They know I'm really arguing with myself, even when I sound like a marriage counselor.

One thing almost all fools have in common is that they are enemies of sex. Christian militants stone it, gender radicals poison it, swingers and kinkos gross us out with it and New Age self-helpers talk it to death. The sexual hypocrisy of right-wing fundamentalists is matched by the infantile peek-a-boo pornography of the flaming Left fringe. Sexuality and sexual identity have inspired more wretched prose and wretched thinking than any subject this side of religion. This is a country where infinitely more energy is expended prying people apart than bringing them together. The best thing to do is ignore everything except your own instincts. If they don't arrest you or come to your house with torches and pitchforks, you're probably going to be all right.

*Married men in their forties still think about sex even more than basket-
ball. But they begin to feel that the gap is closing.*

Do You Believe in Magic?

We were sitting up late in the back room of a bistro in Greenwich
Village, the lawyer and I, nursing the last of the wine and talking
in an unguarded late-night way about sex and marriage. The newspapers had been full of the spectacular and ultimately fatal sex life
of the great basketball player Earvin "Magic" Johnson and the new
autobiography by Earvin's apparent role model, basketball immortal Wilt Chamberlain, who claims in his book to have enjoyed the
sexual favors of approximately 20,000 women.

Wilt scored over 30,000 points in 14 years in the NBA, but if we
figure two points for a field goal we find that he claims more
women than field goals and free throws combined. (He once scored
100 points in one game, and 12 women at one birthday party.)
Numbers like these are bewildering to men—and presumably
women—like me and the lawyer, who have been married for most
of our adult lives. But even the sexual adventures of our single
friends had left us pensive. If we were missing out on something,
what was it exactly? If variety is such a shallow, adolescent
approach to human sexuality, why do so many people risk everything, including their lives, in its pursuit? What's normal out there?
Are they sick and jaded, men like Johnson and Chamberlain, or
are the rest of us timid and stunted?

These are honest questions. Most of the news stories that capture
the public's imagination—Clarence Thomas and Anita Hill, Willie
Smith, Jimmy Swaggart, The Little Rascals Day Care Center, Jim
Bakker and Jessica Hahn, Gary Hart and Donna Rice—are about
sex. But when Earvin Johnson tested positive for the virus that causes
AIDS, it cast a different kind of shadow. It wasn't only that one of
America's most wholesome images was suddenly linked with what
had been characterized as its most unwholesome disease. It was the
sudden cancelation of the myth of immortality that embraced the
young, the rich, the talented, the beautiful—and the fashionably
promiscuous. Out in the fast lane where many young Americans
hope to travel, there had been a tragic collision with reality.

The first wave of reaction ...as relatively sensible. AIDS activists expressed the hope that Johnson's infection would help to remove the stigma from this epidemic and make it easier to raise money for patient care and research. I think that's a very reasonable hope. I agree, also, that many lives will be saved because young people will be frightened into more responsible sexual behavior.

But as the ripple effect continued—surely no one since Lou Gehrig has had so many column inches dedicated to his illness— narrower politics began to color the debate. The "safe sex" move- ment that recruited Johnson as its champion began to antagonize conservatives who don't believe that all the world's sexual prob- lems can be solved by draping them in latex. Why, they asked, are we making a holy martyr out of a sexually reckless young man who destroyed his life by ignoring Christian morality, and probably infected any number of young women along the way? On the same pages where he had been praised as America's fallen hero a week before, Magic Johnson saw himself denounced as a predatory degenerate.

Beyond the obvious, beyond one athlete's tragedy and its reper- cussions lies the morass, the trackless Great Swamp of human sexu- ality. You might think it takes a lot of courage for me to wade into it, when I have only a few minutes of your attention. But at the very least Magic Johnson set us an example of courage when he came clean, when others might have stalled and hidden. And I can't drown in that Swamp any faster than a lot of pilgrims who came before me.

Sigmund Freud himself has been diligently and ingeniously discred- ited by his own intellectual descendants, but he probably under- stated the case when he blamed almost everything on sex. Sex is the great secret reality, the iceberg of which history is only the tip. The misogyny which informs most of western civilization was spawned by the male's superstitious terror of his own relentless sex drive. Creepy St. Paul and the Christian ascetics who came after him turned their fear into a pathology that still infects the church.

Most churches have not done well with sex, and the Catholic Church has allowed itself to become almost irrelevant, almost ridiculous. Sex is a biological imperative. You can dress it up in Christian marriage and middle-class pieties but it will just get naked again and jump on the furniture, lewd and rude as a Barbary ape. Even the most liberal churchmen have stumbled. When Episcopal bishop John Spong stuck his neck way out to ordain an openly homosexual priest, the man double-crossed him by refusing to embrace monogamy as the church prescribed, and the bishop was forced to back down.

Monogamy wasn't sympathetic to his lifestyle, the priest said. Respect for alternative "lifestyles" is the cornerstone of a liberal's faith. But if a liberal churchman has to respect the lifestyle of the gay priest as well as the celebrity, African-American sporting lifestyle reflected by Wilt Chamberlain and his 20,000 girl friends, does that mean Christian morality only applies to straight, poor, uncoordinated white people?

Impasse, it seems to me. Can one man's pursuit of happiness be another man's mortal sin? Contradiction lies in every direction. A church that reserves sex for married couples—and most of them still do, officially—has fallen so far behind 21st-century realities that I fear for its survival. No church could hope to keep pace with the sexual revolution that was triggered by scientific birth control and the liberation of women.

But the church deserves a hearing because it still takes sex so seriously. And not merely the consequences, but the act itself. It's a conservative influence I've come to applaud. Perhaps the greatest stupidity of the back-to-nature, flower-power movement of the '60s was its self-indulgent conviction that all sex was good sex, that sex was some benevolent organic activity like breast-feeding or mulching the asparagus. Hippies shared it, did it with friends and with strangers, did it in front of their children, did it on acid and did it in the road.

The Aquarians thought they were close to nature, but nature's next trick was herpes, and then AIDS. It doesn't pay to sell Venus cheap. And no one, in my learned opinion, ever really enjoyed sex with someone who thought it was as "natural" as milking a cow. I take my own erotic philosophy from the late Lee Marvin, who said that it wasn't worth doing unless there was a demon sitting on the bedpost that both of you could see. A small demon.

There's a natural progression from that dopey Aquarian self-indulgence to the "safe sex" rallies that followed the Magic Johnson revelation, with athletes and educators tossing free condoms like Mardi Gras trinkets to kids who aren't old enough to drive. Is this where we are, as a society? I understand that the little boogers are doing it like rabbits, mainly because their parents no longer take the time and the trouble to separate them. I don't think their premature rut should be punished with pregnancy, or sickness, or death. I would be, reluctantly, among the parents who voted to install the condom machines in the high-school bathrooms. We have to start by assuming the worst. But of course this sends the wrong message, as the church and the Right have been saying, and it's abandoning territory that we should never have conceded in the first place. Latex is no salvation, no substitute for a functioning brain that occasionally outvotes your gonads.

There's no such thing as safe sex, for two. Sex is too volatile, and the truth about it is elusive. Both extremes have it dead wrong—sex isn't wholesome and it isn't disgusting, it isn't an unqualified blessing or an unqualified curse. It's never clean and simple, like eating leafy vegetables. It's never neutral. And it's not for kids.

Sour grapes, you're free to say, from an aging Puritan whose salad days have long since wilted into compost. On one of those warm, strange nights last week I was sitting on my deck watching the full moon rise over Mt. Bolus, and I felt this strange discomfort, almost like nausea. I thought it was the swordfish steak and then I realized that it was *desire*, that old dumb unfocused kind that makes you want to run along the creek in the moonlight and rub against the trees. It had been awhile.

Laugh if you like. I've suffered from some culture shock, some disorientation. All my life, friends and counselors warned me that I had overweighted sex in the great scheme of things, a miscalculation that would cost me dearly. Then I hear about Wilt Chamberlain and his 20,000 handmaidens, and I realize that I was nothing but a hermit in a cave. But the Wall Street lawyer and I worked out a position we could live with, over the last of the wine. It helped that he was a Roman Catholic, no stranger to restraint.

For all its power and persistence, we decided, sex is like almost everything else an adult has to deal with. It requires a balance between self-denial and self-indulgence—walking that thin line between living an empty life and living one that's too messy, too painful and possibly too short. No one in his right mind really wants a long line of groupies waiting outside his door, fixing their makeup and holding numbers like fast-food customers. But no one wants to spend his life on the wrong side of a locked door, listening to the screams and giggles inside.

If you never listen to that voice from south of the beltline, your life will be less interesting, less memorable, less intense; if you listen too often your life will be a shambles. And the people who never say "no" have made it a lot more complicated for the rest of us.

*You reach an age when you think you have something to contribute, and
you know your kids won't listen. Maybe no one listens, but this is better
advice to the lovelorn than anything I've found in Ann Landers.*

Miss Lonelyhearts Returns

Walter Gibbs, a South Dakota farmer, was 58 when he married
Delores Christenson, who was 18. Ten years later he divorced her
and married her twin sister, Darlene. Through two more divorces
and remarriages to the same women, Gibbs never exactly made up
his mind. Somewhere along in there he married a third woman,
too, but even his friends are confused. When Gibbs was 84, Darlene tried to burn his house down with him asleep inside. Four
months before her conviction for that crime, she and her current
husband—a convicted pig rustler—smothered Gibbs in his bed.
Her twin sister, heir to Gibbs' $178,000 estate, was acquitted of
conspiracy when her lawyer convinced the jury that she was too
stupid to conspire; Darlene, already serving 50 years for arson, was
sentenced to life.

"Walter was a nice guy until he got mixed up with those nitwit
twins," said a friend. "They're crazier than a couple of bedbugs."

But love comes in all flavors, and the winters in South Dakota
are long and hard. To say that Walter loved not wisely seems to
imply that wisdom is the norm. In our hearts we know better. For
every erotic history like Walter Gibbs', highlighted with the black-
comedy violence of the mentally disadvantaged, there are a dozen
middle-class histories so irrational and neurotic they'd have equal
comic impact if they ever went out on the news wires. It doesn't
take a set of bedbug twins to make a fool for love. All the dumbest
behavior of the smartest people is reserved for what we now call
their "relationships."

I'm no exception, and only an idiot would dare to boast that he
was cured. But as I reach the age where erotic confusion subsides
somewhat—perhaps it picks up again later, as it did for Walter
Gibbs—and labor to preserve what appears to be the first "healthy"
relationship of my long demented life, for the first time I have
enough distance to experience amazement at the way relationship
anxieties eat up the lives of American adults. For the dissatisfied,

the unattached and the in-transition, the headlines are only background music. Economic and ecological disaster, made-for-TV
wars, military pageants that would embarrass Caligula—none of it
really distracts them from the painful, time-consuming ordeals that
Americans have made of their mating.

This is, of course, a new development. The arts and sciences of
relationships date only from the decline of male supremacy. "Relationship" recognizes that two people are making choices, an inno-
vation that doesn't go back 100 years. There were always different
kinds of marriages. If a man was neither kind nor intelligent, he
treated his wife like a domestic animal; if he was kind but not intelligent, he treated her like a beloved animal; if he was intelligent
enough to acknowledge her humanity, he gave her rights and dignity. But it was all up to him.

The decay of the patriarchy, along with the rapid decline of
marriage, has given men and women a bewildering array of new
choices—too many for most of them to handle. Instead of the
exhilaration of free and equal mating, many women experienced a
loss of nerve and gave new meaning to "the meat-market mentality" by participating in an epidemic of gross and dangerous cosmetic
surgery. Breast implants are a booming industry that didn't suffer at
all when TDA, a carcinogen derived from the polyurethane foam
covering implants, was found in the milk of a nursing mother.

Men, for their part, responded to the open mating market with
an unprecedented wave of violence against women. Male infantil-
ism and extended adolescence are in fashion now, celebrated by
commercial music. The producers of daytime freak shows like
"Oprah" and "Geraldo!" have documented an astonishing variety
of new sexual hybrids that I, for one, do not view with optimism.
At the very least, these wayward adults are creating a psychological
minefield that few of their children will safely negotiate.

We are poor little lambs who have lost our way. The change has
been too rapid, and almost no guidance is available. Religion is 50
years behind; when the sexuality task force of the liberal Presbyter-
ian church submitted a report asking the church to extend its blessing to homosexual and extramarital relationships, outraged delegates voted it down 534-31. Laws in this country reflect a 19th-
century fantasy of wholesome Christian families. Public opinion is
more hypocritical and conservative than the courts and churches.

Even the 1,212-page *Ann Landers Encyclopedia*, the accumulated wisdom of Eppie Lederer, devotes only 28 lines to Love (under the heading "Love or Infatuation?"), less than half the space allotted to Warts and Wet Dreams. The literature of contemporary relationships is uniformly undistinguished, copious if you read supermarket tabloids, women's magazines, New Age psychobabble and self-help gurus, almost nonexistent if you don't. "The monotonous discovery of common sense," Russell Jacoby called the flourishing self-help industry. Much of its advice to consenting adults is hilarious. I found this passage in *Living, Loving & Learning* by the irrepressible Leo Buscaglia (who used the word "beautiful" so many times I gave up counting after three chapters):

> *Woe be it unto you if you give yourself totally to another. You're lost forever. Maintain yourself as the others maintain themselves. Then you put "They" together and form "Us." Then work on the "Us," and that us gets bigger and bigger while the "You" and the "I" get bigger and bigger and form these enormous concentric circles that grow forever! Intimacy is that wonderful "Us."*

I hear you, Leo. Thanks for sharing that with us. In an emotional wilderness where the only road signs are crazy ones like Leo's, some of the best people I know are wandering aimlessly, wondering what happened to their lives. The popularity of Personals (DWM, 50, seeks any human contact) indicates that some people will take almost any risk in the pursuit of "relationships"; the lucrative phone-sex industry indicates that a lot of other people are just too wounded to go on.

Who will lead these lost tribes out of the wilderness? There's no Moses lurking in the self-help shelves. Would they follow someone who doesn't charge admission? I wouldn't come forward if it didn't seem like such a crisis. But the Miss Lonelyhearts of the '90s needs brand-new strategies, and I've been working on one. I call it Tough Love for Adults. Grownups who learned to stand up to the drugged-out, amoral teenagers of the '80s have to learn to get tougher with themselves.

Start by flushing the hearts and flowers. I'm a candlelight man myself, as sentimental as they get, but when you're starting from scratch the violins just mask the sound of heavy breathing.

Christian counselors and their New Age counterparts will ruin people with all this talk of "fulfillment" and "enrichment." What we're talking about here is mating. Even Dr. Ruth has the good sense to call a penis a penis. Lust is natural, what responsible people call love is supernatural, and they don't even come from the same family of emotions. Lust is just one of a dozen roads—long, winding roads—that might eventually lead you to the other thing.

Confusion between the heart an the hips is the main cause of misery among the mutually consenting (How am I doing, Leo?). I knew a tough woman who wouldn't have turned over her body, her money or her children to a complete stranger at gunpoint; but she turned them over, regularly, to complete strangers who used the words "love" and "marriage."

Remember there's no such thing as living in sin. God never had any interest in the mating rituals of naked apes, or at least no more interest than he had in salmon spawning or the miracle of maggots on meat. Marriage was instituted to minimize the carnage of rut, when competition for females disabled half the hunters in the tribe. It gave the male child a protector instead of a rival for the favors of his mother, and the old ways went underground as the Oedipus complex.

Marriage has lost credibility. Most men made it work to their advantage and it was probably the best thing for the children, but for women it's been a mixed blessing at best. Marriage should be an option, never a goal. If you live in sin for less than two years before marrying, you're crazy; five years is optimum.

Love and marriage—they go together like a horse and carriage, maybe, but they just make the water muddy when you're trying to clarify a promising relationship. Send that old buggy on its way and you'll be standing on your own two feet. Ready to face the last great obstacle to happy pairing, the dangerous illusion of "direction." At some slack point in their lives most men and women, attached or unattached, go looking for a partner with a sense of direction they find lacking in themselves—a human security blanket. But sometimes those farsighted little dynamos of efficiency and self-regard make pretty miserable companions. Life isn't really about direction. I'm old enough to have seen a lot of my friends get everything they ever wanted and spit it up again. Sometimes the easygoing, affectionate, shiftless lovers of our youth are exactly the ones we want back again when we're 50.

"I'm built for comfort, baby," Taj Mahal used to sing, "I ain't built for speed." All you really need is someone who's good-natured and has no plans for you that you wouldn't have had for yourself. (A steady job now and then doesn't hurt either.) And I'm convinced that the people who mate most successfully are the ones who are tough enough to live alone. Be patient, be generous, but be cool. Loneliness is 100 times better than a destructive relationship, a million times better than a bad marriage; if you wear a sign that says "Lord, don't let me be alone" you're going to end up with Delores and Darlene.

One more thing. If you're looking for a decent relationship, or you're lucky enough to have one worth preserving, don't talk about it all the time. One ghastly legacy of the human potential movement and its psychobabble (read *Psychobabble* by R.D. Rosen) is people who talk about "our relationship" as if it were a third person who just closed the bathroom door or stepped out for a pizza. They take its pulse and its temperature on the hour. I never walked out on anyone in my life, but I've never listened to five minutes of relationship analysis without checking the room for a fire escape. If you can't stop talking about your relationship, you don't have one.

When you hear that guys are paying surgeons to restore their foreskins, you know the American male has been pushed to the breaking point and beyond. Whether it's the men's movement or the women's movement, loss of irony is hurting us as much as loss of trust.

A Different Drum

Jackson, Wyoming — Just before sunrise I parked my car on a bluff above the Snake River and picked my way across 200 yards of wild-flowers and prairie-dog holes to where a bull bison was grazing alone. I stopped about 20 yards short of him, too close as any ranger would have told me; the first light was faint and I was mov-ing very slowly, but he knew I was there.

He was a big bull but maybe not big enough to cut much ice with the herd. Several dozen cows and some calves were grazing under the supervision of the alpha bulls a half-mile away. My bull was one of those who wait their turn, sometimes for years, for the chance to mate. Meanwhile they beef up and brood.

I could identify with that. I rested my elbows on an old section of split-rail fence, and as we ruminated together the sun broke sud-denly over the ridge of the Absaroka Mountains behind me. Through the back of my denim jacket I could feel the heat immedi-ately. I was wearing a brand-new Montana cattleman's hat that I particularly fancy, and the fence and my hat and I cast a long, long shadow that cut right across the flank of the grazing bison. A cloud shifted and the awesome Grand Tetons with their razor peaks and glaciers lit up behind him, as if a hidden stagehand had just hit all the lights in The West.

Talk about archetypes. Cowboy, you're onto something here, I told myself. You'll remember this.

I knew I'd received a cue from the Great Stage Manager when I got back to the Jackson Lake Lodge and found Robert Bly eating breakfast at the next table over. Bly, the poet and best-selling author of *Iron John*, is the ranking guru of the American men's movement and, as such, the principal architect of a whole new subspecies of American man. I came to the mountains to think; today's medita-tion, I thought, will be on the recurrent theme of manhood.

Bly and I had met once, in Raleigh where I was a sort of media spy at one of his healing weekends for the wounded white warriors of Wake County. I don't mean to be dismissive. I think several of my friends and acquaintances regard that weekend as a turning point in their lives.

I didn't claim acquaintance with the poet. He's met a million of us. He was sitting with a pair of women, one in her 60s like Bly and one a few years younger. I was born to eavesdrop. The conversation didn't reveal much, besides the trio's itinerary. I can only report— and I report without malice or comment—that Bly addressed his companions as "kids."

I just threw that in to please my wife and the rest of you closet feminazis who think Bly is a suspicious character. I have no bone to pick with the only serious poet who makes a profit in America. Poets moonlight or starve. Bly's basic point, that most American males are ill-prepared for anything resembling manhood or adult-hood, is one of our great tragic truths. His mythology is intriguing, if a little rambling and tendentious, and his emphasis on male initi-ation and tribal responsibility makes sense to me.

I don't hold him responsible for this New Age subculture of drumming, howling would-be wild men who follow in his wake. Men's liberation touched a raw nerve, obviously, and there's no success without excess in the U.S. of A. But again I find myself marching to a different drum. I have seen the men's movement and it is not me. Now and always, I'd rather share an hour with a lone-some bison, who has nothing to say, than with any rhythm section of sensitive, articulate M.A.s and D.D.s trying to resurrect the wild man in me.

You're mistaken if you think this is going to be the testimony of a tough guy, a man who contains his own pain or passes it on to wild animals and small nations. I've just been rafting on the Salmon River with Les Bechtel, who holds six world titles in whitewater kayaking, who climbed Annapurna with his wife. Les is tough. Les's wife is tough. Compared with Les or Les's wife, I'm Pee Wee Herman's little brother. Les took one look at me and assigned me to the big, safe raft with a nice birdwatcher from Virginia who didn't want to get her feet wet.

I'm not a fighter or a killer. I am, in fact, a talker. That shift in male fashions back in the '60s, when grunting machismo went out and words and feelings came in, was probably the only thing that kept me from burying my mating aspirations in a Trappist monastery. A lot of our drummers, I think, were launched by that same wave. But somewhere they lost their confidence.

These are flagrant heterosexuals. Why would they need so much same-sex support unless opposite-sex support was missing? I know that's the most controversial, incendiary thing I'm going to say. But a drummer who claims that his primary relationship is great must be kidding himself, or incapable of the best sort of primary relationship. The men's movement, if it's more than a first-aid station where casualties of the sex wars heal their wounds and revive their courage, seems to smell of retreat and defeat. No one ever said that mating was for the fragile or the faint of heart. My wife writes novels where strong women, devastated by one dreadful man after another, just get up off the canvas, wipe the blood out of their eyes, and go looking for a better man.

Drummers should read these books for inspiration. They should read more books written by women. For men who really take women seriously, it's only women's opinions that count, am I right? Who cares what the guys at work think? My informal poll of sarcastic heterosexual women reveals that women associate drumming with masturbation—reviving the adolescent myth of the "circle jerk"—and even with impotence. That's bad news, boys. Naturally women are suspicious of all these fraternity rites that exclude them as they have for centuries. But there's a strain of condescension this time, and mirth.

Woman are laughing, and not without cause. In an excellent column (with the heartless title "Little Drummer Men") by a Virginia writer, Mariane Matera, I learned that one branch of the men's movement has become an anti-circumcision cult that encourages men to mourn the loss of their foreskins. Psychotherapists help victims of circumcision to relive their infant experience in all its "terror, rage, horror, torture and humiliation." In California, fountain of most New Age absurdity, skin grafts and stretching exercises help the circumcised to regain the lost symbol of their manhood.

This is simply amazing. Of all the things I've lost in this life and long to regain, my foreskin must be at the very bottom of my wish list. It isn't loss of foreskin that defeats these poor devils but loss of forebrain, seat of intellect and irony. God knows the human condition is tragic and ridiculous, but it doesn't need to be slapstick. The humorless self-absorption of the foreskin-seeker completes a perfect circle of defeat. You've got your drums, you've got your foreskin (at least psychologically), you've got your buddies and you've got the whole world of women laughing at you behind your back, which is probably just what you feared the most in the first place.

Where you've got the lost foreskin as The Holy Grail, you've got the worst of the men's movement and the best of the case against it. But it's no revelation that American men feel castrated. In a society of false promises and empty rewards, governed by scoundrels and dominated by malicious voyeurism, competing for a corner office and a better parking space is not living like a man. It's the educated middle class, backbone of the men's movement, that feels most cheated and compromised. Physicians who've lost their compassion, clergymen who've lost their faith, scholars whose passion for philosophy was consumed by nitpicking journals and faculty politics, lawyers who worked 80-hour weeks to make partner in firms they don't respect, journalists who write tepid potboilers for rags we wouldn't read—we are the Hollow Men, Mr. Eliot. Feminism is no threat to a man unless he already feels beaten.

It's not surprising that some of us want to cry on each other's shoulders. If men seem more devastated, psychologically, by disintegrating families and communities, it's because women have never been deprived of the support of other women.

Nor is it surprising that a cream puff like me, who was so happy to see machismo buried with a stake through its heart, finds himself responding to the retro heroes of Larry Brown's novel *Joe* and Robert Earl Keen, Jr.'s *The Road Goes on Forever*—the best country song anyone has written in 20 years (Courtship: "Sonny took his pool cue/Laid the drunk out on the floor/Stuffed a dollar in her tip jar/Walked on out the door."). These are dangerous heterosexual loners, with no family values that Marilyn Quayle could recognize, who manage to live by a certain code. They have their principles—and their dignity.

I've been dealing with my own midlife crisis by tramping the mountains with my dog, like Rip Van Winkle. Maybe I'm hoping I'll fall asleep somewhere and miss the next 20 years, which don't look so good to me. I'm learning the stars again from a book my stepson gave me, sitting up late tracking Vega and Deneb the bright tail of the Swan, and the great tail of the Dragon curling around the Little Bear. I'm avoiding people who talk too much because they encourage me in my habit of doing the same. I'm weary of my own voice, let alone 20 others.

I don't claim to be typical of anything. But it's my suggestion that the men's movement may have fixated on the wrong stage of this tribal mythology they're so fond of. Ritual initiation and integration into the society of men are important. But maybe more important is the step toward manhood that comes just before or after, in many of the tribal traditions that I've studied. It's the spirit journey or "vision quest" that the young man undertakes alone, leaving the tribe and seeking his place in something greater than the tribe—in nature, in all Creation.

This spiritual component is the thing that most modern, urban men have lost entirely. Man alone in the natural world is a balanced man, with his wound healed. Trading war stories and touching each other's scars is a seductive comfort, but it may not be the shortest path to wisdom or self-confidence.

It's easier to regain your balance, even your sense of proportion, than to regain your foreskin. Not everyone can quit his job and move to Wyoming, live in a line shack, spend a year in a fire tower or a lighthouse. But if it's atavism you need, take some of the money you saved for a new drum set (or maybe even for a cape and a hood, I'm sorry to hear) and come out here where the wild ones take real risks. See if you can cut it; try to enjoy it even if you can't. Anything less is just California dreamin' for drugstore wildboys. Note that Robert Bly, on his own vacation, isn't in Santa Barbara reliving circumcisions. He's out here where the buffalo roam.

You shouldn't have to pay admission, wear animal skins or dance naked with your chiropractor to make yourself feel like a whole man again. Just go outside and walk around. Catch a fish. Wear a hat with a wide brim. Smile meaningfully at cowgirl waitresses like Robert Bly does. Shut up for a minute.

I signed up early as a supporter of the women's movement, and I'm proud of a citation from NOW for defending the rights of women in my column. Grassroots feminism is nothing more than justice and common sense, and it's been the most positive revolutionary force in this country in the past 25 years. If a backlash or backslide is setting in, do men deserve most of the blame?

We Shall Overcome

Columnists are human, too. At least we want you to think so. Whenever some mean-spirited, union-busting, poorbox-robbing misanthrope thinks he's just about exhausted your goodwill denouncing welfare mothers, he'll write about taking his boy to the ballpark or his curly-headed granddaughter for a walk in the spring rain.

It's a cheap trick but not always insincere. Fools and SOBs love their children too, a persistent mystery that must be linked to the survival instincts of the species. So I don't need to apologize for saying something about my daughter's high-school graduation. Nothing too sentimental. She was radiant, as they used to say on the society page about every bride who could manage a thin smile. The other kids looked OK, too.

She graduated from a Quaker school where they taught her to question authority. I helped a lot with this education by serving as the authority she habitually questioned. "And just how do you know that, Daddy?" is the single line that defined our relationship, the quote they should have printed under her picture in the yearbook.

Graduation at Carolina Friends School is conducted like a Quaker meeting. There's no commencement speaker, just an amiable, extended silence broken by students, teachers and parents whenever they're moved to speak. It's effective. One parent who offered no advice to the graduates was the one who offers unsolicited advice for a living. I was feeling good, but not expansive.

It's no small shock to find yourself the parent of someone who has been reclassified—however prematurely—as an adult. I remembered the awful example of Kurt Vonnegut Jr., who tried to say something nice at a commencement and ended up telling the graduates of a women's college that the most socially responsible thing they could do was to go and get their tubes tied. The night train that's his habitual train of thought just flat ran over his good intentions.

I was doing a lot of thinking, though. I was thinking of the time a radio interviewer asked me, "Do you consider yourself a feminist?"

"Well of course," I answered. "You know I have a daughter."

She seemed to understand, because she didn't ask me to elaborate. But my answer has lost the self-evident authority it once carried, and even the question is seldom asked of men now, as if the category "feminist" had become gender-specific.

I taped a couple of hours with Gloria Steinem once, about 20 years ago when Steinem and the other celebrity feminists were routinely baited, in print and in public, with epithets like "libber" and "bra-burner." I found the old eight-track tape at the bottom of a mildewed carton, partially unwound and wrapped around a first baseman's glove.

It was a hassle to get it set up, but well worth it. I sound friendly and very young, Steinem sounds patient and very smart. She was just peaking then, at 37. Hearing her talk, I remembered the way she looked.

There's no doubt, in the sexist male world she set out to conquer, that the way she looked gave her a marked advantage over Bella Abzug and Betty Friedan. Steinem was attractive in the chilly, cerebral, what-makes-you-think-you're-man-enough fashion that women-haters hate most of all, and that certain other men—not to mention any names—find almost irresistibly challenging.

She made you want to court her with your brain. In those days my brain didn't have half enough mileage on it to do the job, but Steinem didn't let me down too hard. Unlike the familiar harpies of the early women's movement who were always embarrassing men for making sexist errors, Steinem gave the impression that she was marking your score card privately, according to her own system. It was, of course, about 100 times more effective, if the objective was to make a man behave decently and listen to what she was saying.

She was polite, clever, formidably well-informed. She approved of something I'd written, a venomous piece on beauty contests. The interview was going so well I was emboldened to ask her what she thought of an incident we both witnessed that afternoon. A feminist storm trooper had deliberately embarrassed—probably for Steinem's benefit—a young man who had offered the most tepid, polite sort of heterosexual response to a woman's appearance. His objectionable comment, far from "Get a load of those . . ." was more like "She's certainly an attractive woman."

Steinem shed no tears for the unfortunate boy. Her response, in essence, was "Look, for a long time a woman had to have a great sense of humor to get along. Now it's your turn."

I had a pretty good sense of humor, I told her. But as a writer it irked me to spend three days working on a delicate argument and receive a letter that mentioned nothing but the "sexist language" represented by a politically incorrect pronoun. She witheld her sympathy. But she offered her view that the smart ones might read and live their way into a little more flexibility, and that the movement didn't need the others anyway.

What she didn't consider was that many of the smart ones would read, live and introspect themselves right out of the movement, and leave it in the hands of the pronoun police. The women's movement has been a tremendous force for positive change in the past 20 years. Don't ever doubt it. But reverse sexism, rhetorical excess and destructive infighting, that endemic curse of the American Left, have eroded its political power base to a point where its enemies have begun to roll back its gains. Feminism is still subjected to brutal caricatures—listen to Rush Limbaugh rave about "feminazis" on your radio this afternoon—but its own extremists probably do more damage to the cause. Andrea Dworkin actually exists, though she could have been written by Kurt Vonnegut and drawn to order by Doug Marlette.

Too many recruits who supported 90 percent of the feminist agenda were driven away by zealots who demanded 100. The Equal Rights Amendment has never passed. At the time when she needs it the most, when reactionaries are trying to sell her back into reproductive bondage, the women's movement is no longer in a position to offer my daughter the support and protection she deserves.

In the face of backlash and media hostility, the movement's grassroots heroines have about worn themselves out in the uphill fight for social and economic equality. Maybe it's time for a much larger special interest group to pick up the torch. There are enough of us to change the odds. Feminism is, or ought to be, the natural religion of all fathers and mothers of female children.

Why isn't the movement big enough, and smart enough, to embrace us? Feminism isn't some cult movement like Scientology that was conceived in one woman's brain and slapped to life at the launching party for Ms. magazine in 1972. If that had been the birth I could pass myself off as a godfather, because I was one of a handful of males who were present at the launching.

Feminism, as I understand it, is the permanent pursuit of equality. It began long before Susan B. Anthony, and it doesn't end until every government in the world guarantees equal oppurtunity, equal pay for equal work and a woman's right to control her own reproduction. Women can no more give it up, or de-emphasize it, than black Americans could quit fighting for civil rights and economic justice. It's as basic as struggling to breathe when someone holds you underwater.

The modern women's movement is the logical extension of hundreds of years of struggle. Reproductive rights are the key to everything else. Equality is a joke as long as venal sins, minor indiscretions or even contraceptive oversights can mess up a woman's life in a way they could never mess up a man's.

Feminism isn't essentially radical, or complicated, or intellectually exotic. Feminism is a homely thing called justice. Fairness. I want my daughter to begin her life as an adult with every option open, even the options that seem conservative and timid to her parents. Anyone who tries to limit her options or make any option more difficult, anyone who tries to block any of her paths is my enemy. I'm a physical threat to anyone who tells her that being female means she deserves less control over her body, her money, her time, the company she keeps or the way she chooses to live.

On those issues I take no prisoners. That's feminism, as far as I'm concerned. The rest is a kind of rabbinical commentary on the main theme. And it seems to me that a father's feminism, free of self-interest, is a pretty sincere commitment; maybe more sincere than the feminism of politically correct husbands who act neutered and declawed and run through their catechisms for humorless women who don't really seem to like them.

Feel free to disagree. But when it comes to my basic premise— call it A Father's Commencement Prayer—I don't expect much argument. Less choice is less life, pure and simple. If you want less for your daughter than you want for your son, then you love her less. You value her less. Could a father sit at a graduation, with all its sentiment and symbolism—its hopefulness—thinking, "I can't wait for some big old boy to get her pregnant, take the spring out of her step and tell her what to do like I never could"?

There wasn't a single father who was thinking that. I know it. Though my daughter would reply, "Just how do you know that, Daddy?"

I sat on this column for six months because I knew it would get a mixed reception, even among my friends. I don't think I lost any friends I needed, and I don't think I exaggerated to make my point. The get-even ideology that proclaims rape, battering and incest as standard male behavior is the sickest sexist outrage this side of clitorectomies.

Remember the Lobster Boy

Every conscious American knows exactly what happened to Nicole Simpson, but how many know what happened to the Lobster Boy? A sideshow performer, or what they used to call a "circus freak," the Lobster Boy was born with little arms shaped like lobster claws, as well as stunted legs that confined him to a wheelchair. Two years ago he was murdered in his mobile home in Tampa, shot in the head by an assassin who turned out to be a 16-year-old neighbor.

Police discovered that the youngster had killed the Lobster Boy—Grady Stiles, 55—for a $1,500 fee. The fee had been paid by Stiles' wife and stepson, known as the Human Blockhead for his sideshow specialty of driving nails through his nostrils. Life insurance was the apparent motive.

The Blockhead and the precocious hitman were convicted of murder. But the Lobster Boy's widow pleaded self-defense—the classic battered-wife defense—and convinced the jury, in a trial just concluded, to convict her of manslaughter instead of premeditated murder. Apparently the jurors never doubted that the unfortunate Lobster Boy was capable of the reign of drunken terror the widow described, including assaults with his pincers, head-butts and sexual abuse.

You can probably see where this is going. Admittedly the Stiles family, like the famous Bobbitts and Gilloolys, grew up without the advantages many of us take for granted. But the fate of the Lobster Boy and his wife sets a clear precedent: If a bad relationship gets out of hand and he kills her, he was a monster whose brutality culminated in murder; if it gets out of hand and she kills him, he was a monster who deserved it.

At this rate, murdering husbands will soon be legal and profitable. Bedridden, 90-year-old millionaires, smothered by child brides impatient to inherit, will be portrayed in court as brutes who terrorized their women by spitting baby food and dropping dentures in their handbags.

The new double standard trivializes homicide and tyrannizes the media. I was traveling during the media hurricane that followed the Simpson murders, and I was amazed by the uniform coverage in paper after paper, city after city. Lead editorials decried domestic violence, local victims of violent males were displayed on page one, banner headlines declared "The War Against Women."

It was a powerful spin, apparently orchestrated from some central command post with unquestioned authority. Never mind that only an unethical leak by the DA—a media ploy that misfired—had placed the Simpsons' unhappy history in the public domain. Never mind that no one had broken Simpson's alibi, or that the O.J. Simpsons were about as typical of *anything* as the Klaus von Bulows or the Michael Jacksons.

"A third of women hit by male partner," headlined *USA Today*—neglecting to add that the same percentage of men are hit by their women (hit first, that is). One hysterical talk-show host, estimating that only 10 percent of attacks are reported, calculated on national TV that there must be 60 million battered women in America. But according to the Census Bureau, only 56.8 million women live with men.

In all the mass media, only the intrepid John Leo held his ground against the flood tide of exaggeration and disinformation. Writing in *U.S. News and World Report*, Leo cited a 1993 study of 2,500 women, conducted by the Commonwealth Fund. Two percent of the subjects reported that men had punched or kicked them in the previous 12 months; not one woman reported that she had been choked, beaten up or threatened with a deadly weapon.

A nationwide study by Straus and Gelles, researchers at the University of New Hampshire, found 1.8 million women who complained of violent attacks by their partners—and *2 million* men.

With a fearlessness that takes your breath away, Leo even cited a study of homosexuals in which 46 percent of lesbians reported physical violence in their relationships (three times the rate among gay males and 15 times the standard for heterosexual couples, which holds steady at three percent).

Call Mr. Leo, not me. Statistics are notoriously flexible; corruption occurs when the media trade with only one gang of number-twisters.

No one denies that there's a savage subclass of subhuman males who beat the women who stay with them and shoot the women who won't. New laws are needed to neutralize them. Most men don't relate much to this little fraternity of Cro-Magnons. No more than most women relate to Frances Lipscomb of Gastonia, N.C., who doused her husband with rubbing alcohol and set him on fire, or to Helen Carson of Kingsport, Tenn., who bit off her husband's tongue when he tried to kiss and make up.

Any way you slice up the facts and figures, they won't add up to "The War Against Women." People are violent and cohabitation often brings out the worst in them. Angry men tend to cause more serious injuries. But when it comes to murder—when deadly weapons level the playing field—things even up considerably. Among white couples, men kill women more frequently by only a 60-40 split. For blacks it's almost even, 53 female victims to 47 males.

So why have juries and editorialists begun to assume the guilt of males and the innocence of females? Why do even the movies I like keep telling me that evil is gender-specific? From many angles this is still a conservative, sexist country, dominated by men in gray suits. Radical and even liberal ideas go begging. Just one radical program is selling well everywhere. It's the program of the militant victim cult, which holds that rape, battering and incest are inevitable paradigms for the unequal relationship between men and women.

Victim theology is no secret covenant between angry women. It's in your face. Marilyn French, an unskilled writer of ponderous phallophobic tracts, has spelled it out: "All men are rapists and that's all they are." Instead of a place with history's ostracized bigots and hatemongers—a place with Joseph Goebbels and the author of *The Protocols of the Elders of Zion*—the author of these words seems to hold her place as a guru of the feminist Left.

Practical feminists, who dominate my board of advisors, advise me never to rise to such bait. They warn me that a man seeking justice in this court is like a coon trying to reason with a coon hound. Let the flaming fringe consume itself, they counsel; the real victims of victim theology are its true believers, women too corroded by bitterness to recognize equality if it comes.

I know this is sage advice. But how easily someone managed to shift that indictment from O.J. Simpson to men as a group. If gender radicals are so few, why are they so effective?

And then there was this letter, from an anonymous reader. Seems I had infuriated her by declining, mildly, to applaud the castration of John Bobbitt. She was an educated woman entirely convinced that men without exception are vile, infantile, half-bestial creatures any sensitive human being would avoid.

"Men," she wrote, "will go to any lengths to use women, to objectify and abuse us." As evidence she cited three separate incidents in New York, when men masturbated in public to offend her. Apparently drugs, alcohol and mental illness weren't factors she considered, in a city swarming with homeless mental patients and junkies. It was a disturbing illustration of the way a fixed idea accumulates the selective data it needs to perpetuate itself.

"We shouldn't pretend to tolerate men anymore," she concluded. "We should claim our rage. You deserve it for all these centuries of male power abuse in the form of violence against women. Can't you see you've created—and maintained—a society where women are afraid of you? It's obvious you males prefer to keep it that way—so stop whining when one of us cuts the cord."

How did this letter make me feel? It made me feel terrible—like a black spy at a Klan rally, like a Jew hearing "Heil Hitler!", like a Palestinian listening to Meir Kahane. Like a feminist in Bangladesh.

It taught me, a privileged Anglo male, just how black men felt when some cracker said that all any of them wanted was white women and watermelons. A valuable lesson for me, no doubt. But after that, what's accomplished?

Some feminists argue that the demonization of men is a political necessity, vital to "the deconstruction of the patriarchy." Political necessity is a euphemism for intellectual terrorism. You're a terrorist if you attack people who have never harmed you, and wouldn't harm you, because they share race, gender, or nationality with others who may have harmed you.

Terrorists justify it by declaring that no one in that other group is innocent. They're all guilty, all inferior—and all the same. Waged with lies or with pipe bombs, terrorism is a moral and intellectual dead end. It's where civilization stops and the jungle closes in.

I don't mean to embarrass my reader, a woman totally sincere and almost courteous in her fury. Traumatic experiences, usually far worse than watching derelicts masturbate, breed irrational fears and feed stereotypes. Victims need therapy and sympathy—not disciples.

I've taken the feminist side in every social, political, legal and sexual debate since the '60s, beginning with a sarcastic send-up of beauty contests when I was a cub reporter. It's all in the morgue somewhere, if anyone cares to look it up. But what progress is served, what self-respect have I retained if I offer aid and comfort to fanatics who peddle hideous stereotypes of a group that includes me? Men who don't protest deserve the withering contempt of *Time* essayist Lance Morrow:

"Here we see the descendants of the ancient priests of Cybele, who as part of their initiation would castrate themselves and sling their testicles into the earth mother's pine tree."

A man has to draw the line, when he hears rhetoric that follows a logical path toward sexual apartheid or exposing male infants at birth. I guess I understand why they're saying these terrible things about men, and why they think they have to. I'm no Candide. But there's something truly sick and irresponsible about confusing ignorant young women with outrageous lies about half the human race—the half that includes their own brothers and fathers.

There's only one useful generalization about men: An overwhelming majority of them want to have sex with women. They're stubborn about it. If you can live with that, most of them are relatively harmless. You can domesticate one with the same techniques that work on a dog or a child. Use affection liberally, be firm but fair, establish the rules at the beginning and never back down.

Never let the sun set on any notion about male prerogatives. If his mama spoiled him and his daddy raised him on macho-myth (if he's Southern, some people would say), you might encounter serious problems. But never generalize from your failures. That's what dumb men do. Stereotypes not only make you sound like a bigot, but—to everyone who knows better, male or female—they make you sound like a chump.

When was the last time you heard anyone stand up for innocence? The only fan letter came from a nun. But there's a strange war on childhood in this country, and it begins with dimwits like Lu Ann Dippy peddling sex manuals in pre-schools.

Songs of Innocence

They sequestered me in the little room that the doctor had decorated for much younger patients. The walls were covered with Misterogers posters and Smurfs, and drawings in crayon by the doctor's children. I was envying him the passionate declarations of love, printed in black and red crayon, from a daughter who must have been about seven. I could barely remember when my daughter was that age and that demonstrative, though of course I've saved all the crayon documents somewhere, in folders and scrapbooks.

I picked up the only magazine in the kids' rooms, which was a *National Geographic* with a wonderful photograph on the cover. It was a blonde Viking maiden beautiful enough to inspire sagas, her face lit from the lower left as if by firelight—the illumination was identified inside as the midnight sun. The girl is an Icelander with a name, Ingibjorg Bjornsdottir, as romantic as her portrait. In enlightened Iceland a daughter carries her father's name and the stamp of their relationship all her life. When *Geographic's* Bob Krist photographed her, Ingibjorg was nine years old. The expression in her eyes is remarkable. There's trust and curiosity—she's nine, after all—but there's also suspicion and a trace of something you could characterize as intrigue.

When does childhood end? Ingibjorg and the crayon mash notes to Daddy focused me on one of my idiosyncratic notions that's always been unpopular with the progressives and post-Freudian moderns with whom I seem to have spent most of my life. I always maintained that innocence was a precious commodity in and of itself, independent of any attitudes about the wonders or terrors of human sexuality. You might be surprised to see how much that offends and threatens certain psychological sophisticates, and how far they'll go to shatter these harmless old-fashioned illusions that I seem to harbor.

I've even been reminded, in a fairly shrill voice, that those brief, magical years when a daughter can't get enough of her father are merely a displacement of the raging sex drive that she's nurturing, and as yet has nowhere else to go with. As for the affection the father feels in return, that's best left unexamined.

"I'm sure that all goes double for my mother and my brother," I reply. "So what and why mention it? Who cares if old Jim was a little too fond of Huckleberry Finn? Did Freud liberate us or did he lock us in another kind of prison?"

There are people, I believe, who despise innocence and need to spoil it for the usual reasons, out of spite and envy, because they've lost it themselves or missed it altogether. That innocence exists and that it's beautiful hardly needs to be demonstrated. It's what we find touching about children, animals and fools. It's what makes us grin when we see an infant or a kitten pulling at a toy that it doesn't understand. Innocence is what I find charming when my stepson asks me about that book "by Alex Haley" when I had recommended Aldous Huxley. If he were 25 it would only be ignorance, and inspire no affection at all. Innocence in others is what brings out the best in those of us who have lost it. It's what makes us protective and generous instead of competitive and wary.

We invented childhood, in this particular culture and quite recently, against a tradition of 12-year-old girls who started having babies and 10-year-old boys who went to the fields and the mines. I think it was one of the good things we invented, this period of grace between infancy and grim adult responsibility, when the sex drive and all the other drives could be sublimated and harnessed into helping us learn something about the world before it swallowed us up.

Sexual innocence is only one aspect of childhood, and maybe not the most critical. But I don't applaud the progressives who would eliminate childhood by eliminating its proper mysteries, and I'm honestly appalled by a six-year-old armed with a complete sexual education against the drooling army of perverts and child molesters that her parents see lurking at the end of their driveway.

I object to creating adult sexual awareness among preadolescents, not because sex is evil or even unsafe and unsanitary, but because it's so powerful. Once it gets a firm grip on you, it may never let go. To say that it's a serious distraction for these teenagers is to deal in humorous understatement. I've watched adolescents go through sexual relationships equivalent to the ones most of my generation experienced in our 20s. The cost in time and energy, if only in arranging trysts, is almost debilitating. Is it better to go on sublimating, at least up to the 11th grade? All I know is that I did more reading proportionately as a teenager, before the pursuit of sex and its social ramifications overtook me, than I ever did again in my life. Almost any modern teenager knows ten times as much about sex as I knew at the same age, and demonstrably less about everything else.

It's the advocates of preschool and virtually prespeech sex seminars who seem to have the least respect for Eros and its power. They could be talking about needlepoint, or navel hygiene. A registered nurse from Florida with the unfortunate name of Lu Ann Dippy recommends sexual orientation for two-year-olds, and prepares courses for children under five. The Surgeon General suggests thorough sex education classes no later than the third grade. These theories produce tiny gynecologists with medical vocabularies who frankly give me the creeps. And for all their technical education, the kids show little improvement in sexual common sense. Nearly a third of our 15-year-olds have had intercourse, an unthinkable statistic in the '50s. But two-thirds of these sophisticates practice contraception irregularly or not at all. Asked why they didn't, 40 percent replied that they just didn't feel like it.

Should innocence be laughed out of our culture for such a poor harvest of practical results? I don't deny that ample sexual fuel is always present in these cubs of ours, almost from the cradle. I just think there should be some debate about when it's sensible to light a match.

It's a debate I expect to lose. Now that AIDS has entered the equation, there's no way we'll be able to protect our darlings from Lu Ann Dippy or from those other kids whose parents issue them condoms and diaphragms when they're 14. We reactionaries may have to fall back on another aspect of childhood and innocence that the new hurry-up culture is eliminating just as rapidly and self-righteously, and with equally depressing consequences.

A college freshman sat in my office last week and told me that teachers had treated her with amusement bordering on contempt because she was one of the few students in her class who hadn't declared her major and her lifetime vocation. I went into my patented rage and explained that there was something seriously wrong, in most cases, with anyone who *can* make a confident choice of her vocation when she's 18. At 18 you don't know who or what you're going to be; you don't have a clue. A profession chosen by a college freshman is exactly like a marriage contracted by a college senior—it will almost certainly end in divorce or terrible unhappiness. Any better result is blind luck.

With the collusion of our educators, grasping corporations are reaching deeper and deeper into the years of innocence to start shaping the curious clones that suit their often-nefarious purposes. Cutthroat competition for prime university places is encouraged as early as junior high school, and a university freshman is expected to have all his identity crises behind him. The grim workplace casts a shadow over undergraduate innocence from matriculation to commencement.

School days, another happy invention of our affluent Western society, were intended as a grace period of pure learning and suspended responsibility, when the young men and women lucky enough to get them could ignore the feeding frenzy outside the campus walls. The workplace and the marketplace have no place at our schools. Let corporations, as well as professional sports leagues, run their own training programs at their own expense.

Innocence is brief and getting briefer, and there are few besides me who mourn its passing. It's a useless thing, like an orchid. And after innocence comes the breeding and the feeding. First sex gets you, then work. A girl from Rochester lit a match to my slumbering libido in 1960 and the fire hasn't gone out yet. But when it was only sex that owned me, I still found time for a lot of other interests, well into my 20s. Then along came working for a living and trying to act like a man in the world, and I've never been able to get back to the things I put off, like learning the names of plants, and some decent Spanish so I could read Cervantes in the original.

Maybe someday. But as far as I can see, sex and work are the time-consuming and self-consuming things that never end. All we control is the beginning.

X

$\mathcal{P}$ersonal — Stages of the Journey

Standards erode, institutions crumble, our private lives go on. But it gets to be a problem when everyone's lost, because there's no one to give you directions that will get you where you want to go. Where do you turn for guidance in a poisoned postmodern society where William Bennett sits in judgment on our virtue and Connie Chung sits on the throne of Walter Cronkite? Where a president's daughter makes nude kick-boxing videos, an agent books personal appearances for John Bobbitt and Joey Buttafuoco, and every woman under 60 who makes the news gets a big offer from Penthouse to take her clothes off? And finally, where Richard Nixon gets to make a hero's exit?

I stumble on alone. A tranquil middle age must be just ahead of me there somewhere, just over the next hill. But the path is mined and crisscrossed with tripwires. And every few miles they've camouflaged a major pitfall, a tiger trap with those sharpened stakes at the bottom. Sex is the toughest trap to escape alive. But there are others, deep ones, and the groans of the poor devils impaled down there never seem to warn us in time.

When I was a young man, alcohol was the Number One enemy of the American journalist. Today I think it's cynicism.

In a Dry Season

As between the evils of alcohol—cirrhosis, cancer, etc.—and the aesthetic of bourbon drinking, that is, the use of bourbon to warm the heart, to reduce the anomie of the late 20th century, to cut the cold phlegm of Wednesday afternoons, I choose the aesthetic.

—Walker Percy

In his eulogy for Jimmy Wallace, former mayor of Chapel Hill, columnist and Carolina alumnus Ed Yoder created a charming portrait of an unusual man whom he much admired. But even in so indiscreet a place as his syndicated column, Yoder was unable to ignore the principal cause of Wallace's death: "A few too many wee drams of the elixir his Scottish forebears brought to America."

Behind this graceful euphemism there were, of course, melancholy volumes left unwritten. Some people's virtues are inseparable from their signature vice. Last June, at a wedding in Massachusetts, some of us who had worked with and around the late Pete Axthelm engaged in similar reminiscence. Pete's death was a more tragic and premature variation on Jimmy Wallace's, and there were few memories of Pete that didn't involve a wee dram, or a dozen. Our colloquy turned morbid, turned into a body count of all our old friends and colleagues who had died of drink. The toll, in 20 years, was alarming.

Naturally there were glasses of whiskey in our hands as we mourned our dead. Writers and journalists, as a community, have suffered much from alcohol, and suffered also from making romance of it. Usually the ones who suffered most from the drinking were more talented than the ones who loved the drinking stories. I was pleased when my stepson, after reading a book by a writer we both admire, asked me if so many drinking stories were really necessary.

He had seen through a sophomoric variety of male glamour that had me, at his age, entirely in its grip. I told him that we used to tell the stories mainly because we were fools, half in love with reck-lessness and dying young. If we still tell a few at my age, I told him, it's because we survived somehow and still fear the bullet that we dodged. We're whistling past the graveyard.

The romance of alcohol is a false romance, and the humor—remember Frankie Fontaine as Crazy Guggenheim?—is always in bad taste. The methodical destruction of brain cells and liver tissue is no lyric poem and no laughing matter. Doctors, who used to pre-scribe a dram or two for "medicinal purposes," are turning against the tradition of the harmless social drinker. Drinking drivers are the targets of a national vigilante movement. Even the mythical link between drinking and creativity has been discredited. Faulkner and Hemingway, prodigious drinkers at their worst, both insisted that every decent line they wrote was written sober.

"One of the disadvantages of wine is that it makes a man mis-take words for thoughts," wrote Samuel Johnson.

The One Hundred Years' War between America's "wets" and "drys" was supposed to have been resolved, in favor of the wets, when Prohibition was repealed in 1933. H.L. Mencken died believ-ing that the Temperance movement would never recover from the corrosive effects of his contempt. But the spiritual descendants of Carry Nation are staging an unmistakable comeback. The average American adult has reduced his annual consumption of hard liquor by a full gallon since 1975. The wine rage that peaked in the '80s has subsided with five years of falling sales, and America's folkloric beer drinkers have been seduced and betrayed by strange carbonat-ed eyewashes that are beer in name only.

The social norms that govern drinking are changing rapidly. Office Christmas parties are going dry and even welcoming spouses and children, a development that would have amazed Pete Axthelm as much as H.L. Mencken. Traveling with the Ghost of Christmas Past, I tried to imagine a Time Inc. Christmas party with kids and Cokes and cookies, with my martini-powered senior editor reading "The Night Before Christmas" to someone's moppet, but I could not; the vision would not come.

The president of an all-dry advertising agency told a wire service reporter, "It's a developing attitude, just like no smoking."

Liquor and cigarettes make a tenuous analogy, it seems to me. They're both potent threats to your health. But nicotine is too cruel an addiction, too swift a killer, too disgusting and antisocial in its routine consumption to compare with a protean drug like alcohol that shows every face from the most satanic to the most benign. I think the greatest difference is that every smoker honestly hopes to quit. Coughing, wheezing, panting, turning yellow, stinking like toxic waste and failing insurance physicals is just no way to live this brief life we're given. Even smokers are smart enough to dream of something better.

The time will come, soon enough, when cigarettes will virtually disappear. There will be even more shame attached to their manufacture, and no profit in it. Those who predict a similar fate for alcoholic beverages are poor students of history and human nature. For a significant minority of drinkers, alcohol in any form is a one-way ticket to the morgue; in their AA meetings and support groups it's necessary for them to speak of all these beverages as if the devil bottles them in hell. But the majority, who've been able to drink for many years without losing families, jobs, equilibrium or liver function are, by and large, quite grateful for the privilege.

One man's poison is another man's sturdy crutch. It's hard to say which drinkers are the lucky ones. In a smoky taproom somewhere, in one of the lairs of the lost, there must be at least one living witness to an occasion when I myself suffered a loss of dignity under the influence of drink.

I offer my case with proper humility. Like every drinker who's getting old and plans to get older, I drink less every year. I never believed that real men and women could hold their liquor, while weaker creatures stumbled. Above the age of 16 I never saw drinking as an ongoing test of my manhood; above 30 I never saw it as a poetic way to die. But self-consciousness and pessimism seem to have dogged me from the cradle, and alcohol was the first medicine I found that banished both. It was only an over-the-counter remedy, a quick fix perhaps and no cure. But it offered so much relief I could live with the side effects. And I have.

To the pure of heart and sweet of breath, this is the pathetic confession of a drug addict in denial. I know the rhetoric. It seems to me that the simpleminded challenge of alcoholic machismo—"Do you think you're man enough to handle this?"—is coming back at us from the other side, in a different form: "Are you man enough to face your life stone sober?"

If that's the game, if the temperance tribe is saying that they're tougher, cleaner, made of finer stuff, I concede it. I'm not made that well. I'm easily discouraged by Baptist ladies who hiss "Nigger!" at 13-year-old boys in Christmas pageants (are there really Christians so stupid that they believe in heaven and believe it's segregated?). I despair when my countrymen deep-freeze their girl friends, bake their babies and film sex acts with day-care toddlers—all items in last week's papers. I'm not at all sure that large, complicated brains in anthropoids will turn out to be one of Mother Nature's most successful experiments.

I'm bewildered sometimes. Last weekend I was driving through an expensive neighborhood in Chapel Hill, searching unsuccessfully for a friend's house where there was a Christmas party. It was 11:00 a.m. I pulled over to ask a woman on a bicycle for directions. She threw up her hands, screamed, "You don't have a prayer, sucker!" and pedaled off shouting and snarling, I swear. What was she thinking? Even without my little blue blazer and Christmas tie I look more like Captain Kangaroo than Chuck Norris or Jeffrey Dahmer.

I was shaken. I drove right to the ABC store and did some last-minute Christmas shopping, comforted just by the presence of all those bottles. Our lives are painful and puzzling. It seems that almost anyone who could drink, would drink, at least in a pinch. The late Walker Percy agreed:

"What, after all, is the use of not having cancer, cirrhosis, and such, if a man comes home from work every day at 5:30 to the exurbs of Montclair or Memphis and there is the grass growing and the little family looking not quite at him but just past the side of his head, and there's Cronkite on the tube and the smell of pot roast in the living room, and inside the house and outside in the pretty exurb has settled the noxious particles and the sadness of the old dying Western World, and him thinking: Jesus, is this it? Listening to Cronkite and the grass growing?"

Some people who can't drink choose to drink anyway. Some of them are very clever, like Jimmy Wallace and Pete Axthelm. They didn't see themselves as victims, but as men who made a very frightening choice. So we bury them, fearing all the while that they'll be replaced by sober people with no mercy for drinkers or smokers either—by some new, horribly healthy, functional sort of corporate person who never cries or dreams.

If that's the future, let's drink to the past. My brother and I amused our family this Christmas by giving each other identical bottles of bourbon. Whiskey has been our traditional exchange, and I don't think it's because we subconsciously, archetypically seek each other's destruction. But a drinker lives with ambivalence. The poet Robert Burns, one of Jimmy Wallace's distinguished "Scottish forebears," died at 37 and immortalized the elixir that helped to kill him as "a cup of kindness." Out of respect for his memory, I would never toast "auld lang syne" with tap water.

Each of us has a private devil that whispers to him in a voice more seductive than all the rest. If I had been St. Anthony, every one of those demons in the paintings would have been waving a pork chop.

The Way of All Flesh

Richmond, Virginia — It was a lesson in humility, finally; a lesson in the way our highest and (so-called) lowest impulses are quartered so close together that you can't embrace the one without waking up the other.

A poet drove me to it. Duke's Jim Applewhite, intending no harm, read his poem "How to Fix a Pig" for an audience of writers and creative writing students at Virginia Commonwealth University in Richmond:

> _When that vinegar and wood ashes_
> _smoke starts rising,_
> _And blowing in a blue wind over fields,_
> _It seems like even the broom straw_
> _Would get hungry . . ._

Several hundred were charmed by the poem; one was undone. One had been carrying—burning in his pocket like a forbidden woman's phone number—a flyer for the World Invitational Rib Championship at the Virginia State Fairgrounds. It might have remained there until, like so many meaningful scraps of paper, its hour of possibility was past. But Applewhite's eloquence started a salivary chain reaction on a level far deeper than will or reason, in the region "under sleep," in Eliot's words, "where all the waters meet."

Without ever making a conscious decision to attend the World Invitational, I found myself at the fairground gates at 11:30 Saturday morning, the second car in line. The gates opened at noon.

I can't say what I expected. What I found, in a cloud of hickory smoke and airborne cholesterol no poet could properly honor, was like nothing so much as a red-light district in some foreign port where sailors come on shore leave.

If you know New Orleans' Bourbon Street or Baltimore's Strip you have a sense of it. There's no point in feigning innocence or indifference here. No one comes to window-shop in the Rib District. They know you when you come.

"Hey, step over here. This is the place, Mac."

"Try some of these."

"Just take a look, that's all."

"Free samples. One taste, sir?"

Beckoning from the shadows, framed by the flames of the cook-fires, the rib runners are like pimps or Bourbon Street shills, like St. Anthony's demons. The Prince of Darkness is Cleveland's Lemeaud "Hot Sauce" Williams, a handsome black man wearing skintight black pants like a wet suit, wheedling seductively from a thick cloud of hickory smoke.

"It's hot, hot, hot," cackles Hot Sauce. "You like it hot, don't you, Jack? Hey, you in hog heaven now. High on the hog. Come get it while it's HOT."

Under Hot Sauce's awning, under Hot Sauce's beaming, crooning, proprietary scrutiny, I made short work of a half rack of baby back ribs smothered in a sweet, electric-red sauce with a deep jalapeno burn that operates on a five-second delay. Across the table, another big white man, with a big gold chain, was on his second rack.

"These are good, but try the Iowa tent," he offered, mopping hot sauce from his mustache. "Their mustard sauce is . . . unique."

Like lonely men in a brothel, passing in the hall, we exchange guilty glances and helpful tips but never look each other in the eye. Gluttons and lechers share the furtive camaraderie of the damned.

The glutton has one advantage, though: He can sample almost every attraction on the street. The Rib District's 20 alchemists, at their fires ringed around a sandy no-man's land of woodpiles and electric cables, were transmuting mere meat into rainbow delicacies I'd never dreamed of, in every color at the warm end of the spectrum, from near mahogany through burgundy to gold and hot pink. Smoked and soaked and purified by fire, the ribs become something almost mythic, more than flesh. "Meta-meat," a friend suggested. If Hot Sauce Williams was my Rubicon, the Australians were my Ides of March.

"Over here, myte—you. Free tyste. Don't pass this by."

The Aussie's greasy napkin cradled something that once was meat. It was beef, I think, no rib attached. He said it had been marinated, smoked and cooked slowly for two days. The first bite awakened impulses from the collective unconscious, racial memories from bloodstained ancestors crouched by their cookfire a million years ago, while giant hyenas fought in the darkness for the castoff bones.

I'm a man of some willpower who rises at 6:30 to run three miles, who once lost 90 pounds, who lets years elapse between one piece of cheesecake and the next. I've been training to become a vegetarian, gradually and successfully eliminating red meat from my diet. My relapse in the Rib District naturally brought me shame. My body felt mutinous, my pulse sluggish, as if fat cells that recently belonged to hogs were building roadblocks and damming streams in my arteries. I looked at the demon rib chefs themselves, at 300-pound Billy Bones from Red Keg, Michigan, and 350-pound Ray Green, the swollen football lineman whose Sweet Meat Cooking Team from Euless, Texas, won the 1989 grand prize for Best Ribs in the World. The life of the flesh takes its toll.

But there's a wisdom beyond shame in the Rib District. A man must come to face his limitations. In spite of my hypochondria, in spite of my belief that animals have rights, I'll never talk that vegetarian rot again. It's like boasting that you're a good husband who would never cheat on his wife; as long as you know there's one woman who could always trip you up, you're nothing but a hypocrite blowing smoke.

Besides uniting the most vermilion of rednecks and the most soulful of soul brothers in a rare common passion, the Invitational serves as a great leveler of all our pretensions. There's a sensitive side of me that objects to rib-eaters cheering for Robinson's Racing Pigs while the contestants' luckless littermates are reduced to charred bones a few feet away; it objects to Little Piggy puppet shows for kids with sauce and hot fat still staining their T-shirts. The World Invitational is spectacularly low-rent, a visual dialectic on the difference between "tastes good" and good taste, between tasty and tasteful.

But when did I start assuming that high-rent was where I belonged? In shame in the Rib District, I sensed that I was spending too much time with people who talk about houses and careers. And though I honestly enjoy them both, maybe too many evenings eating poached scallops and drinking Vouvray. You can't live on scallops and Vouvray any more than you can live on Mozart—the well-nourished spirit cries out for Mose Allison and B.B. King.

Worst of all, I had fallen into one of the self-worshiping heresies of the Reagan generation. I wasn't caught by the acquisitiveness, the hunger for wealth and possessions. What I'd absorbed was the accompanying myth that rich people don't ever have to die and give it all up. There's a connection between greed and fanatical good health, between earning more dollars you won't need and more days on earth you won't enjoy.

In the Rib District, a different voice whispers that you need meat; it whispers that you are meat. It whispers that the Lord wouldn't have made the meat so sweet and the swine so fine if he hadn't wanted us to enjoy them. Is that voice the Lord, the devil or Hot Sauce Williams? Do I care? Ask me if I'd trade six months of my life for what I received at the World Invitational. If they were healthy, full-speed months in my 50s, maybe not. If they were medicated, couch-potato, TV-lounge months in my 80s, I'd turn them over in a heartbeat. If a long life is so great, why are more old people killing themselves than ever before? (A 25 percent national increase between 1981 and 1986.)

At this existential moment the Jukebox Naturals, the quintessential redneck band this event demanded, wailed their opening anthem across the fairgrounds:

> It's later than you think, son
> Better have some fun
> Time marches on
> Soon you be dead and gone.

I took it seriously, as an omen. I'll go on running at 6:30 and avoiding butter. I'll never be as wide as Billy Bones or the Sweet Meat man mountain from Euless, Texas. But excommunicated by the vegans and shunned by the fastidious, I may grow bigger. Lord willing, I'll never again be a sanctimonious cholesterol cop, shaming others for their greasy diets. Moderation in all things, my late, meat-loving arteriosclerotic father counseled. Even moderation should be practiced in moderation. Show me the great poetry that celebrates the mortification of the flesh.

You can't really write about depression until you manage to beat it a couple of times, and some writers never do.

Deep Blues

There was an article in the paper about depression, an interview with a professor of psychiatry at Duke who estimates that there are about 15 million undiagnosed depressives in the adult population. The professor's remarks were straightforward, but as usual depression came out sounding like something you can pick up off a toilet seat or a dirty shotglass. You "have" depression, like you have acne or influenza.

I read this a few days before I left for New York City, where I once had a fairly intimate relationship with clinical depression. It went on for the better half of a decade. Since everyone agreed that I had nothing to complain about, perhaps a good deal to be thankful for, I was willing to pay top dollar to find out what was wrong with me. Psychiatry was as common as marijuana and peace signs among the people I knew then. Nine of the 10 people who worked in my section were in therapy or analysis. Our secretary dispensed prescription tranquilizers like typewriter ribbons. One of my best friends visited the doctor twice a week by himself, twice with his wife and once on Saturday with his wife and daughter.

All of them were trying to discover what sickness, what internal deformity kept them from enjoying a coveted career in the world's greatest city. Some of them are still trying. I was one of the lucky ones. I ended up with a psychiatrist named Wheat, a tall gaunt customer from Louisiana who resembled Vincent Price. For about a year he said almost nothing, or so it seemed to me. Then he said, in so many words, "Maybe there's nothing especially wrong with you. You grew up on a village green someplace and you hate New York. I don't much care for it myself, I'm just more adaptable than you are. Quit whining and get out."

I probably owe him my life. There are other Big Apple psychiatrists—so it seems to me—who have been trying to hammer square pegs into round holes so long that the poor pegs they've been working with have no shape left at all. In New York there are people who have been in the same therapy group for 10 years, still snapping and snarling and truth-telling and ostensibly prodding each other toward the light at the end of the tunnel.

I haven't won any Mental Hygiene beauty contests, but that was the last time I was depressed *all the time*. I'm skittish and spacy when I visit New York, like a Marine revisiting Iwo Jima.

For some unhappy people, it isn't just New York. When Truman Capote died last week, most of the obituaries lamented the waste of talent, the books that might have been written. Loss to the world, etc. I didn't care for the tone of that, as if Capote had been some rare lab animal who had unfortunately died before we'd run all the tests and milked him dry. What about the poor bastard's life?

". . . A full, deep and rich life," eulogized Artie Shaw, at Capote's memorial service. Will you play that again, Artie? Capote was a lifelong depressive—for good reason. If you think the world is a bad fit for you, put yourself in his size-3 sandals. An unwanted and almost parentless child with an excess of imagination, brilliant, a tiny bird-voiced homosexual with a tendency to fat, insecure to the point of hysteria. He started out as a literary celebrity and a gay sex symbol, ate and drank and made a fool of himself until he was a literary and sexual curiosity, and ended up as a lap dog for rich women.

If Scott Fitzgerald's fascination with the very rich was enigmatic and troublesome, Capote's was pathetic. It's ironic that he ended up as a pet in the home of Joanne Carson—as rich as any of his ladies if the stories are accurate, but a big drop in jet-set prestige from Babe Paley, Cee Zee Guest and Jackie O. The unresolved anguish at the center of his personality is obvious in the most superficial consideration of his work. At his most objective, at the greatest remove from his own experience with projects like *In Cold Blood* and *Handcarved Coffins*, he's matchless. In his creative fiction, after the near-perfect *Other Voices, Other Rooms*, the clear, clean prose is sometimes clouded by his demons. At his most autobiographical and self-indulgent—for example, the "night thoughts" ramble in *Music for Chameleons*—he's awful and pitiful.

Alcohol and drugs can't cure the self-pity that comes from knowing you're in the wrong place, especially if the wrong place is everywhere. Most of us can make ourselves more comfortable than a tiny genius who resembled an overfed parakeet. But if you're *never* depressed, you're not normal and admirable and well-adjusted.

You're a zucchini. An ornamental gourd. All it really takes to achieve depression is unrealistic expectations (for some people, almost any expectations are unrealistic), a couple of sense organs—you hardly need a full set—and a brain just good enough to beat Gerald Ford at chess.

Look around. Is this what you had in mind? The three worst ideas human beings ever had were nationalism, sectarian religion and the worship of private property. And all three of these ideas are flourishing so extravagantly, in this country and all over the world, that in many places there isn't room for any other ideas. Too many humans with too many bad ideas are chewing up the landscape to a point where it will make little difference, in 50 years, whether they blow it up or not. Most of the "exciting careers" that big corporations are selling so aggressively to gullible kids (and educators) would have been the stuff of nightmares if any novelist could have imagined them 50 years ago.

And yet only 15 million American adults are suffering from clinical depression. I think we're doing real well. The ones who go to bed and won't get up are going to have to be analyzed and medicated, but I think the rest of them could benefit from a change of perspective. If you think everyone's out of step but you, don't despair. You may be right. Some of the saddest victims are the ones who enrich generations of psychiatrists and psychologists because they think their normal depression is curable. I remember a friend of mine, a priest, who had just added liver cancer to his fairly long list of depressing prospects.

"All you can do is concentrate on the things that work for you," he said. "Try to give help instead of asking for it. Don't expect any miracles."

For a lot of sensitive, valuable people, life is New York City. When it gets to be too much, though, they can't leave it through the Holland Tunnel.

Kurt Vonnegut's greatest contributions to human understanding are the concepts of the granfalloon—a false, meaningless brotherhood—and the karass, a true one. In spite of George Bush, I still believe left-handers are members of a karass, with something profound and mystical in common.

My Left Hand

I believe the thing about marijuana that causes a stoner for people is that the majority of the population is right-handed. This means they think with the left side of the brain. When they get high they become aware that they are using the wrong side of their gray matter, and this tends to disorient them. But left-handers, such as yours truly, are used to using the right side of the brain. The correct side. The smoke puts us totally in sync with nature, and we have no trouble handling it.

— Bill "Spaceman" Lee, noted left-hander

I've been told, not always with approval, that everything about me—my politics, prejudices, aesthetics, temperament, friends and enemies, loves and losses—can be explained by the fact that I'm left-handed. Never mind heredity, childhood trauma, education or my Aries sun sign; the first time I reached up with that little wrinkled left fist and tried to tear off my mother's earring, my path was clearly marked from the cradle to the grave.

Certainly no one has been more severely conditioned by the limits of left-handedness in this right-handed world. There's nothing ambidextrous or borderline about my case. My right arm has been accurately described as vestigial. It's half as strong as my left and only two-thirds as thick. With great patience and difficulty we've trained it to manipulate a fielder's glove and those hellish scissors, and in a pinch a salad fork. Otherwise it just takes up space inside my shirt.

When you're as left-handed as I am, you can't help noticing the trait in others. The left hand/right hand–right brain/left brain split has generated a lot of promiscuous generalization, in my opinion. My impression is that right-handers come in absolutely every color of the rainbow—and left-handers in, well, many colors. There's just one kind of person who's never left-handed, and that's the straight-ahead unquestioning conformist governed only by herd instinct and whatever-Daddy-said. If you know such a person, I guarantee you that he grips his little monogrammed attache case with his little right hand. And don't try to refute me by pointing to the last three Republican presidents of the United States, three left-handers with less than a single fully formed original idea among them. Left-handers think—are forced by the world to think—that they're special. Presidents are invariably people who have always thought of themselves as mighty special—even if, as in these cases, it was more in the sense of the Special Olympics.

Each left-hander suffers alone, without benefit of lobbies, support groups or antidefamation leagues. In almost every language, the words for "left" have insulting connotations and double meanings; the French *gauche*, the Latin *sinistra*, even the Spanish *zurdo*, which also means malicious. In English idiom the sins against us are many and grievous, most of them compounded by the King James Version, which is presented to discouraged left-handed children as the Word of God itself. I antagonized a Sunday-school teacher when I was eight by complaining about Jesus who "sitteth at the right hand of God the Father." Ever since I've been waiting to hear someone, anyone, praise his left-hand man.

The most common second meaning of left-handed is backwards, upside-down, inappropriate, as in left-handed compliments and left-handed approaches. But this poisoned language is a light burden compared with the ancient cultural prejudice that poisoned it, the primitive hostility toward all deviants that stigmatizes left-handers to this day. A reporter at the *Washington Post*, a right-hand Nazi named Malcolm Gladwell, recently began a paragraph, "Because left-handedness is correlated with low intelligence . . . ." I'm not kidding. And Gladwell still has his job, as far as I know, and has neither been suspended nor exiled to the obituary desk for life.

I never heard a word of protest. Imagine the tidal wave of fury if Gladwell's slur had been directed at blacks, women, Koreans or even some minuscule minority like cross-dressers or electricians. They'd have disemboweled him. And I spit on any proffered statistics that may seem to support his outrageous statement. If you think culturally biased IQ tests handicap blacks and Hispanics (they do), try to imagine a hapless lefty going in backwards—and right-brained—against those infernal labyrinths of wheels and pulleys that are supposed to gauge mechanical intelligence.

For me it was like trying to fix a watch in the dark, with gloves on. Somehow I got into college anyway. And among the practical-minded left-handers who were able to overcome this tremendous mechanical handicap were Leonardo, Benjamin Franklin and Albert Einstein.

Other famous left-handers were Alexander the Great, Julius Caesar, Charlemagne and Napoleon. I have no doubt about their motivation for conquering the world and putting whole provinces full of right-handers to the sword. It was anger that drove them, left-handed resentment pure and simple. Oriental histories are less detailed, but no doubt Genhis Khan, Attila the Hun and Tamerlane were also southpaws. (Jack the Ripper and the Boston Strangler came at you from the left side, too.)

Most of us have learned to live with it, the way individuals blind from birth find blindness normal and bearable. We have a queer left-handed confidence of our own that compensates for the lemming smugness of The Right. But now, out of deep left field, comes a bombshell. A study of 2,000 deceased Californians, published by a Canadian psychologist, indicated that the right-handers lived *nine* years longer than the lefties, on the average—and the average difference among males was a full decade.

I laughed at first because I saw that fatal accidents—five times as likely for left-handers—were responsible for most of the discrepancy. Lefties know they shouldn't try to fix right-handed power mowers. Inanimate objects lie in wait for us; just five minutes earlier I had fallen, hard, over a lawn-chair barrier I'd set up to keep the puppy off the living-room rug. I grinned through my pain. No fracture this time. But then I began to reflect. Ten years is an eternity, if you've already lived more than half your life. Ten years is the difference between a ripe old age and an ugly scene at the funeral parlor.

I doubt very much that there's anything definitive about this fatal study. You'd have to study something more substantial than Californians to convince me (I have no prejudices). Everyone knows that left-handers are particularly drawn toward alternatives, and who knows what dangerous substances and self-destructive activities have seduced left-handed Californians? Hang gliders and acid don't mix, guys. And I've been saving, for gloating purposes, a September 1989 study that asserts just the opposite—that it's left-handers who live longer.

The early study (conducted, oddly, by another resident of Vancouver, B.C.) based its conclusions on the death certificates of 4,479 major-league ballplayers, certainly a more reliable sample than that crowd from Southern California. It found that lefties born after 1910 lived 2.1 years longer, an advantage that projected to 3.7 years for players still alive.

That sounds better. I'm more comfortable with the ballplayers because I have my own record books to cross-check, and because I think left-handed baseball pitchers were the source for the original stereotype of the zany, doomed left-hander. I think it all began with Rube Waddell from Bradford, Pa., just down the road from where I lived as a kid. This turn-of-the-century fireballer was the genuine article—paralytic boozer, alligator wrestler, fire-engine chaser—and he died at 37 after stacking sandbags in an icy, flooding river.

But I checked the *Baseball Encyclopedia* entries for six other left-handers who were prominent in Waddell's day, and found that they lived to an average age of 85. Doc White and Nick Altrock, star lefties of the Chicago White Sox "Hitless Wonders" world champions of 1906, lived to see 90 and 89, respectively. And all of them were ordinary citizens (except maybe Altrock, who ended up as the fat half of a Laurel-and-Hardy team of baseball clowns, with Al Schacht).

One bad apple. It's true that Lefty Gomez was known as Goofy, but the Cardinals' Gashouse Gang of Lefty's era pitched Dizzy, Daffy and Dazzy, all right-handers. And Gomez outlived them all. Lefty Sam McDowell may have been modern baseball's most outrageous drunk, and the San Francisco Spaceman, Bill Lee, was the shaman of its Flower Children. But neither of them could lay a glove on their contemporary Dock Ellis, a right-hander who wore his hair in curlers in the clubhouse and pitched a no-hitter on LSD.

I'm typing up my research and sending it to Vancouver. But maybe it would be better, for the time being, if everyone believed the latest study, the one that says we're doomed. Though we make up 10 percent of the population, lefties have never attracted any sympathy as a minority, never acquired any clout. But if it's true that we're innocent victims of our genetic package, tragically condemned to an early grave no less than victims of sickle cell anemia or Huntington's chorea, then we become a *disadvantaged minority*, with all the rights and privileges attached.

One of the principal rights, exercised to the point of nausea by all the other disadvantaged minorities, is the right to choose a name for ourselves and compel the media and all politically correct individuals to call us by that name and that name only. And we have a right to change it as often as we like, without notice.

At last I'm in the driver's seat. And I don't really like "left-hander" at all. It's too much like "left-winger," which is the same as "communist" in this country, and the same goes for "lefty." "Portsider" is no good, it makes you think of alcoholic beverages and it sounds off-center. "Southpaw" combines the negative images of the American South with "paw," which sounds positively subhuman. Save "southpaw" for Brer Bear.

Someone suggested "gaucho-American," but the Indian word *gaucho*, unrelated to the French *gauche*, means "vagabond." "Contra" has been ruined. We're working on it, in the little time we have left. In the meantime you can refer to us, along with the rest of the handicapped, as "differently abled."

Parenting is the hardest thing we can undertake in our lives, and the most important. The most unpopular thing I ever said—on a public radio talk show—was that there ought to be a law against double-income yuppies who try to raise children in their spare time. The phone wires were smoking for hours. But I'd say it again.

A Father's Blessing

Tomorrow is my daughter's 20th birthday. It's a time for sober, possibly tearful reflection and a time for letting go. A father's anxieties end only in his grave. But when she reaches 20, he ought to keep them to himself, if he can. By letting go I mean giving up the illusion that anything can be forbidden, that throwing fits and making threats will do more good than harm, that the grown woman in question can still be molded and edited to conform to the father's design. I retain some financial leverage, but I've sworn to use it sparingly, if at all. She can count on the checks, with no lectures attached, as long as I'm confident that she won't use the money to hurt herself.

I guess it won't be long before I'm sitting on the sidelines with another generation of grandparents, irrelevant and obsolete, practicing love without leverage, watching helplessly while my worst mistakes are repeated and amplified. But I never go quietly. Before I put on my slippers and creep over to the rocker by the fireplace, I have a few valedictory observations for parents who remain on active duty.

This is a terrible time to raise kids. Everybody knows that. When some friend sends us a happy letter announcing a welcome, hard-earned pregnancy, my wife has to intervene to make sure I don't respond with something like "Tough break" or "Are they sure?" instead of "Congratulations." I'm not against reproduction. I know someone has to do it, the same as military service. It's just that I like most of these people, the odds are stacked against them, and I don't think most of them are tough or clever enough to beat the odds.

Half of them, at least, will be led like lambs to the slaughter. Well-meaning couples from the white middle class are especially pitiful. They tend to be blinded by sentiments and traditions that no longer apply. In an urban ghetto most parents know what they're up against; out in the subdivisions most parents don't have a clue. First they're hopelessly innocent. Then they're in denial. And then, for many of them and for many of their children, it's like trying to patch up Humpty Dumpty.

I heard some more stories this month, stories about children of people we know. You wouldn't believe these stories. You'll never hear them in time to benefit from them, because the parents only tell their stories to counselors and to other parents with similar stories. The suffering of middle-class families has become an oral tradition, recorded only in confidential files.

Down the rabbit-hole, was the way I described it in a column about drugs. In the blink of an eye. One day she's Daddy's little girl, the next day she's got more experience of a certain kind than any woman Daddy ever dated. You've still got the picture in your wallet, with the braids and the two teeth missing in front, but the person you're looking at is a troubled woman you may never be able to comfort or understand. The boy who looks like a Xerox of you has deliberately or accidentally pushed himself so far from your experience that you need an intermediary to approach him.

There's never been a gap between generations like the one we're facing now. For an American born in 1950, it would be easier to understand a person of his own class born in 1650 than one born in 1975. Divorce, women's liberation, TV and the mass media explosion, drugs, legal abortion and the autonomous, tribal teenage culture have altered the social landscape almost beyond recognition, all in my own lifetime. I can't imagine how it looks to the few members of my grandfather's generation who are still alive and sentient.

Statistics have become cheap currency. But in Neil Postman's *The Disappearance of Childhood* there's a fact—supported by statistics—that I keep coming back to: Before 1950 there were no crimes committed by children. Or not enough crimes to show on the charts. Last year in Washington, D.C., 15 juveniles were arrested every day (and every day 26 children were reported abused, and 1,300 slept in shelters).

When we were kids, the whole family gathered to watch "Father Knows Best." In real life two of the actors who played the children had serious drug problems; Robert Young, who played Father, became a drunk in his old age and recently tried to kill himself.

This is rich metaphor. Now kids the same age watch heavy-metal junkies humping on MTV, and make holes in themselves for jewelry (in places besides their ears).

When your child reaches a certain age—12 isn't too young to start—the experience gap between the two of you is growing so rapidly that you have to hold whatever you're doing, right there, and make damn sure the gap doesn't become unbridgeable. Just when the child wants to communicate less, you have to communicate more. Just when the child wants more freedom, you have to be prepared to offer less. Just when your babies begin to resemble adults, you have to begin to watch them as if they were babies again.

A permanent gap can open in an instant—a gap that means a lifetime of silences and forced conversations, family holidays with both generations sneaking glances at the clock. Or much, much worse.

The gap can become permanent when the child takes a fatal step into a range of experience that you can't comprehend. Intravenous drugs, psychedelics, rehabs, felonies, sex with multiple partners, venereal disease—these are radical experiences that may move a 14-year-old right out of your league. The child may recover, but your relationship may not.

There's only so much that can be forgiven or forgotten, on both sides. Sometimes forgetting is easier than forgiving. The greatest challenge for any parent is to be there to forestall the unforgivable, to head off the worst before it happens. Some of the best-intentioned parents fail miserably. You have to be a snoop and a tough cop, sometimes a bastard. When the kid's peers begin to replace you, you have to fight back. You can only get so much mileage from a child's affection, or a child's conscience. Fear and surveillance have their place. Don't even talk to me about anything as stupid as *trusting* your teenager. I was a teenager.

I wouldn't say these things if I didn't believe them, if I didn't have personal experience to back them up. If you can get your kids into their late teens relatively untraumatized, you may end up a winner. They'll never again be as stupid as they were at 13.

On the other hand, your best efforts may be thwarted. There's a critical mass of undertended teenagers out there, waiting to swallow your kid. Sophistication may not save you, any more than kindness. The best families lose children. There was a national scandal when the police in the Bronx discovered that Eliezer and Maria Marrero had chained their 15-year-old daughter to a radiator, for a year. But it turned out that the Marreros were loving parents who were trying to save their daughter's life. Every time she went out the door she went straight to a crack house. Parents everywhere experienced an involuntary shudder of sympathy and recognition.

Those 15 years between the baby pictures and the Marrero Maneuver will pass more swiftly than you can imagine. I offer these words of caution from concern, not from the smug position of a retired father who's patting himself on the back. Don't confuse me with Bill Cosby, who sold millions of books on fatherhood before they discovered that he had a daughter on drugs. (I recommend Cosby's book for three things though—for admitting that having a baby is totally irrational, for asserting that the worst thing you can do to grown children is to let them live at home, and for confirming that nearly all children lie compulsively, like horse traders.)

When people praise my daughter, I don't take a lot of credit. I was never the stern, vigilant father a girl needs these days. I don't know if I ever told her anything that helped her. I certainly wasn't there to guide her every step.

She's gone her own way, and she tells me stories that make my blood run cold. But she claims that a certain native caution always held her in check, even when it wasn't evident to her parents. Maybe she has me to thank for that, or at least my chromosomes. I was blessed, or cursed, with the same lurking caution. The worst scrapes I ever got into, I always had one eye on my father's blood pressure. It shames me to admit it, but most of the worst stories about me are wild exaggerations.

If she was sometimes less than a model child, I was always less than a model father, which gives a certain balance to our relationship. We ended up sort of even, without going to extremes. Unlike so many fathers and daughters who went through divorce, remarriage and all the trimmings, neither of us ever did anything that's real hard for the other to forgive. Of course she'd have to confirm that. But forgiveness is the key issue in most families. You wouldn't believe what some of these poor parents are being asked to forgive.

I'm letting go of my daughter without my fingers crossed. But as I recall, the last present I gave her was a heavy silver bracelet from Taxco—only one, no chain attached. Maybe some time when she's feeling impulsive she'll look at that bracelet and think of me, and of Eliezer and Maria Marrero.

Insight thrives in solitude, withers in a herd. The italicized quote from Wendell Berry just about sums up this book, and everything I believe in.

Happy Trails to You

Panther Junction, Texas — This trail up Pine Canyon was rated "medium difficulty" in my guidebook. But this same guide had sent me off on ghost trails in the desert, where flash floods had erased every trace of human passage; it had steered me to "intermediate" mountain trails where tiers of switchbacks designed for Sherpas disappeared into the clouds. At about three o'clock on a chilly, overcast afternoon of intermittent drizzle, I stopped to wipe my glasses and reconsider my assault on Pine Canyon.

The guide told me how many hundred feet I'd have to climb from the trailhead to the top of the canyon, but it didn't mention that I'd climb them all at the end of the trail. For the past quarter of a mile the trail had been as steep as a tenement staircase, and my heart was rehearsing a familiar solo by Buddy Rich. "Never surprise your heart," a cardiologist told me when I was much younger, and I've made it one of my rules to live by.

The ticker sounded mildly startled, and mutinous. I know my limits. But a mountain never lets you know how much more it's going to ask from you, how your best effort is going to match up against the task at hand. I wasn't packing a pedometer; the top could have been just around the next boulder or another half mile straight up. I sat on a log in a grove of Texas madrone, those shocking naked trees the Indians called lady's legs, and stared up into the mist. A minute before two bearded backpackers—the only other hikers I saw all day—had passed me climbing hard. In the perfect silence of the high Chisos Mountains, I couldn't hear anything from up there in their direction, not a cough. They must, I thought, be far above me already, on the way to the distant waterfall that I would never see.

With me the machismo factor is rated intermediate; the curiosity factor is powerful, always. I convinced myself to sweat for one last ridge, and quit if the trail from there just kept on climbing. It would take some Texas-size stretcher bearers to carry me out of this canyon, but at least the guys ahead of me could tell them where I went down.

Of course the climb ended on that ridge, where I could see the top of the canyon, 100 level yards ahead. I hadn't heard the back-packers because they were stretched out on their backs staring up at the 250-foot cliff and its fragile waterfall, observing a religious silence as outdoor people often will in the presence of unusual beauty. Still breathing hard, I joined the easy brotherhood of Those Who Stuck It Out.

"North Carolina? They've got some pretty fair mountains in North Carolina, don't they?"

"Not like here."

"I'd like to see them, though. Nothing like mountains."

"That's the way I feel."

"People don't think of mountains when they think of Texas."

We lay up there, mostly quiet, for another 20 minutes. Then they wished me luck and started down. Low clouds shifted and cov-ered half the cliff face, until the little waterfall seemed to be falling directly from the clouds. A wind came up and moaned around in the pinyons and the naked madrones. Pine Canyon is a place of great power, as Castaneda's Don Juan would have said, a place where the spirits are strong. Chisos means "ghost" in one Indian language, and according to Indian legend a great chief named Alsate still haunts the high Chisos, tricking mortals with the glow of huge campfires that disappear when they approach.

It's not a place you'd want to miss by 100 yards because you were faint of heart, not when you'd walked half a day to get there. The lesson was clear and familiar: Never give up, never sell yourself short—your goal is just over that ridge. But what if the plot had gone differently, with the pilot of the rescue helicopter smoking half a pack of Salems down at the mouth of the canyon while a team of burly, cursing medics wrestled my beefy carcass down the mountain on a stretcher? Then the lesson would have been more like, "Know when to hold 'em, know when to fold 'em." Learning when to quit and when not to quit is a much more sophisticated lesson than "I think I can, I think I can . . . ."

I work with lessons, you see. A friend said once, without malice, that I have an incurably pedantic mentality. He meant that I turn everything that happens to me and around me into some kind of lesson—as if the universe existed for my personal education. "That'll teach me," I say four or five times a day.

This habit of thinking isn't surprising, considering that both my parents were teachers, and that the classroom and the pulpit were the only careers I considered seriously before I stumbled into this one. It isn't pathetic or immoral, I don't think, as long as you don't try to keep all your lessons for yourself.

But it is, according to the same friend, utterly futile. The only important lesson we ever learn, in his opinion, is that our lives are finite. He adds, for emphasis, that most people learn no lessons at all. Generation after generation they genuflect to the same falsehoods, mate with the same lack of foresight, adopt the same absurdities and platitudes as the immutable truths of their lives. They scheme to make fortunes without skills or knowledge, they elect liars and parasites to lead them, they offer their lives in indefensible wars. They march like lemmings, as if they never heard the splashes ahead of them. They abuse the same debilitating substances and buy the same meretricious products that support the same destructive conglomerates.

His is a hard message for the pedantic (I prefer pedagogic) mentality to accept. I prefer glib optimists who make good cases for progress: We conquered polio and smallpox, we freed our women from the bondage of their wombs, we photographed Mars at close range. But Progress, once an almost universal article of human faith, has become a more specialized, sectarian faith— even a highly gullible theology.

If the sum of human wisdom is represented by the way we control our reproduction and care for the planet that sustains us, the Church of Progress should be full of empty pews. On a clear day in the Chisos, you can see mountains in Mexico 60 miles away. A few decades ago, according to a marker in Big Bend National Park, you could see a mountain 250 miles away. On the clearest day of the winter, I looked across the Rio Grande from the Chisos and saw an oily haze over the Sierra del Carmen. It comes all the way from LA and Mexico City, a ranger told me. And smog from the oil fires in the Persian Gulf has already spread halfway around the earth.

My pessimistic friend sees exceptional people as martyrs, worms writhing on the double-barbed hook of human hopelessness. Edison, Steinmetz and Einstein pioneered amazing technologies to save human beings from primitive drudgery, only to see their discoveries transformed into nightmare weapons orchestrated by fat generals in fatigues. Medical science has learned to protect children from almost every disease except their parents. Duke Ellington's descendants play rap on their boom boxes.

This subversive message is becoming more seductive to me, somehow. But up in the Chisos, out in the Chihuahuan Desert, disillusionment skirts despair and resolves itself in a shift of focus. Each of us has a life of his own, after all. The brilliant but sometimes contradictory Wendell Berry, whose essays I took to the desert with me, expends a lot of passion on the primacy of community but ends up making a better case for himself as a solitary man of principle.

"Now it is only in the wild places that a man can sense the rarity of being a man," Berry writes in *Notes from an Absence and a Return*. "In the crowded places he is more and more closed in by the feeling that he is ordinary—and that he is, on the average, expendable.

"You can best serve civilization by being against what usually passes for it." (My italics.)

Must be a lesson there somewhere. Berry offers plenty of useful instruction in the art of living, but his best advice is probably this, in essence: Plow your own field the best you can, and never mind if your neighbors make a botch of theirs. A solitary commitment is no less moral and no less constructive, as long as you begin by making the right choices. It's just that the choices are infinitely more critical when you make them alone. "Never give up" is a useless, even a dangerous principle if you weren't on the right trail in the first place.

Epilogue

Heroes

A friend of mine, a good woman who takes politics seriously, looked tired and depressed after watching Newt Gingrich crowned with standing ovations in the House of Representatives. "So what now?" I asked her.

"There are always individuals," she said. "There are always a lot of exceptional individuals who care and commit themselves."

And so there are. My generation was brought up in a tradition of admiration; we were taught to find heroes and role models and to study them seriously. This last section features some of the individuals I have admired, for a great variety of reasons. These essays probably reveal more about the writer than any of the others in this book. I'm sorry to see that so many of them were inspired by obituaries.

Hal Crowther

Petra Kelly: Death of the Green Queen

If you look out for yourself, assiduously, with any luck you'll live to a ripe old age. If you look out for others, especially *all* the others, you'll probably die young, and violently. Conspicuous altruism is life-threatening. This is not a rule; it's a pattern that impresses itself, as the years go by, on an observer who struggles against the mortal sin of pessimism.

In an endless succession of examples, the most recent is the short, unhappy, exceptionally worthwhile life of Petra Kelly. Kelly was not well known in this country, where the wretched science of self-promotion long ago replaced measurable achievement as the passkey to renown. The most thorough account of her death was published in *Vanity Fair*, a wildly schizoid slick that covers AIDS and famine back-to-back with Fifth Avenue furniture auctions. In fact *VF* ran Kelly's picture back-to-back—overleaf—with a photo of its covergirl, jet-set model Claudia Schiffer, whom it billed as "Germany's most famous woman."

It's doubtful that Petra Kelly was ever Germany's most famous woman. But at the zenith of her influence, in 1982, *The Guardian* called her "the second most powerful woman in Europe," next to Margaret Thatcher. Since Europe is the place where women seem to achieve the most political power, you don't have to deplore Thatcher as much as I do to suggest that there was a time in the '80s when Kelly may have exerted more *positive* influence than any other female on the planet.

Tabloids called her "The Green Queen." As a founder and president of Germany's Green Party, as a member of the German Parliament, as one of the decade's most outspoken and tireless champions of human rights, deep ecology and nuclear disarmament, she was a major factor in shaping the liberal conscience of the West. In an age of semiliteracy, no writer or artist could have tipped the scales as many degrees as this hands-on revolutionary who believed, like Rosa Luxemburg and the proto-radicals she revered, that nothing cleared the mind and cleansed the conscience like another rousing arrest.

When I read that Kelly had been found dead in her house in Bonn, shot through the head with a .38-caliber bullet, I picked up an envelope full of color photographs and went out to sit in the yard. I

took the snapshots in September 1991, at an environmental conference in Morelia, Mexico. I found her in just one. We were at an outdoor market along the wharf at Lake Patzcuaro. In the foreground is
my friend Faith Sale; in the center, grinning, is Peter Mathiessen. In
the background, under a row of handwoven sweaters, is Petra Kelly.
There's no symbolic foreshadowing of tragedy, though morbid Mexico
is always crawling with skeletons and death's heads. The sweater that
hangs directly over her head depicts a brilliant rainbow.

It would be misleading to say that I knew her, fair to say that I
made her acquaintance. She and her lover Gert Bastian, who
apparently shot her before committing suicide, occupied the room
next to mine at the Hotel Villa Montana. Kelly seemed a little
embarrassed by the hotel, sumptuous by Mexican standards, a
sprawling hilltop extravagance that reminded me of some of the
fancy homes in Beverly Hills. One beautiful night she sat with us
by the pool after dinner, looking down at the lights of the city. But
after a few minutes she cast a worried look at Bastian and he took
her inside. She wasn't cold, I don't think. It was just a counter-
revolutionary setting, if there ever was one.

Like many of the sincere revolutionaries I've encountered, Kelly
was soft-spoken and self-effacing, almost shy when you took away
her bullhorn. You could make her laugh if you worked at it, but her
eyes were tired. She was an attractive woman, with better bones
than Claudia Schiffer's. But she didn't look healthy. She was pallid,
and there were dark circles under her eyes from a kidney disorder.
She suffered a heart attack in 1982, when she was only 35. She
gave the impression that she was using herself up very rapidly, and
you would shrink to waste a minute of her time with small talk.

Most of us felt protective toward Kelly and deferred to her in
conversation—we would wait an extra beat or two to see if there
was something she wanted to add. She carried the authority of total
seriousness, the only kind of authority that people like me are
forced to recognize.

She was deeply pessimistic, she said, about the future of the
earth.

"I don't see any political will that's going to coalesce in time to
save us," she told the assembled writers and scientists. "Where is it,
do you think?" And she reminded them that the end of the Cold
War, the liberation of Eastern Europe and the reunification of Germany were minor events compared with what she characterized as

"the biological holocaust." Peace between the superpowers might be a blessing for Europe, but it was almost irrelevant to the wretched populations of the Third World. A false hope, she called it, and she quoted someone: "When elephants make war, the grass gets trampled; when elephants make love, the grass gets trampled."

Gen. Bastian, once the commander of Germany's 12th panzer division, was a handsome man with formal manners who held Kelly's elbow when they walked, and rarely let her out of his sight. His manner was more guarded than hers, but there was a gentleness about him, if "gentle" is ever the right word for a general officer from the regular army who fought for the Third Reich. We said good-bye to them at the taxi stand in front of the Camino Real, in Mexico City. Petra left us with the standard Green farewell of the moment: "See you next spring in Rio."

I didn't make it to the Earth Summit in Rio de Janeiro. I assume, without checking, that Kelly and Bastian were there. A year and a month after we parted in Mexico City, Bonn police found both of them shot in the head and in an advanced state of decomposition. Kelly, 44, was lying in bed.

Like radicals everywhere, in Bonn or in Chapel Hill, their friends were quick to suspect a political assassination. There were any number of enemies to choose from, any number of lethal agents who would have been pleased to see the last of them: the CIA, the new Nazis, the German government itself, the South Africans, the Chinese who have been embarrassed by Kelly's support of human rights in Tibet.

But the facts of the case—the powderburns on Bastian's hand, for instance—don't lend themselves to any of the more paranoid scenarios. Kelly's influence had diminished since voters turned the Greens out of Parliament in 1990. No one will ever know whether she was a party to her own death. But it isn't hard to build a case for exhaustion, discouragement and despair.

The resurgence of the German Right, with the accelerating attacks on foreign workers and refugees, would have been very painful for Petra Kelly. (Though to give the Germans their due, 200,000 of them showed up to protest the attacks, a demonstration of good will such as the United States has never mustered against its native bigots.) The partition of Czechoslovakia would have been difficult for her, and the negative role of the United States in

Rio de Janeiro, and of course the post-Communist horrors in what used to be Yugoslavia.

Sophisticated as she was, Kelly knew that ethnic warfare and political fragmentation could deal a death blow to the Green agenda. Smaller countries, weaker governments and feeble economies mean more passive reliance on the multinational corporations whose power will eventually outstrip every political entity. It's much harder to bargain with presidents who answer to stockholders instead of voters and reckon their success in profits instead of the quality of human lives. Business goes on as usual. Even as American environmentalists were congratulating themselves on the ascendance of Al Gore and Bruce Babbitt, the Commerce Department was giving BP Chemical the green light to sell a $100 million poison-gas factory to the *Iranians*.

It isn't easy being Green, which I think is a quotation from Kermit the Frog. It takes a lot of optimism, because this effort to save the human race from itself requires an almost religious belief, a belief in the possibility of a kind of cooperation that has no historical precedent. That one of the most relentless idealists of the 20th century may have run out of optimism before her 45th birthday is a sobering thought, on this sorry gray day in January.

I'd rather think that the spirit was still willing, in Petra's case, even if the flesh had had about all it could take. The Dalai Lama, her close friend, declared his faith in her fighting spirit when he gave her a special Buddhist dispensation to neglect repose and meditation. "Go on fighting," he is supposed to have told her, "I will meditate for you."

I don't know if the future is as hopeless as Petra Kelly may have concluded. I know the media are hopeless, when 50 percent of American schoolgirls could probably identify Claudia Schiffer, and 95 percent could identify Madonna or Demi Moore—all women whose only known function is to be photographed. Not one in a hundred could identify Petra Kelly, who according to my criteria was the most convincing heroine of the postwar generation. Let us meditate on that.

Hal Crowther

Lewis Mumford: View from a High Place

I recently made a substantial pilgrimage—to Lakeville, Conn.,
1,000 miles as the crow flies—to attend a memorial service for
Lewis Mumford. I made no attempt to recruit other pilgrims in
North Carolina. Yet I was saddened, more than surprised, to find
people who had never heard of Mumford, others who knew the
name but could not place it.

At the memorial service Kirkpatrick Sale, the author of *Human
Scale*, stared hard at his audience—as if to invite a challenge—when
he called Lewis Mumford "the greatest thinker of the 20th century."
To Malcolm Cowley he was "the last of the great humanists." To me
he was nothing less than an Old Testament prophet, Isaiah in a
tweed jacket. I'm not the scholar to tell you which of his ideas were
absolutely original and which ones were brilliant amplifications of
his intellectual ancestors. But in his books you will find, I believe,
everything you need to know about the world you live in.

To some extent Mumford, who died at 94 in January, outlived
his fame. But his fame at its high-water mark was a limited fame.
At one time all serious, literate people were aware, at least, of his
work and his concerns. At one time there were a lot more serious
people. The audience for a writer like Mumford has been steadily
shrinking throughout the turbulent century that contained his life.

To describe Lewis Mumford in dust-jacket fashion, with a list of
the professions and disciplines he encompassed, is to diminish and
insult him. Between 1922 and 1982 he was the author of at least 27
published volumes by my best count; he was best known for *The
Myth of the Machine*, *Technics and Civilization* and *The City in History*,
and for his column "The Sky Line," which ran for over 30 years in
The New Yorker. He began his career as a journalist.

I think I describe him best as a writer who believed that we can
read the future in the lines of cities, as a palmist reads your future
in the lines of your hand. He saw things that frightened him; Mumford's romance with the American city, with New York in particular, is one of the tragic love stories of the 20th century.

This was the man who wrote, in *The City in History*, "the city
should be an organ of love" and who saw in the metropolis "a great
mysterious will" as inspiring as the one he found in nature. In
Sketches from Life, he describes a prospect of New York from the

Brooklyn Bridge that moved him as profoundly as "the wonder of an orgasm in the body of one's beloved." (At the service, it was no small wonder to hear that passage read and to observe the unembarrassed pleasure of the beloved in question, his 90-year-old widow Sophia, a gallant woman who wears her snow-white hair in a modified flapper bob not unlike the one she wears in the photographs of their courtship.)

Like his mentor Patrick Geddes, the Scottish urbanologist who established himself in a tower high on Edinburgh's Castle Rock, Mumford relished views of the city from distant heights, and believed that the fate of the city was the fate of a civilization itself. Yet he came to write, at 73:

"No small part of this ugly urban barbarization has been due to sheer physical congestion; a diagnosis now partly confirmed by scientific experiments with rats—for when they are placed in equally congested quarters, they exhibit the same symptoms of stress, alienation, hostility, sexual perversion, parental incompetence, and rabid violence that we now find in Megalopolis."

Most telling of all, the lover of cities spent the last decades of his long life in the tiny (pop. 1,157) rural community of Amenia, N.Y., which greets visitors with a sign, "Welcome to the Hamlet of Amenia." (Purists point out that Mumford actually lived in the tinier hamlet of Leedsville, a suburb of Amenia.)

Mumford's career, like the careers of most visionary thinkers in the 20th century, was a series of intellectual triumphs and practical defeats. He was the first writer to explore the connection between totalitarianism and technology, tracing the roots of fascism and human regimentation back millennia before the Industrial Revolution, to ancient civilizations like Egypt in the Age of Pyramids— "an archetypal machine composed of human parts."

"As for the great Egyptian pyramids," he wrote in *The Myth of the Machine*, "what are they but the precise static equivalents of our own space rockets? Both devices for securing, at an extravagant cost, a passage to Heaven for the favored few."

Mumford's horrific Megamachine provides an organizing principle for all our most urgent fears and forebodings about the path on which we have set ourselves in this century.

"Our present civilization is a gigantic motorcar moving along a one-way road at an ever-accelerating speed," he wrote in a surge of fearless metaphor. "Unfortunately, as now constructed the car lacks both steering wheel and brakes, and the only form of control the driver exercises consists in making the car go faster, though in his fascination with the machine itself and his commitment to achieving the highest speed possible, he has quite forgotten the purpose of the journey."

Thirty years ago, when even liberals were reluctant to listen, Mumford deflated the grand sham of the Cold War and the nuclear arms race that held us on the brink of annihilation for half a century:

"By imposing a permanent state of war this elite constructed a vast megamachine, extravagantly supporting and inflating with public funds an assemblage of private corporate megamachines, operating on a the same principles, pursuing the same ends."

His cynical approach to technology—he called The Machine "the new Messiah"—gave hope and purpose to neo-Luddites like me, but he persuaded us that skeptical perspective was better than blowing up plants and laboratories. Whenever I needed an idea to make a connection, or authority for a favorite idea of my own, I turned to Mumford; he rarely failed me. But above all I'm indebted to him for the example he set. Mumford boasted always that he was a generalist, and claimed as his spiritual fathers the great generalists like Geddes and Samuel Butler, all the way back to Leonardo.

In a culture that places the highest premium on specialists I always recoiled, almost by instinct, from the pressure to become one. It was a pressure that I interpreted as the malignant will of the Megamachine trying to assert itself over me, my friends, the poor children who are supposed to choose a major and a profession the day the university absorbs them. To give in, it seemed to me, was to give up a critical measure of your free will and independent mind. A specialist who never struggles to outgrow his specialty is always a mere moving part, rather than a master or even a critical observer, of the stupendous machine.

By text and example Mumford encouraged the few of us, the stubborn holdouts, to view life, like the city, from a high separate place where you could see all around it. He was the patron saint of the vanishing American generalist.

That's what I owed Lewis Mumford and what I knew about him. At his memorial service I learned, among other things, that he was a man who took himself very seriously, and expected no less of his family. His daughter Alison Morss remembered when he had contradicted something one of her teachers told her, and she had complained of it.

"A teacher is just a teacher," her mother had remonstrated. "Your father is a great man." No levity relieved the impact of this revelation.

Later some of us discussed this, whether it meant that Mumford was a man for whom we might have felt little affection. I stood up for him. It was a different generation, I argued. Today we have so many self-important chimpanzees parading in public, so many Lee Iacoccas, that we've come to prize a phony sort of talk-show humility, a product perfected by Ronald Reagan. In Mumford's day people with talent took themselves and other things very seriously, and they often made serious contributions. Today no one but an idiot would call himself a great man; so we have no great men, and few good ones.

We assembled to honor Mumford in a New England village hours from the nearest city, in the chapel of the famous Hotchkiss School, where generations of future Yalemen have begun their intellectual journeys. Mumford would have noted the architecture —high vaults of dark blue held aloft by white pillars, a design to make schoolboys think of God. The chapel was almost full, a congregation of environmentalists, architects, enlightened philanthropists, publishing people from New York, country neighbors of the Mumfords.

It was, of course, no youthful congregation. Walkers were in evidence, and hearing aids. No schoolboys were present. Outside they went about their business. One in a T-shirt opened the side door for an instant and backed out in embarrassment, startled by this parliament of ancients in the sacred center of his school. We were honoring the only ideas, the only kind of perspective that could possibly salvage the foundering civilization this boy is stuck with, but to him we must have looked like some arcane geriatric cult at its ritual. We almost seemed like that to me—a defiant but obscure remnant of a secret society that once, like the Knights of the Temple, held great sway.

What impresses them, these schoolchildren who haven't read their fathers' books and cannot, waves of studies tell us, find Africa on the map? Do they contemplate the passage of time? Would it impress them to know that the man we were gathered to remember was as old as the school itself, much older than television or nuclear energy, older than radio, airplanes or automobiles, older even than the astonishing century that's rapidly drawing to a close?

I wonder if it would frighten them to know that this old man, who saw so much and was justly honored as a prophet, wrote to a friend in 1969, "I think, in view of all that has happened the last half century, that it is likely the ship will sink."

Mumford also said that he would die happy if his tombstone read, "This man was an absolute fool. None of the disastrous things that he reluctantly predicted ever came to pass." Even as his hopes for the city and the earth were repeatedly dashed and his prophecies became increasingly pessimistic, he ended every book and most chapters on a note of optimism. He published an award-winning autobiography at 87. In extreme old age he declared that his unifying theme was human purpose, a defiant refusal to give up or give in. His biographer Donald Miller writes that his favorite line of poetry in those last years was from Tennyson's "Ulysses": "Come my friends, 'tis not too late to seek a newer world." (By pure coincidence, I had been reciting those verses myself for months, as I faced what I perceived as middle age.)

Despair was not in him. *The New Yorker*'s Brendan Gill, speaking at the service, cited him as the highest example of a man who set his course and never wavered from it. Lewis Mumford taught us to stand apart, in a high place, and look at the whole thing; he taught us by his example to work and to persevere in spite of everything. We can learn these lessons well and still lose the game, but what else do we need to know?

Randy Shilts: Strike Up the Band

According to my wife, who saw a few seconds of the tape on CNN, there were hostile demonstrators at Randy Shilts' funeral. I wonder what they were trying to say. You wouldn't expect a thing like that to happen in San Francisco, where public protests against homosexuals have been uncommon—and unsafe—since the city's politics were revolutionized by the Gay Liberation of the '70s.

Maybe the demonstrators didn't hate Shilts, dead of AIDS at 42, because he was a homosexual. Maybe they only hated him because he was a journalist.

It's a tough life when you belong to two of the most reviled and endangered minorities in your society, and then spend your last seven years on HIV's Death Row. But this was a very tough guy. A special case.

So many AIDS obituaries have been written, in cities like San Francisco and New York, that there's a perfunctory quality to some of the writing, as if the horror and misery of these deaths needed no further explication. Homosexual writer, tragic victim, survived by his companion, future square in the AIDS Quilt, which by now must be big enough to cover San Francisco like a comforter from the Golden Gate to Candlestick Park. A grim, familiar litany that doesn't come close to telling us what we ought to remember about a singular character like Randy Shilts.

The gay political establishment, which didn't always appreciate him, was generous in its eulogies. Even playwright Larry Kramer, one of the movement's most unforgiving militants, admitted that Shilts' best-selling *And the Band Played On*, published in 1987, was the most important single factor in educating this country about the AIDS epidemic.

Most homosexual activists and HIV carriers acknowledge the debt they owe to this relentless reporter, who developed full-blown AIDS in 1992 and completed his last book in a hospital bed with a collapsed lung. It's the fraternity of professional journalists that may not understand what it owes him, or why he should be presented as a role model for beat reporters yet unborn.

Shilts took his leave from a profession in crisis. Diminished by a tabloid infection that spreads as rapidly and ruthlessly as a retrovirus, outflanked by press agents, drawing paychecks from callous profiteers who deal in toxic or worthless information, most main-stream journalists sign over their honor without a murmur. Even Dan Rather, in a recent jeremiad at the Columbia School of Journalism, warned students that entertainment—he calls it "Holly-woodation"—is overwhelming professional journalism and everyone who believes in it.

When they sacrifice their dignity and authority for entertainment dollars, mass media journalists create a very cynical audience. An English columnist, bidding his readers a bitter farewell, complained that the worst thing about them was that they always assumed he was beating the drum for one side or the other. Apparently more readers believe in angels than in the possibility of objective journalism.

I've experienced the same frustration. My readers are fair and thoughtful, for the most part. But some of them seem to live in a world of dueling propagandists, a battlefield of mechanized warfare between high-tech spin machines. Power is contested by editorial inches, minutes on the evening news, advocates on talk shows, books sold, homes reached, votes influenced. These people don't believe in free agents. Support them and you're a brother, contradict them and you're a Nazi.

When there are no reputable wholesalers in the marketplace of ideas, it reverts to the law of the jungle—might makes right and shrillness and repetition make what passes for truth. The jungle is a lonely place for independents. If a journalist craved popularity and the security of group-think, he'd feel tremendous pressure to join a team and wear its T-shirt. But then he'd know he was in the wrong profession.

No one faced more pressure than the late Randy Shilts. There's a passage in The Mayor of Castro Street, his biography of Harvey Milk, that brought Shilts' position into focus for me. He indulges in some mild sarcasm at the expense of Warren Hinckle, the most radical of San Francisco's straight journalists and a loyal supporter of the gay rights movement.

Hinckle had theorized about a conspiracy in the assassination of Milk, the gay community's first representative on the city's board of supervisors. But when the local media offered him no encouragement, Shilts writes, "Hinckle had to make a living and he soon found other subjects to fuel his ongoing fires of moral outrage."

I can sympathize with Hinckle. It's hard to hold a bead on one target when every headline represents another outrage. But it's easy to see why Randy Shilts resented Hinckle's freedom. For Shilts there was no closing the book and moving on to the next assignment. From the beginning, when the *San Francisco Chronicle* hired him from the all-gay *Advocate*, the homosexual community was his beat, his responsibility, his family.

For Shilts, the challenge was objectivity. He "came out"—declared his homosexuality—when he was an undergraduate at the University of Oregon, and his roots were in advocacy and interest-group journalism. He was totally immersed in the history and politics of San Francisco's gay enclave, known as The Castro, long before it was ground zero for the AIDS explosion. The third-person narration of his book on Harvey Milk is anything but detached and impersonal. Milk's story often becomes a vehicle for expressing Shilts' own central torment: Why the straight world insists on making life so difficult for homosexuals.

No one expected much objectivity from a reporter whose friends were dying all around him. But Shilts discovered, under the pressures of this AIDS story he was uniquely qualified to tell, that he had a weakness for the hard stuff—the unvarnished truth.

The Castro applauded when Shilts reported that the Reagan administration and the medical establishment were playing politics while people died. It snarled when he reported that gay groups were guilty of the same thing, lobbying to keep the homosexual bathhouses open when everyone knew they were a primary source of infection.

"People died while gay community leaders played politics with the disease, putting political dogma ahead of the preservation of human life," Shilts wrote in *And the Band Played On*. In The Castro, people he knew spit at him on the street.

Shilts persevered, in the conviction that the public, jaded with the heavy traffic in partisan rhetoric, would recognize and respect the truth. He tried to live up to the standard he set for himself in the introduction to *The Mayor of Castro Street*: "I tried to tell the truth and, if not be objective, at least be fair; history is not served when reporters prize trepidation and propriety over the robust journalistic duty to tell the whole story."

Shilts insisted on the mordant irony that Rock Hudson's death, in 1985, did far more to call public attention to the AIDS epidemic than all the deaths that preceded it and all the stories Shilts had written. But most historians of the '80s will assert that the turning point was the publication of *And the Band Played On*, which the *New York Times* celebrated as "a heroic work of journalism."

Sometimes life has a funny way of saying "congratulations." On the very day that he delivered the manuscript for *The Band* to his publisher, Shilts learned that he'd tested positive for HIV. He made a secret of his illness as he'd never made a secret of his homosexuality. It was nearly six years later, when he was literally on his deathbed, that he admitted he was suffering from AIDS.

"Every gay writer who tests positive ends up being an AIDS activist," he said in an interview. "I wanted to keep on being a reporter."

That's a level of commitment you don't encounter much anymore, in our business. Let's not hesitate to claim him. The AIDS epidemic has had so many victims, martyrs, heroes to memorialize. Journalism, in its late Hollywood phase, has so few candidates for its highest honors—almost none among the younger generation. I think it would be appropriate, and in line with Randy Shilts' wishes, if the guard of honor for this memorial service could be chosen from the Fourth Estate.

Spike Lee: In Your Face

Anything I write about sex or race will infuriate 10 readers for every reader it pleases. Why do I do it? Maybe because I'm getting too old to drive fast with the lights off, stay out late in dark angry places, swim a lake at night, climb a mountain alone. Opinion isn't a high-risk racket, but sex and race are still combat zones where you fight for a beachhead and keep your head down. Monetary reform and recycling don't do the same thing for me, somehow.

Why defend Spike Lee, for instance, when he doesn't need it and wouldn't appreciate it? The key scene in Lee's *Malcolm X*—the most controversial scene, by any measure—is when the white girl comes up to Malcolm at Harvard and asks him what a decent white person can do to help his movement.

"Nothing," says Denzel Washington as Malcolm.

If you asked Spike Lee the same question, what can a white person do? I don't know if he'd say, "Nothing." But I saw him enduring an interview on TV, and when the reporter asked the black film-maker how he really feels about white people, Lee grinned owlishly and said "I call a spade a spade." It gave him special satisfaction, he told her, that he had finished the film—which ran way over budget—by soliciting cash from black millionaires like Bill Cosby, Michael Jordan and Oprah Winfrey.

"These weren't loans or investments," Lee said. "They were gifts. This was black money, and black people helping each other."

The young woman at Harvard reminds many of us of ourselves in the innocent '60s, when Malcolm and Martin Luther King, Jr., were recent martyrs and white liberal guilt was at flood tide. Some of the memories are embarrassing. Most of us weren't used to close contact with black people. We were horrified by the assassinations and the events in places like Selma, Ala., and the only behavior that seemed appropriate was the kind my Lab Gracie displays when she approaches another dog in the street: We rolled over on our backs and stuck our tongues out.

Some of the black people who were subjected to this spectacle were mercifully kind. Others, for good reason, were scornful. The scorn must have had its effect. I don't know that scorned white liberals went back to the racism of their parents, in any significant numbers. But among my own generation, there was a lot more passion for civil rights in 1965 than I could find in 1985, or in 1992, either. The Big Chill brought backsliding, more than back-lash. It takes actual character to stand up for the other fellow's rights when your own are secure, especially when he isn't begging you or thanking you for your support.

At the time of his death, Malcolm X was coming around to a view of the future that included reconciliation and cooperation between whites and African-Americans. But he came to it on his own, after a pilgrimage to Mecca, not as a result of any overtures or olive branches he received from penitent whites. If you read the same publications I was reading in those days, you know that Malcolm carried a pretty sinister image compared with Dr. King, who preached nonviolence and welcomed whites. "Uppity," as applied to black Americans, really means "ungrateful" rather than cheeky or disrespectful. The animosity of active racists probably harms black leaders less than the resentments of petulant liberals who didn't get the hugs and kisses they expected.

It's this second kind of martyrdom, ostracism by the "well-mean-ing" white middle class, that may be waiting for Spike Lee. Lee and the black angels who saved his picture are members of a tiny but revolutionary new black aristocracy of athletes and entertainers. Favorable changes in their industries, mostly a flood of television money, have blessed a few of these performers with more personal wealth than almost anyone in the white establishment.

Scrutinized as they may be, these black celebrities are free in a way that no black men or women in this country were ever free before. The only catch is that their good fortune depends, to a cer-tain extent, on the good will of the American public—affluent white consumers. And this public, expressing its will through the mainstream media that regulate the celebrity culture, still demands an occasional show of deference.

They don't ask for a full shuffle, just a tip of the hat and a happy field-hand's salute to Uncle Sam, Aunt Jemima and George M. Cohan. Like when they forced Michael Jordan to play in the Olympics and act as if he loved it.

Nobody gives them less satisfaction than Spike Lee. There's a high-powered black academic I know—he'll probably recognize himself—who breaks some of the unwritten rules of faculty primo-geniture by acting just a little too sure of himself, a little too impatient with well-meaning whites who are boring. I get a kick out of him because I see him as a walking litmus test for latent racists.

That's the way I see Spike Lee, only much more so. I get a kick out of him, too. If "In your face" is what he's saying, I'm not sure it's an inappropriate attitude for a black artist to assume. Oprah and Michael Jackson might be buying up small countries and bailing out the savings-and-loan industry, but a huge section of black America is worse off now than it was in the '60s. For 12 years, conservative Republicans have been laboring diligently to cancel everything that was accomplished by the civil rights movement. The leader of a powerful Republican faction, Patrick Buchanan, is a more dangerous racist than George Wallace in his prime. I'm still not sure that Supreme Court Justice Clarence Thomas, nominally the highest-ranking black man in America, wasn't chosen solely for his surname by belly-laughing right-wingers who thought the joke was too good to pass up.

Should Lee be singing "God Bless America"? It worries me to hear liberals knocking him because he's so venal, with his TV commercials and the full line of "Brand X" products he's been selling to promote his movie. I didn't realize that "too commercial" was still a valid criticism of anyone in this country, where President Reagan sells a $2 million after-dinner speech to the Japanese, the highest government officials auction themselves off to conglomerates and foreign governments, and everyone but J.D. Salinger does commercials.

I don't think a white artist would attract the same criticism. Remember what Lee remembers always, that even 10 years ago it would have been impossible for any black to tap into this mother lode of easy money.

He's redistributing the wealth according to a master plan of his own. And more than Leona Helmsley or Donald Trump, more than any of the other black superstars he runs with, he seems to be plowing most of his money back into projects that deserve respect. His next film, he told the interviewer, will be based on Toni Morrison's *Song of Solomon* or Zora Neale Hurston's *Their Eyes Were Watching God*. That's a far cry from the wasted talent of Eddie Murphy and *Beverly Hills Cop VIII*.

Lee has become a force to reckon with, and certain elements seem to be circling for the kill. It's one thing when a film critic is making the call; a black, political director like Lee should be judged by the same critical standards as any other. But *Malcolm X* has been getting the treatment from national columnists disguised as Pauline Kael. The firing squad includes a couple of the pundits who spent the '80s trying to make us feel good about being white and well-to-do.

"Light Hollywood entertainment"? "Not biography but hagiography"? Compared with what, *PT-109? The Babe Ruth Story?* Is this a less truthful film than *JFK*, a more worshipful film than *Gandhi*? Apparently Lee shuffled the facts to make Malcolm's parents seem nobler and more mythic. Certainly the last part of the picture is a little intense and theatrical; the last part of Malcolm's life was intense and theatrical. But do these "critics" honestly mean to tell us that they weren't impressed?

The heroic eulogy we hear at the end—"Malcolm was our manhood, our living, black manhood . . . our own black shining Prince!"—wasn't written for Lee's movie. It was actually delivered at Malcolm's funeral by Ossie Davis, whose voice we hear in the film. Whites, well-meaning or otherwise, make a grave mistake if they dismiss *Malcolm X* as cynical, commercial entertainment. They need to read Eldridge Cleaver's "Initial Reactions on the Assassination of Malcolm X," written in his cell at Folsom Prison on June 19, 1965. ("We shall have our manhood. We shall have it or the earth will be leveled by our attempts to gain it.") I guess there's a generation now that hasn't read *Soul on Ice* or *The Autobiography of Malcolm X.*

Lee isn't kidding us with this picture. He isn't hustling. By all reports Malcom X was a remarkable individual, who has become an enduring symbol of black pride. This is a black thing and a very serious thing, and whites who don't understand it have been embarrassing themselves in print.

I have no quarrel with the cocky, gifted little agitator who filmed *Malcolm X.* I don't covet Lee's affection any more than he covets mine. In a profoundly racist country, he makes films that are never vehicles for hatred. He can speak eloquently to both races, as anyone who has seen *Do the Right Thing* or *Jungle Fever* will concede. His films are original, relevant and usually intelligent. Which American filmmaker, working regularly, is making a more positive contribution to the medium?

I'm not sure why so many white people are getting tired of his act. Race is crippling this country, and real black leaders are in short supply. Why do we want to silence the smart, subtle ones— Malcolm was a subtle one, too—and then curse our luck for the furious ones who follow after?

Tom Seaver: Of Tom and the River

I don't know where you can find a prettier train ride than the Empire State Express from Albany to Buffalo, across the New York that no one in the South has heard of, nearly 300 miles of lakes and rivers and red-brick mill towns and long unbroken stretches of hay and cornfields of such a sweet midsummer green that they beg for a soundtrack, that they make music conspicuous by its absence. Between chapters of *The Unbearable Lightness of Being*, I saw a deer and two herons and what's left of the Erie Canal. And an obscenely fat midsummer woodchuck in a field that the setting sun saturated with a color to which only the late V. Van Gogh could do justice.

I didn't see the two things I strained hardest to see. South of the track between Canajoharie and Little Falls is Lake Otsego, James Fenimore Cooper's Glimmerglass. At the other end of the lake is Cooperstown, where in two days they were holding the Hall of Fame ceremonies that I was going to miss. I thought if I caught just a glimpse of the lake from a hilltop, it would be almost as if I'd looked in for a moment and paid my respects to Enos Slaughter and Hoyt Wilhelm, and Lou Brock. But there was no hill, and even though the air was as clear as spring water the lake was too far away.

Two hundred miles later the train passes just south of Albion, N.Y., and the Mt. Albion Cemetery tower, a 19th-century Gothic curiosity that used to command the whole county. From the top, on a fairly clear day, you can see across ten miles of orchards and the Old Ridge Road to Lake Ontario. In the shadow of the tower my father is buried, and his father and his father. I thought that if I could see the tower it would be like tipping my cap, touching base—touching home. But it was later in the evening and there was more haze, and maybe they've built some high-rises in the meantime. Albion was indistinct.

I was thinking of my father because my purpose in Buffalo was an Old-Timers' Game that featured Bob Feller. My father was a student in Cleveland when Feller arrived in 1936. More than anything else, it was that experience—seeing a 17-year-old boy with a fastball that made Lou Gehrig wince—that hooked him on baseball for the rest of his life. (It was late July now, when my father would be at the dining room table after dinner running through his earned run averages with a speed that awed me; that was a lot of earned run averages to update every day, all the pitchers in the National and American Leagues and the International League as well. Early in the season, when he was rusty, he used up a lot of No. 2 pencils, but by August he barely had to look at the box score. He slid the numbers and decimals around like a croupier. He was never wrong because I often checked him; that ability to do long multiplication and division in my head was the only part of his logical, legal, hard-edged mind that I inherited.)

With an Old-Timers' Game, it's important to control your expectations. This one was promising, with Brock, Slaughter and Wilhelm joining Feller and a whole crowd of the very best: Hank Aaron, Warren Spahn, Johnny Bench, Robin Roberts, Ernie Banks, Brooks Robinson, Early Wynn. The stadium, Buffalo's ancient War Memorial, is the place where they filmed *The Natural* with Robert Redford, the bank of lights on the right-centerfield roof the same one Redford ignited with that imaginary home run. War Memorial was a tumbledown travesty until the movie company renovated it. Now it has shabby dignity and a brand new Triple-A franchise.

An Old-Timers' Game is like visiting your grandmother in the nursing home at the very end of her career—the respect and affection you feel are the same, and the memories are worth the trip, but it's painful to stay long because she's not quite Grandma. Mickey Mantle avoids the old-timers' circuit because he can't run anymore, and he says he can't bear to see Aaron play at 215 pounds. In this game Feller, who at 67 can just get the ball to the plate, was ripped for a couple of long balls by Brock and Bobby Thomson. Slaughter, exhibiting his legendary feistiness at 69, dashed around dangerously and stumbled once. Wilhelm can still throw his knuckleball. It was about the only effective pitch five Hall of Fame pitchers could muster. What I remember best was Bob Feller standing alone at the end of the dugout, removing his glasses and rubbing each of his eyes very slowly with a handkerchief before he jogged out on the field to be introduced.

I'm pretty good at controlling my expectations. When Tom Seaver went to New York to try for his 300th major league victory, I paid my money and followed, knowing and accepting that I might be a week or a month or even eight months early if the players' strike canceled the rest of the 1985 season. There may be nothing you can count on, but there are people you can bet on. I saw Tom

Seaver pitch his third or fourth major league victory in 1967, 30 years after my father found Bob Feller, when I was the student and Tom was the rookie sensation. Aside from the fastball, Seaver was nothing like Feller. Feller was a farm boy from Iowa, almost literally in overalls, rough and wild and naive. Seaver was a middle-class college boy from USC, the son of the best golfer in Fresno, Calif.

He was smart, disciplined and cheerfully cocky, and whatever else he may have learned at USC, he had already learned how to pitch. Someone pointed out that his whole generation of Mets pitchers looked the same on the mound—that long, low driving motion that takes so much of its power from the legs. But it's uncertain whether they all learned it from the same coaches or whether the others copied Seaver. Either way, by the end of the season Seaver and his old Mets teammates Nolan Ryan and Jerry Koosman will have won nearly 800 games, and counting.

I met Seaver when I covered the Miracle Mets in 1969, and I've been known to kid him in print. I wrote once that I preferred his USC teammate Bill Lee because Lee, like me and unlike Seaver, was left-handed, bearded and a little turned around in the head. But where's Bill Lee now? I chided Seaver for some mild over-confidence when he told me that the big difference between us was that he could do my job (he studied some journalism as a Trojan) but I couldn't do his. Point taken, or at least half a point. If I ever win the equivalent of my 300th game, there won't be network camera crews or 60,000 paying customers. Tom Seaver won't fly in from North Carolina to catch my act.

Unlike Mantle, Mays, Ruth and most of the heroes before him, Seaver arrived in New York all grown up and in full control of himself. His career has proceeded just as we expected the first time we saw him pitch and listened to him in the locker room. His maturity (a word I hate but acknowledge) and steadiness have deprived him of a measure of fame. He wasn't deep country like Dizzy Dean or Catfish Hunter. Kinky Friedman couldn't write a song about him. He wasn't a matinee idol—he's a shade too stocky and cherubic— or a troubled pop-off like Jim Palmer. He was just always incontestably the best, and as the years went by he became my physical *doppelganger*, that athlete your own age to whom you link your mortality. I despaired of him a couple of years ago and prepared our rocking chairs. But we made some adjustments and 1985 has been a good year for both of us.

Everyone knows what happened in New York last week, but I didn't read many accounts that did justice to it. The working sports press sees too many games to see any of them clearly, even the ones that make history. Some poor drudge reported that Seaver got a 4-1 lead and "held" it, like you "hold" your mother's coat. Listen. If cameras could have recorded that game in Yankee Stadium just as it happened, with every nuance, it would make *The Natural* look like a driver education film. You don't "hold" a three-run lead in Yankee Stadium, with the short rightfield fence and seven left-handed hitters in the Yankee lineup. You clench your teeth and hang on for grim death. Every pitch is like checking your gas oven with a lighted match.

The setting alone was epic. A crowd of 54,000, half of them there for Phil Rizzuto Day (they gave The Scooter a "Holy Cow" named Huckleberry with a halo fastened to her horns), not an empty seat that I could see. A perfect day, cool and bright like World Series weather. The loathsome Yankee mercenaries with their loathsome partisans, some of them so vile they booed and cursed Tom Seaver.

The Yankee starter, Joe Cowley, had nothing, but the White Sox were overeager and kept giving up baserunners: an unsuccessful steal, an unfortunate attempt to take an extra base, a double play. Seaver gave up a run on two clean singles in the third and still trailed 1-0 after five. In the sixth the White Sox got him four, the last two on a single by Brian Little, who played at Louisburg College (the pitcher Little victimized was Brian Fisher, who in his brief run with the Durham Bulls two years ago was the Bob Feller of the Carolina League). There was no more scoring, but that was when the serious baseball began.

The game had been delayed more than an hour by the Rizzuto ceremonies. By the seventh inning it was after six o'clock and the stadium shadows were creeping. Home plate was in shadow and the pitcher's mound in sunlight, the arrangement pitchers love. It might have carried Seaver through the eighth, when he struck out the Yankees' best athletes, Rickey Henderson on a called strike that he disputed and Dave Winfield swinging on a low changeup that wasn't in the strike zone. They were classic confrontations classically mounted. Baseball fans don't just hoot and scream continually like football crowds; they fall silent and groan or gasp in unison. Imagine 60,000 people taking one deep breath before the giant Winfield swung and missed the 3-2 pitch with two men on, two out.

By the ninth the outfield grass had gone from green to lemon to almost butterscotch, and the wheeling shadows of the Stadium pigeons carved it up, the only things moving on the field when Seaver paused at the top of his stretch. Now the stadium shadow had moved out and decapitated him. The rooftop scalloping was patterned on his shoulders and only his head was in the light. He had been coasting, the occasional fastball with that smooth motion still looking like 90 miles per hour (his catcher says it still is sometimes), but here he was tiring fast.

The left-handed hitters were finding him. There was an account that said "Dan Pasqua singled." The single was a 330-foot line drive that hit the fence two feet short of a home run. The same account mentioned that rightfielder Harold Baines made "a leaping catch" of another drive by Willie Randolph. Baines, a great athlete giving something extra in the service of history, went so high and had such a hang time, and had his body so wrenched around by the effort that we couldn't tell, holding our breath, if he really had it until he held it up. For sheer athletic ability, there's rarely been a greater catch. A moment later Don Baylor flied out routinely to left. Seaver had it and we had it, and we hugged and high-fived and we believed. The Yankee fuhrer George Steinbrenner stormed from his box in a fury, and Tom Seaver, with a 1969 grin, was hugging his wife and his daughters and his catcher.

The perfection of it all was reinforced when the strike was called but settled in two days. In baseball things are settled sometimes, the way they're never settled in Lebanon or South Africa or Ireland. Sometimes it turns out well, and the wicked are punished and the good are rewarded. Sometimes it's just the way you imagined it, just the way you wanted it to be.

Georgia O'Keeffe: When the Blind Lead the Blind

"To see takes time, like to have a friend takes time. . . . There are people who have made me see shapes—and others I thought of a great deal, even people I have loved, who make me see nothing."

—Georgia O'Keeffe.

Sometimes a journey will unexpectedly acquire a theme. I don't spend much time in New York, which I fled many years ago and never missed. Occasionally I go back for some culture, or more often for a baseball game or a tennis tournament. This time I was in New York to have my eyes examined by a doctor in Greenwich Village.

I'm nearsighted beyond the point of joking about it comfortably. In junior high they called me Mister Magoo. I wear high-tech trifocals, and I used to have a recurrent nightmare about learning braille. Stumbling along 14th Street with my pupils fully dilated from those drops the doctor uses, literally blinded by five o'clock sunlight, I was focused forcefully on the miracle of sight—"the highest bodily privilege, the purest physical pleasure which man has derived from his Creator," in the words of the 19th-century English essayist Sydney Smith.

Through a glass darkly—a pint glass of Guinness in a dark cave of a saloon where shapes began to reassemble themselves—I reviewed the privations and sorrows that blindness would bring. The blind miss the paintings of Georgia O'Keeffe. That alone would be ample reason for them to shake their fists and curse their darkness.

The exhibition at the IBM Museum on Madison Avenue is called *Two Lives*. It features some of the best work O'Keeffe and her husband, the photographer Alfred Stieglitz, produced while they were most intimate and exerting the most influence on each other as artists. The exhibition was organized to invite direct comparisons; often the painter and the photographer are rendering the same subjects—a tree, a porch, a skyline—and alongside O'Keeffe's paintings are many of the remarkable photographs in which she served as her husband's model.

As a portrait of a marriage, the show presents an inexhaustible range of psychological nuance. As art history, it takes us back to a time when the argument between abstraction and representation was fresh and fascinating, and embodied in the development of groundbreaking artists like O'Keeffe and Stieglitz. But to a layman with an open mind and an unjaundiced eye, it presents two artists of genius carrying on a passionate dialogue about what it means to *see*.

I couldn't escape this theme. New York offers a formidable Chinese menu of images, a thousand choices in its galleries and museums as well as in its streets. At the Metropolitan Museum there's an exhibition titled *The Waking Dream*, which chronicles the history of photography from the first barely discernible, pre-camera images on treated paper, recorded in the 1830s, through tintypes and daguerreotypes to the 20th-century innovations of Alfred Stieglitz and the futuristic abstractions of Man Ray. It ends, chronologically, on the eve of the Second World War. The cumulative experience of this powerful show is like placing your eye behind a single lens and watching a new world come slowly into focus.

But there was still another museum and another exhibition I wanted to see. In this case, word of mouth was overwhelmingly negative. In the judgment of the director and curators of the Whitney Museum, its Biennial exhibition represents the most interesting new developments in American art over a 24-month period. Robert Hughes, the cruel and canny art critic for *Time*, labeled the 1993 Biennial "a fiesta of whining agitprop" and "a saturnalia of political correctness, a long-winded immersion course in marginality."

As Hughes concedes, there are a few artists at the Whitney who may deserve to be plucked from the path of the great tidal wave of his contempt. The show isn't absolutely devoid of inspiration or of humor. But it is, in fact, a dispiriting demonstration of the awful hash that ideological contamination can make of an artist's or a museum's best intentions.

Hughes describes the new aesthetic in his book *Culture of Complaint*: "I am a victim: how dare you impose your aesthetic standards on me? Don't you see that you have damaged me so badly that I need only display my wounds and call it art?" (His specific target was the notorious, howling Karen Finley.)

Painting is vanishing from these shows, Hughes explains, because painting is suspected of "mastery"—or craft, or accomplishment or by definition of "art" itself—and mastery is associated with the oppressive white males who dominated art and mankind. To avoid the seduction of mastery is to embrace the marginalized victims who were never allowed to achieve competence or eloquence.

In other words, art succeeds by being wretched and inept. Stripped of irony or any suspicious cleverness, political and "conceptual" art becomes a flea market of used slogans, serving a captive audience that agrees with every word. It verges on simple-mindedness when you see it in the Whitney at its worst. It amounts to artists telling the rest of us how to think before they themselves have learned how to see.

The result is degraded anti-art, because artists lay no legitimate claim to political or social clairvoyance, and never have. They've never changed the world by screaming at it—only by patiently holding up a mirror to the world until it began to see itself in a different way. The pathetic decline of the arts when they were co-opted and politicized by socialist dictatorships might have served as a warning. But it never registered in Manhattan. And there's no scowling commissar coming to inspect them at the Whitney. They've done this to themselves.

I'm trying to imagine what the Whitney victim-worshipers would say about Georgia O'Keeffe. O'Keeffe became a feminist icon because she succeeded so splendidly and stubbornly on her own terms, in an era when the art world was more phallocentric than Karen Finley could imagine. But she was also the lover, model and protege of the magnetic Stieglitz, an exuberant heterosexual who was notorious for his romantic infatuations long before he met O'Keeffe. Though his behavior was scarcely out of the ordinary for an artist-sage of his generation, most modern feminists would take him for a satyr, and condemn his relationship with the young painter as gross exploitation.

But everything we see in *Two Lives* belies that simplistic formulation. The works of art themselves argue that this was a historic collaboration, a romantic and creative partnership that has never been equalled. When O'Keeffe's affair with the married photographer became a scandal, "They wrapped themselves in voluminous black capes against the world and the weather," as biographer Beverly Gherman poetically records.

I love that line because it's such an image of defiance against a world where no one seems to offer much hope for men and women together anymore. O'Keeffe was devoted to Stieglitz and never minimized his role in her growth as a painter. Even after they parted ways in their artistic theories, and O'Keeffe turned to the Southwest for inspiration that Stieglitz never understood, their regard for each other never diminished.

And O'Keeffe won her gamble. At great risk to her independence, she accepted the love and patronage of a powerful, willful man who was light years ahead of her when they met. But you have only to look at the works in this exhibition to see how she finally outgrew and surpassed him. She saw more, finally, and cut deeper into the heart of light.

Who was the victim, if the woman took more than she gave? You wouldn't attempt to measure them that way unless you were a convert to the most cynical and inhuman of the postmodernist heresies—the belief that all human impulse, including sex and art, reduces to plus-minus transactions with power as their currency.

A fastidious loner by nature, O'Keeffe took the leap of faith across the deep chasm of gender, just as hopeful fools of both sexes have leaped for a million years. You could argue that she became a far greater painter because she dared. It's by no means mystical nonsense, this business about the collective power of the yin and the yang.

I'm sure it scandalizes the Whitney whiners to note that these works by O'Keeffe and Stieglitz, encompassing a period of world war, worldwide depression and unprecedented political upheaval, are serenely free of political or social comment. O'Keeffe had an aversion to placing human figures in her landscapes; Stieglitz devoted several years to photographing the sky.

Was this insensitivity or humility, a humility about their own limitations that's now almost extinct among artists? They both held strong opinions—O'Keeffe blamed an extended clinical depression, a year when she couldn't paint, on anxiety over the general human misery of the '30s. But they never confused their opinions with their work.

They committed their lives, and their life together, to learning how to see. They still teach us what they learned, and that's why we admire their work 50, 100 years after it was executed. And that's why no one outside the maintenance crew in the Whitney's basement will ever see this Biennial rubbish again.

Eubie Blake: A Century of Ragtime

Many years ago—at least 15—when I was a very young man taking myself seriously in New York, some friends took me to a jazz performance at the Overseas Press Club, a benefit for something or other. It was an important black musician, Thelonious Monk, I think. I can't recall for certain. There were a lot of celebrities and media big shots in the audience. Just before the first note a bunch of people came in with a very old black man, not supporting him exactly—he looked fairly spry—but surrounding him on all sides so he couldn't bruise himself on anything or fall more than a few inches in any direction. The old man looked amused.

"God, that's Eubie Blake," said a man in the next row. "I think he played with Scott Joplin. He must be 100 years old."

None of us had ever heard of Eubie Blake, a ragtime pianist and composer who retired before we were born. But about seven years later, when a man from the QRS Music Roll Company called my newspaper and asked me to send the music critic down to interview Eubie Blake, I remembered the night at the Press Club and reserved the assignment for myself. It isn't every day you get to meet a 107-year-old musician.

It turned out that Eubie was only 91, still active and in the middle of a comeback. QRS, the only surviving manufacturer of player piano rolls in the United States, was hoping to cash in on the ragtime revival by getting Eubie to repunch the master rolls he'd cut for the company in 1912, the year my grandfather graduated from college. The rolls were getting a little ragged after 60 years, but luckily the original artist was still available to update them.

It was a perfect setup, the ragtime equivalent of having Arthur Rubinstein come and play in your parlor. A bright winter afternoon, a beautiful old red-brick factory, Eubie sitting in the sunshine beneath a 15-foot window at the enormous recording piano that must have been at least as old as he was. He played off and on for three hours for an audience of five—his wife, QRS president Ramsi Tick, one technician, my photographer and me. I felt guilty about the critic I didn't bring along, a man who understood the music and its history. Eubie had to explain syncopation to me and demonstrate it repeatedly before I began to catch on. He must have wondered why they sent him a musical illiterate. But Eubie Blake live was as much a visual as a musical experience, and I told myself that a tone-deaf film critic might appreciate some details that the man with the good ear would have missed.

You could start with the artist's skull. No hair had grown there in the 20th century, as ancient photographs attest. The skin that caught the sunlight had acquired a kind of permanence, a metallic sheen that seemed to have nothing to do with human flesh. Eubie's head looked like a priceless bronze, a Tang dynasty heirloom that a loving curator removed from its glass case and polished till it burned.

It was the second most arresting thing about him. The legendary hands with their 12-key span really had to be seen up close—I sat on the same piano bench—to be believed. Twelve keys is almost a foot, a couple of inches more than any other pianist could manage. The fingers weren't only supernaturally long but bizarrely spatulate, as if nine decades of pounding keyboards had flattened them almost to the bone. I have to invoke E.T. to give you a real image of those fingers. But it seems insulting to Eubie to yoke the mechanical darling of a single season with the human achievement of a century. It's enough to say that the nature of ragtime piano is to play a syncopated melody with one hand and a regularly accented accompaniment with the other, and that with another 20 years' practice Eubie Blake might have played them both with the same hand.

At 90 the weird fingers still moved as fast as he asked them to, and they weren't the only things that moved. Ragtime isn't sitting-still music, and he rarely sat still when he played. When he felt he was getting hot he'd stick out his tongue a little and bounce up and down and back and forth on the bench, the bony old body looking frail enough to break if he came down any harder. He got hot and cooled off again a half dozen times during his session at QRS. He rarely missed a note. Just once or twice, resting between songs, his mind would drift a little—once he started singing "Waitin' for the Robert E. Lee" softly to himself while his wife was talking—and we'd be reminded that he was older than we were. And just a year younger than the late Franklin D. Roosevelt.

He and I had rapport, I think—about as much as you're going to get between a 90-year-old black man from Baltimore and a 30-year-old white man who was born in Nova Scotia. At the age when Eubie started playing piano in a Baltimore whorehouse, I was shocking the sixth grade by dropping out of the Methodist Youth

Fellowship. He told me his favorite joke about why black pianists learned to play ragtime, which relies heavily on the black keys: "Back in those days there was so much Jim Crow we were afraid to hit the white ones." He admitted that Scott Joplin might have had an edge on him as a composer. He told me that neither he nor Joplin could play the piano like another black man whose name I've forgotten, a musician with classical training who was forced into ragtime because America, still fond of its minstrel shows, wasn't ready for black fingers playing Mozart in Carnegie Hall. When he talked about the color barrier, which he did freely, it was without any edge and in the deep past tense.

The only secret of his longevity, Eubie said, was his wife. If she hadn't taken him in hand he'd have killed himself years ago chasing skirts and breaking up saloons. He used to be pretty good with his fists, Eubie told me, and held up a fist to show me. I'd never seen a fist made up of eight-inch fingers about as thick as a praying mantis's forearms. I'd have laughed if it hadn't seemed disrespectful. I don't think he was kidding.

When we said good-bye he gave me his card, as if I might need a pianist for some lodge clambake or wedding reception and should give him a call. The card has been in my wallet ever since, along with lawyers' and agents' cards and the cards of people who tried to sell me insurance:

Eubie Blake
Pianist-Arranger
Composer of *Shuffle Along* & *I'm Just Wild About Harry*
Lou Leslie's Blackbirds & *Memories of You*

I wrote a long story that read more like art appreciation than music criticism and made a weak joke, as it seems to me now, about Eubie trying to get the music rolls right because he wasn't sure he'd be around in 60 years to do them again. As if he was obviously on borrowed time. Eubie went on to an astonishing comeback, playing concerts and television with some of the best young musicians in the business. He became twice the legend he'd been when he and his partner Noble Sissle integrated Broadway in 1921. Last year there was a new Broadway musical celebrating Eubie Blake and his music. He was in the audience opening night. He outlived his wife.

Last week I finally had to take Eubie's card out of my wallet and file it with the cards that for one reason or another have gone inactive. He hadn't been feeling well enough to attend his birthday party, a lavish celebrity affair at the Kennedy Center. Five days later he died, perhaps of old age. This time he was really 100 years old.

Celebrity obituaries aren't an exalted art form. Local columnists often use them to pass along tired myths and to give themselves a little glamour by association. Years ago, when I was writing about films and TV and celebrities on a regular basis, I set down some guidelines for eulogies. I had to have had some personal contact with the deceased, I had to have had a moment or two with him that wasn't shared by other notebook jockeys and I had to admire him a good deal. I went through ten years of articles and columns and I found only two entertainers who'd qualified: Groucho Marx and Jack Benny.

Fast company. But not too fast for Eubie. I leave his place in history to be decided by other musicians. I just pass along what I was sure of in his company—that he was an authentic American landmark, an irrepressible, indestructible bald-headed package of talent and endurance that doesn't come along even once in a century.

For the Poets: A Cobbler's Petition

When the news is unbearable I like to spend an hour rummaging through the family archives, of which I have become the principal keeper. There's an anodyne effect from fading letters in antique script, commencement programs, wedding invitations, newspaper obituaries worn tissue-thin, marbled photographs of turn-of-the-century cousins whose names will never be retrieved; a yearbook dedicated to Miss Lillian Achilles (true), school librarian, a maiden lady with a pince-nez, wrapped in fur, her black voile dress gathered above her bosom with a cameo head of Athena.

The most surprising thing I ever found, I found in a high-school literary magazine dated 1930: an eight-line poem, unrhymed, attributed to my father. Poems, to the best of my knowledge, had never been his style. I won't subject him to the cruel scrutiny of modern critics by reproducing those verses. His inspiration was autumn leaves, an invitation to the obvious then and now. He was 16, after all.

But in the concluding lines he apologizes for distractions that blinded him to beauty:

> *I reveled through in uglier sights*
> *Machines and noisy man-made things,*
> *That now in weariness I flee.*

The revelation was that it sounded exactly like me, and nothing like my father. He loved cars and clothes, big bands, big productions. I'm the born Luddite, anchorite, forest hermit, destroyer of telephones. When was he weary? But the poem connected me with a piece of my father that opened him up to reinterpretation, more than any of his lectures or the few letters he wrote, more than his diaries, which I have. It made me feel more securely that I was his son.

I mean psychologically, Mom. Every poet is obliged to shed his everyday voice, trained to hide things, and find that other voice that gives things away—not always the same things the poet set out to give away. Even the most mannered, conventional verse may shed more light on its author than a dozen earnest letters to the editor. An honest poet, with or without great skill, is like a house with no curtains.

People can see in, if they bother to look. And that, at most times in most communities, is considered bad form. Never worse than now. Poet Dave Smith, editor of the *Southern Review*, claims that poetry's "lyrical effusion" is an embarrassment to the stage managers of Southern literature ("SoLitCrit doesn't like art personal, effused") and accounts for its exclusion from the inner circle.

Emotional exhibitionism has become a cultural misdemeanor, while educated readers root through haystacks of minimalist text for needles of insight. The decline of poetry, like the decline of language itself, has been well documented. I was one of the few to lodge a protest, three years ago, when the *Los Angeles Times* and the *Washington Post* banished poetry reviews from their book pages. A street-corner survey showed that the average American is unable to name a single living poet; half of the subjects thought Shakespeare wrote novels, and a significant minority thought Chaucer was an early astronomer; the one who claimed to know Robert Penn Warren identified him as the Chief Justice.

When newspaper prose aspires to television and both of them pay homage to the *National Enquirer*, the language of poets recedes rapidly in the rearview mirror. As they lost readers on the high side and on the low, poets huddled together for survival, holed up in universities and writers' colonies, published in small magazines and small presses that Waldenbooks doesn't carry. Their work naturally took a turn toward opacity and solipsism, and little of it filtered out.

In the absence of poets, prose rules carelessly. As readers in the mainstream, we lose the habit of poetry. One of my Christmas gifts from my wife was a new collection of poems (*The Transparent Man*) by Anthony Hecht, who has been my single favorite poet ever since James Dickey, in person, scared the daylights out of me in New York in 1969.

It was Hecht's first book since 1979, and I opened it with something close to erotic anticipation. But I wasn't ready. Dulled by that rank Ganges of literal-minded prose, the "news" that helps me to make a living, I'd lost not only the habit of serious attention but even the habit of play. Here in "Curriculum Vitae," the first poem, what does he mean that children in winter "manufacture ghosts"? I grope around for some psychological handle and then thump my empty head in humiliation: He means their breath freezing, in clouds above their heads. And "ferned and parslied windows," that

I stumbled over without comprehension, that's just frost on the window.

Our capacity for language shrinks rapidly if we don't exercise it, and poetry is the only exercise that engages every muscle group. Hecht is a true poet, and a true poet's words take up more space than any other words—more space on the page, in the memory, even in that limpid millpond of the air that the bard will set to rippling with his shouts.

In the best poetry the words are breathing, like Hecht's children, and they manufacture ghosts and pictures. Real poetry is luminous and numinous, but best of all it's precise. In the best hands, its precision is awesome. Novelists release floods of words and then go back over them like inspectors on an assembly line, looking for defects and duds. Journalists choose their words as carefully as we can, under the circumstances, under the clock. But a gifted poet in his pride will never release a word he's ashamed of, and his best choices can cut like a laser.

I have to call attention to an essay by Dave Smith. First he asserts the superiority of poetic expression, and then he pulls the trigger: "the rest [of literature] is mostly information *cobbled* together" (my brackets, my italics). *Cobbled.* Can you see us poor prose monkeys there in the dim light, hunched over our little benches with our little hammers, working stiff leather with stiff fingers? *Cobbled.* It's a choice so devastatingly correct there's no rejoinder, no defense. After that verb, the room falls silent. The poet has spoken.

Or take "Common Form," from *Epitaphs of the War* published by Rudyard Kipling in 1919, when poets were still public men and the last war of all had just been fought:

> *If any question why we died,*
> *Tell them, because our fathers lied.*

Poets have every right to their arrogance, to their wounded tribal pride. They have been neglected, quarantined, reduced to an audience of "mostly magnolia maidens and academics," according to Smith. But the rumors that alarm me are the rumors of separatism, of deliberate secession during the verbal collapse of a waning civilization. It's nothing new, this conviction that poets should write only for other poets. Robert Graves and his lover Laura Riding shared it passionately, 60 years ago.

"True poets will agree," Graves sneered, "that poetry is spiritual illumination delivered by a poet to his equals, not an ingenious technique of swaying a popular audience or of enlivening a sottish dinner party."

Curse you, man. To me this sounds like desertion under fire. Who ever finds the audience that he thinks he deserves? The language is slipping away from precision, toward manipulation and concealment, vulgarity and chaos. When we lose precision we lose meanings; when we lose enough meanings we lose our perspective, and our sanity. We fight wars and talk gibberish to defend them. The hour is late.

Call this a cobbler's petition, to poets who may be sulking in their tents. Don't abandon us, don't give us up. Sometimes your erudition is too much. Even if we had the learning for it once, few of us have maintained it. We haven't kept up. But we're still listening, still counting on you. The plague is spreading fast, and what becomes of us if the last few physicians will only treat each other?

Hal Crowther

Death of a Bard

He knew
Himself to sing, and build the lofty rhyme
He must not flote upon his watry bear
Unwept, and welter to the parching wind,
Without the meed of som melodious tear.

— John Milton, *Lycidas*

Just at dusk on Christmas Eve, I drove past a lot where a man in a Stetson was removing the letters from his sign — Final Sale, Any Tree $5 — and turning off the lights on a half acre of little fir trees laid out on their sides in the rain like the innocent victims of some forest catastrophe.

I thought that was the saddest thing I'd encounter this Christmas. But an hour later at American Legion Post 808, where half the town was warming itself on the free Tom and Jerries that the bartender has been dispensing on Christmas Eve since time immemorial, they told me that the village bard was dead.

It isn't given to every local versifier to die like Byron, surrounded by freedom fighters in a camp bed at Missolonghi, or like Shelley in the azure waters of the Gulf of Spezzia. Dr. Possum, as he was known to his friends and disciples, died in his bathtub. He lived alone and it was several days before they found him.

It was known for certain that he was a retired railroad man, rumored only that he had delivered the valedictory at his high school graduation, back in the early '20s when even rural scholars hat to read something more than computer terminals and crib sheets. In his creative prime he was an alcoholic. Draft beer was his drink. "Another dish, Lucy" was the cry that punctuated his rambling epics. Empty glasses formed a triple wall between The Doctor and his audience. The woman who filled them, the innkeeper's wife, was emaciated and wild-eyed. No one but Dr. Possum ever called her his muse.

Like Swinburne, he curbed his drinking to accommodate his failing health and lost his inspiration. A colostomy and ulcerated calves were included in the price he paid for his years of malt and music.

324

Inglorious our Milton may have been, but never mute. He worked in an oral tradition, like the ancient Greeks, and delivery was his greatest strength. He had a large voice, deep and imperative. Any number of startled deer hunters or traveling salesmen could be seen to spin on their barstools at his fortissimos, thinking the old man in the engineer's cap had challenged them or ordered them from the room. He dealt in obvious rhymes and urgent rhythms. Some of the verse could be traced to Robert Service and John Greenleaf Whittier. Most of it was either original or derived from sources so obscure that I could never track them down. Some of it was ribald, and none of it was precious or dull.

At his table, by invitation, you would find almost anyone in the community who has a passing affection for the language and a passing tolerance for strong drink. The group was never large and it wasn't predictable. There were dairy farmers who quoted him and English teachers who disdained him. No one competed with him. At the corner table with the forest of empty eight-ounce beer glasses, only Dr. Possum could invoke the muse.

I may be accused of exaggerating The Doctor's genius, but I can't exaggerate the significance of his passing. They tell me that the poets in Wales are like kings in their native villages, courted by everyone and subsidized by the government. Boris Pasternak, in *Dr. Zhivago*, tells us that the Russian people always loved their poets. Even in the cultural wasteland that the Communists have created, bureaucrats defer to Yevtushenko.

It was never so in this country. Walt Whitman may have been the last poet in any way attuned to the national *zeitgeist*, and America never embraced him in his lifetime. "To have great poets," he wrote, "there must be great audiences, too." Since then there has been an almost conscious conspiracy—aided by many poets— to dismiss poetry as effeminate, irrelevant and an unfit distraction for the sort of clear-eyed hale fellow who makes this country tick. The campaign has been so successful that serious American poets are known only to other poets and teachers. The public supports doggerel-mongers that even Dr. Possum would despise for their feeble rhythms and mawkish insights.

The week The Doctor died, *Time* magazine named the computer its Man of the Year. In a country that pays homage to mechanical memories, the memory of a Homer or a Dr. Possum is a quaint amusement. They never made a bard who could compete with an SRQ-1127. The oral tradition is dead and language itself is mortally ill.

That night we heard he was dead, The Doctor's surviving admirers lifted a few dishes together at the American Legion. The hotel where he had held forth was closed for the holidays, as if in appropriate mourning. We recited what we could remember of his verses, but our memories proved to be poor ones compared to his. A few fragments really, nothing more. I noticed that everyone who was trying to quote Dr. Possum was over 35. The younger people at our tables paid very little attention, dismissing us as noisy drunks just as so many of their parents had dismissed our master.

There isn't anything very unusual about my hometown. It has a village idiot, a village drunk, a village bully and a village whore. It even has a village historian and a village philosopher. Like many other villages, it used to have a village bard. He was an old man, and sick. His position is open now. It won't be filled.

Samuel Beckett: Play It Again, Sam

I couldn't let him pass without a word. The pedants have said that a great writer belongs to everyone. But Samuel Beckett belonged to a smaller number, and those of us who held a share in him held it with a particular pride and passion. His death at 83 in a Paris nursing home will expose his life and work to a furious round of posthumous scholarship, the search for hidden meanings and significances that he so loathed and mocked. I should merely like to note that he died at the winter solstice, on the shortest and darkest day of the year.

To offer a literary assessment or even deliver a literary eulogy for Samuel Beckett would be to reach above my station. Modesty was a virtue that Beckett admired and exemplified. This is a personal testimonial. Above all, superseding and qualifying anything else that can be said of me, I am a reader—a member of the dwindling cult for whom the primary stimulus is the printed word. And this gaunt Irishman with the spiky hair was the writer who offered the first interpretation of the world that I could fully comprehend.

Our English professors lingered interminably among the Victorians, modernized us reluctantly with *The Waste Land* and sent us forth as finished products with a semester of *Ulysses*, as if all English literature had ended there on Joyce's desk about the same time the Great War ended, and ended with the word "Yes." No one who has read *Ulysses* with a competent scholar has ever failed to get drunk on it, to take it like a drug. But some of us needed black coffee afterwards. The artist as magus, impresario, lord and wizard was not for us the final incarnation; "Yes" was not for us the last word. It's a matter of temperament. It took a resounding "No" to get our attention.

That's where Beckett came in—literally, in the late '20s, carrying Joyce's books and bags. (With characteristic self-deprecation Beckett denied the popular myth that he was Joyce's secretary, insisting that he was just one of many friends who read to the half-blind novelist and did odd jobs at his home.) Beckett admired Joyce's work and his integrity, but he knew from the start that Joyce's voice, which he described as "tending toward omniscience and omnipotence," was not the kind of voice he would attempt.

"I work with impotence and ignorance," he said.

Waiting For Godot and *Endgame* had made him a famous drama-tist, but English departments ignored Beckett into the '60s because he had, after all, let down the side when he abandoned his native tongue to write in French. I'd never seen either play nor read a word of Beckett when a friend, a Catholic scholar, handed me a paperback of *Malone Dies* with a mixed endorsement: "I can't read this wretch, but he ought to be right up your alley."

That alley I share with Beckett and his tramps is the only alley where I've always felt at home. "Ah, if no were content to cut yes's throat and never cut its own," he wrote, in *Texts For Nothing*, and I responded "Yes I said yes" as fervently as any Molly Bloom. This was my man. I learned that Beckett, too, had been raised in a com-fortable, progressive family where children were valued and encouraged.

"My parents did everything they could to make a child happy," he recalled, "although I had little talent for happiness."

A few of us understand. It offends me to hear Beckett described as an apostle of despair. Despair to your ear may be honesty to mine. The most terrible burden any creature was ever compelled to endure is the sure knowledge of its death; all human civilization—but especially religion—testifies to the ingenuity and tenacity of our denial.

Like any real philosopher, Beckett was less appalled by the trap itself than by the relentless savagery we practice upon each other in our struggle to ignore it, and to defend the illusions that keep our knowledge at bay. In his work and in his life he tried to set an example, to show that you can live with *no* illusions without losing your humanity or even your sense of humor. That's the hardest trick of all, and one of the few worth attempting.

Beckett's kind of honesty isn't for everyone. In a century where advertising has become the dominant medium and commercial and political deceit have so polluted the stream of human discourse that honesty is seldom rewarded and scarcely recognized, Beckett became a kind of last mastodon of whom a few naturalists strained to catch a glimpse.

He set the best example; he validated my most unacceptable feel-ings and perceptions in that droll, deliberately emaciated vernacu-lar that seemed to stumble into eloquence as inevitably as his sight-less, senseless derelicts stumbled into ditches. Other writers seemed as painfully aware of the human condition as Samuel Beckett. But I met one or two, and I couldn't understand why their boundless contempt for humanity's self-importance didn't contain a small corner of contempt for their own. If we are all spit on a rock, in the cosmos, how is it also true that the artist is a privileged agent of the sublime?

Beckett alone seemed free from the distortions of ego. Of course I never met him—few were so fortunate—but it goes without saying that he reserved his rudest gestures (rude indeed) for the cult of the artist as priest, prophet and Promethean hero. His window overlooked the exercise yard of a prison. In his 50s he referred to his work as "this rubbish" and his mind as "stony ground" and no one questioned his sincerity. He lobbied against his selection for the Nobel Prize in Literature, and refused to go to Sweden in 1969 to pick it up. Whatever his self-image might have been, laurels from the inventors of dynamite didn't fit into it. The man and his work were all of a piece.

Such testimonials nauseated Beckett. Rubbish or not, the work was everything, he insisted, and the wretch who created it "devoid of interest." He cringed at the cult of celebrity that degrades and corrupts the writer even as it enables him to make a living. (I have in my possession a questionnaire mailed to published authors by *Esquire*, an American magazine with literary pretensions, that inquires among other things into the writer's sado-masochistic preferences and frequency of orgasm; I like to think that *Esquire* waited for Beckett to die before they sent it out.) He suffered his art like an affliction, a compulsion to write that he cursed and belittled but could never stifle.

In Beckett's unholy trinity of human curses, loquaciousness ranked right alongside hope and the knowledge of death. He considered himself among its most pitiful victims. To him the mind was an infernal machine, the tongue and the pen its deadly appendages. His constant theme is the voice that cannot be stilled. Even death may not deliver us into merciful silence. "And at the same time I am obliged to speak," says the narrator in *The Unnamable*, who seems to be dead. "I shall never be silent. Never." And 123 pages later he concludes "You must go on, I can't go on, I'll go on." Beckett's last fiction, about the length of this column, was published a year ago and titled *Stirrings Still.*

His is a voice, strangely, that terrifies some and stabilizes others.

The landscape where I wander may bear little resemblance to the desolate landscape that Beckett populates, sparsely, with starving vagrants and cripples. But until I had seen Beckett reduce the human landscape to its barest essentials, I wasn't sure that I belonged there at all. Until I'd seen him reduce literature the same way, I wasn't sure that it was more than a seductive intoxicant. You don't read Beckett to vindicate your depression; you read him to vindicate your sanity. If that's the way reality appears to such a sane man—and he was eminently sane—then you, an optimist by comparison, must be all right.

He had other virtues. To a polemicist he might seem the least political of writers. But it was Beckett who taught me that the difference between enough to eat and not enough is an enormous, significant difference, and that the difference between having enough to eat and being emperor is very small: the merest membrane of vanity and illusion. It was a truth I'd always suspected, but had no emperor to verify. It's the fundamental political truth. Once you know it, the rest is easy.

Heroes are the most pathetic of illusions according to Beckett, a writer who never consciously created one. He must have found grim satisfaction in the way the ghouls of biography devour dead heroes. Who will look at a Jackson Pollock the same way now that we know the artist was an impotent bisexual alcoholic who beat his wife? I doubt that Beckett's grave will yield any humiliating trophies to these vultures, but I wouldn't read the stuff anyway. There are many corroborated stories of generosity, humility and courage, and they should suffice.

It's clear that Beckett never lost his humor or humanity. It's uncertain whether he truly lost heart. We don't know, either, whether the great pessimist was ever happy. But I know that I have been, from time to time, in part because Samuel Beckett was doing the hard work for all of us, standing the long watch on the side that faces the dark.